Recovery and Management of Neuropsychological Impairments

Recovery and Management of Neuropsychological Impairments

Edgar Miller

Addenbrooke's Hospital and University of Cambridge

JOHN WILEY & SONS

Chichester · New York · Brisbane · Toronto · Singapore

Library of Congress Cataloging in Publication Data:

Miller, Edgar.
  Recovery and management of neuropsychological
  impairments.

  Includes bibliographical references and indexes.
  1. Brain damage. 2. Neuropsychology. I. Title.
RC387.5.M54 1984   616.8'046   83-21582
ISBN 0 471 10532 5

British Library Cataloguing in Publication Data:

Miller, Edgar
  Recovery and management of neuropsychological
  impairments.
  1. Mental Illness—Physiological aspects
  2. Neurophysiology
  I. Title
  616.89'1   RC455.4.B5

  ISBN 0 471 10532 5

Printed and bound in Great Britain

Contents

Preface

For a long time the clinical contribution of neuropsychologists has centred on diagnostic assessment. With the advance of other techniques, especially radiological methods such as computerized tomography, neuropsychological assessment is rarely a crucial element in diagnosis although it may still contribute some useful additional information. On the other hand, people with some form of damage to, or disease of, the brain do suffer significant psychological handicaps which are often permanent, and they have to try to adapt to normal living as best as they can.

It is the main assumption behind this book that the most important potential contribution of clinical neuropsychology is likely to be in the field of rehabilitation rather than diagnosis. Once neuropsychological impairments have occurred there is usually little that can be done from a medical standpoint in order to relieve them. Those afflicted still have to learn to cope despite their handicaps. It is at this point that the psychologist ought to be able to make a unique contribution.

In recent years there has been an increasing number of reports of attempts to ameliorate neuropsychological impairments. This book attempts to review and evaluate these. It also attempts to set therapeutic intervention in the context of the normal spontaneous recovery and adaptation that occurs after brain damage. Although there may be some permanent impairment, deficits are not necessarily static, and spontaneous change does occur, particularly over the first few months after the injury. From this follows another emphasis in this book which is that real progress can only be made if therapeutic interventions are set against the background of these spontaneous processes leading to recovery.

As always the author is solely responsible for his own writing. Nevertheless a book like this is not written in a vacuum. Many of the issues covered have been discussed with colleagues and friends in Cambridge and elsewhere, and these discussions have influenced and modified my thinking. The list of people would be too long to name individually but I would particularly like to thank Dr G. E. Berrios and Dr M. F. T. Yealland who gave useful comments on parts of the text.

Cambridge
April 1983

Acknowledgements

Thanks are due to the following for permission to reproduce various figures from their original sources: Elsevier Biomedical Press (Figure 1); University Park Press (Figure 2); the Editor of *Archives of Neurology* (Figure 3); Mouton & Co. N.V. (Figure 4); Oxford University Press as publishers of *Brain* (Figure 6); and the Editor of the *Journal of Neurology, Neurosurgery and Psychiatry* (Figures 8 and 9).

CHAPTER ONE

Introduction

Traditionally neuropsychology has dealt with a range of issues. Until recently it has largely ignored another aspect which is arguably of equal theoretical interest and probably greater practical relevance. Extensive investigations have been made in an attempt to define the kinds of functional disturbance that are likely to occur after lesions in particular parts of the brain.' This approach has an anatomical bias. Alternatively neuropsychologists have adopted an approach that is more centred upon functions. They have tried to determine the kinds of change that are produced in such functions as memory or language but with little emphasis on the type or locus of the lesions responsible for the impairments. There are thus anatomical and functional biases in neuropsychology.

When neuropsychologists have tried to relate their work towards problems of direct relevance to clinical practice, as opposed to pursuing issues of mainly theoretical importance, the emphasis has been very much upon assessment. Considerable energy has been devoted to developing tests alleged to be sensitive to the presence of 'brain damage' and in localizing such damage within the brain (see Lezak, 1976). In just mentioning and then passing over the topic of assessment it is certainly not intended to imply that psychological assessment has no part to play in the practical management of patients with neurological disease. What must be noted is that the increasing sophistication and efficiency of radiological techniques (including computerized tomography—CT) surely means that the value of psychological tests in deciding whether there is a lesion, where it is located, and the nature of the pathology, is severely limited. Even in the unlikely event of the psychologist's skills becoming well enough developed to match those of the radiologist in answering these questions, the surgeon carrying out an operation is likely to prefer the three-dimensional visual impression that can be obtained from angiography and the CT scan. Psychological assessment does have significant roles other than that of diagnosis (see Miller, 1980a) and these still remain valid for neuropsychology, but this is not the place to extend the argument further.

Whether inspired by theoretical or practical considerations most work in neuropsychology has tended to ignore the fact that the psychological consequences of brain damage do not remain static. The effects alter with time and typically, if not always, there is some recovery of disturbed functions. That this is so would be difficult to glean from some neuropsychological writings. Walsh's (1978) otherwise admirable introduction to neuropsychology does not specifically deal with recovery, nor do other recent texts by Dimond (1980) or Williams (1979). Of the major texts that have appeared to date Hecaen and Albert (1978) and Heilman and Valenstein (1979) manage to devote a chapter to the question of recovery. Even here the way the topic is presented does not give the reader the impression that it is of central importance.

Fortunately the situation is now changing quite rapidly. The first significant signs of change appeared within the literature on physiological psychology. Finger (1978a) edited a book discussing many aspects of the problem of recovery from brain damage in relation to work on animals. Eidelberg and Stein (1974) record the proceedings of a symposium on this topic, and Cotman (1978) has presented a collection of papers on the related issue of neuronal plasticity. Some reviews of the application of psychological techniques to the remediation of impairment after brain damage in human patients have also started to appear (e.g. Diller and Gordon, 1981; Miller, 1980b; Powell, 1981; Trexler, 1982). Despite this it is still fair to say that, as judged by the contents of its most popular texts and major journals, recovery from the effects of brain damage is far from being a crucial issue for human neuropsychology as conventionally practised.

The relative neglect of recovery is of significance for two reasons. From a purely academic point of view where the concern is with understanding brain–behaviour relationships and the ways in which the brain controls behaviour, the power of the brain to adapt to insult and to regain, either partially or fully, the ability to achieve certain goals must be of considerable theoretical importance. At the practical or clinical level it can be argued that the greatest potential contribution that psychology could make to relieving the problems caused by neurological disease and disability is in the field of rehabilitation. The individual with significant brain damage has to try to adapt to the situation and learn to live as satisfactory and independent a life as he can despite his handicaps. It is in this situation that psychological skills and techniques ought to be at a premium.

The major aims of this book are, firstly, to review what is known about the process of recovery and the mechanisms that make it possible. Secondly it is hoped to draw out of this review whatever conclusions might be justified that are of significance for the management and rehabilitation of neurologically impaired patients. Finally, there is a discussion of the literature dealing with possible means of influencing recovery from deficits or ameliorating their consequences. With regard to this last aspect there has been an extensive and long-lasting concern with the treatment of aphasia, although remarkably little has been done in the way of attempting to evaluate the suggested techniques. Recently interest has started to grow in the possibility of finding therapeutic interventions that will be of value in the management of other kinds of impairment such as in memory. It is hoped that this book might draw together what has been achieved so far and stimulate others to join in this important and exciting work.

Before passing on to other matters the reader ought to note a significant bias in the preparation of this work. The writer is a practising clinical psychologist and not primarily a teacher or research worker. Ultimately his concern is motivated by the need to resolve clinical problems and directed towards the better management of those who have suffered disease of, or damage to, the brain. Within this general orientation there is no intention to neglect theoretical aspects. It is accepted that a better understanding of the basic processes that underlie recovery is likely to have a significant spin-off in more appropriate and better-designed management programmes. Fundamental issues will not be avoided but the writer's clinical background does mean that some theoretical issues will not be pursued as diligently as might be the case if the interest was largely academic. This will be the case especially where the direction followed seems unlikely to lead to any conclusions of possible clinical significance. The other side of this coin is that the discussion of possible practical applications may be taken further than the less clinically oriented reader may feel is necessary for his purposes.

Before commencing the major task there are some other points that need to be clarified. Neuropsychological research as a whole raises a number of conceptual and methodological problems. Some of these are especially acute when it comes to dealing with the problem of recovery. The next section of this chapter will be devoted to such issues. They will not be considered in great detail but at a depth which, it is hoped, will be adequate for an understanding of the main themes of this book. In the concluding part of the chapter there will be some more general comments upon the overall approach adopted in the rest of the book, together with an outline of possible criticisms and limitations. It is intended that the rest of this chapter will 'clear the decks' to some degree and also help to avoid the tedious repetition of certain basic points and qualifications throughout the later chapters. Alternative, and in some instances more extensive, discussions of many of the basic conceptual and methodological issues can be found in Finger (1978a) although written from the rather different standpoint of more fundamental research with animals.

DETERMINANTS OF THE EFFECTS OF BRAIN DAMAGE

Any examination of the recovery of function after brain damage must assume that the injury or pathology of the brain has produced some form of functional impairment. The exact nature of this impairment is determined by a number of factors. It also appears inherently likely that the factors which determine the nature of the original impairment will also have a bearing on its recovery. Unfortunately the absence of suitable evidence means that this point cannot be followed through in later chapters with the detail that it might deserve. Nevertheless the factors determining the nature of the consequences of brain damage present a suitable topic with which to start the examination of the fundamental issues underlying the main part of this book.

It is strange when looking back into the literature that many psychologists were quite content until relatively recently to consider the effects of 'brain damage' as if these followed a standard pattern regardless of the type or location of the pathology. In investigations published as late as the 1960s many examples can be found of the lumping together of all 'brain-damaged' patients into a single group with the presumed expectation that they will all behave in a similar way. With few exceptions it is now generally realized that the pattern of functional disturbance in patients with brain damage is capable of almost infinite variation and that the old unitary view is naive in the extreme.

In a paper describing the effects of head injury the eminent British neurologist Sir Charles Symonds made the very apt comment that 'the symptom picture depends not only upon the kind of injury but upon the kind of brain' (Symonds, 1937). This statement identifies two highly significant sets of factors determining the functional consequences of brain damage. These are the nature of the damage or injury and the characteristics of the subject who sustains it.

Nature of the injury or damage

The most significant variable here is the anatomical distribution of the lesion. This may be diffuse, as is the case with the neural damage produced by severe head injury (e.g. Strich, 1961) or the pathological changes associated with Alzheimer's disease (e.g. Tomlinson *et al.*, 1970). Alternatively the lesion may be more focal in nature, as in the case of an area of infarction resulting from a stroke or a well-circumscribed tumour. (It must of course be remembered that lesions as well defined as those that can be placed in experimental animals are rarely encountered in human clinical material. Also even apparently localized lesions may have more general effects. For example, any space-occupying lesion will create increased pressure in the whole of the cranium.) In very general terms whether the lesion is anterior or posterior, or within the left or right hemisphere, is likely to influence the nature of the functional impairment produced (e.g. Reitan, 1964).

This latter statement begs the question with regard to what is probably the oldest controversy bearing upon neuropsychology. This is the degree to which there is localization of function within the brain. The extent to which it is possible to localize the so-called 'higher functions' is not an issue that can profitably be argued here. For present purposes it is sufficient to note that there is ample evidence that the effects of lesions in different parts of the brain are not the same, and there must be some localization of functions (e.g. Walsh, 1978). The strong association between aphasia and lesions of the left hemisphere is only one of the more specific lines of evidence that might be cited in support of this assertion. By the same token it must be acknowledged that the evidence also indicates that there is certainly no simple punctate relationship between individual higher functions and particular parts of the brain. A form of latter-day phrenology with the functional terms translated into more up-to-date psychological jargon and placed over the surface of the cortex rather than the skull should clearly be eschewed.

Another variable which determines behavioural outcome is the rate at which the injury occurs. This issue will arise in a slightly different form in a later chapter (Chapter 4), but the general finding is that slowly progressive lesions cause less disturbance of behaviour than lesions which produce the same amount of damage but which occur suddenly or develop quickly. It is also sometimes found that malfunctioning tissue causes more disturbance than the complete ablation of the same amount of tissue (Miller, 1972). Finally, there is evidence that the consequences of lesions in the same general area of the brain may vary according to the type of pathology that produced them (Reitan, 1964). It may well be that differences between types of pathology will reduce to the fact that the detailed anatomical consequences of, say, a tumour in the parietal lobe are not the same as that of an occlusion of an artery that produces an infarction in the same general area of the brain. Despite this, knowledge of the kinds of impairment produced by the various types of pathology may still be of practical value.

Nature of the subject

Age is by far the most potent variable here. It is well recognized that the effects of comparable lesions in young children are commonly not as drastic as those in adults. Because it relates closely to the problem of recovery a more detailed discussion of the effects of age will be deferred until the next chapter. Other subject variables can be related to the consequences of brain damage. Handedness is of these (e.g. Subirana, 1958) and there is accumulating evidence that there are sex differences in the consequences of brain damage (McGlone, 1980).

Time as a variable

The nature of the brain injury or pathology and the status of the subject are well recognized as being influential variables in neuropsychology. A variable that is less readily taken into consideration is time in the sense of time elapsed since the damage occurred. Since this book is concerned with recovery of functioning, and recovery that can only happen over time, then the time dimension is central to present considerations. In fact one of the first topics to be dealt with in the next chapter is the detailed relationship between the extent of the functional disturbance on the one hand and the time elapsed since it was first produced on the other.

The factors determining the consequences of brain damage are therefore complex and have only been given the briefest of outlines above. More extensive accounts have been provided by Miller (1972) and Lezak (1976) amongst others. Although the present concern is with recovery, or changes associated with the passage of time, the other factors cannot be entirely forgotten. In fact they will emerge again and again in various disguises as different aspects of the major topic are introduced and discussed.

CONCEPTUAL PROBLEMS

Any discussion of 'recovery of function' after brain damage raises a number of conceptual points which could lead to confusion. The most immediate example of these lies in the fact that neither of the terms contained in the phrase 'recovery of function' is as simple and straightforward as might be considered at first sight. In order to avoid ambiguity later on it is important to explore the variations in meaning that can be denoted by these terms and to ensure that in future discussions the exact meaning intended can always be made clear.

In neuropsychology it is commonplace to talk about 'functions'. The concept of 'function' is unclear or ambiguous in at least two ways. One of these has been elaborated by Luria (1966) who describes two possible alternative uses of 'function'. The first is to refer to the activities of small units. Thus it is commonly accepted that the 'function' of the rods and cones in the retina is to be selectively sensitive to electromagnetic radiation of certain wavelengths. A corollary of this usage is that 'functions' are strongly localized, almost by definition. The other use of 'function', according to Luria, is to refer to complex activities like memory, perception, or language. In order that they can be easily differentiated Luria prefers the term 'complex functional systems' for the latter type, and this emphasizes the dependence of such complex activities on the operation of a range of functions of the former kind. Visual perception requires an adequate level of functioning of the cells in the retina, the transmission of information along the optic tracts, the operation of the visual cortex, and so on, as well as requiring contributions from other complex functional systems such as memory. It is logical to expect that complex functional systems can never be strictly localized to one part of the brain. In the following chapters the term 'function' will be almost exclusively used in the sense of complex functional systems.

The second source of ambiguity relating to 'function' again emerges as two alternative ways of viewing the concept. On the one hand, it can be used to refer to some kind of overt performance such as being able to supply the date '1066' when asked when the Battle of Hastings occurred. On the other, the 'function' involved could be assumed to be some sort of hypothesized ability, such as memory, considered to be necessary for adequate performance in tasks requiring the exposition of previously learned historical information. Following Laurence and Stein (1978) it is possible to consider these as functions relating to goals (i.e. actually stating the correct year) or as relating to means (the underlying memory process).

The term 'recovery' is ambiguous in exactly the same way as 'function' in relation to goals and means. Recovery in an amnesic patient may be considered solely in terms of meeting certain goals. In this case it might be a return to a state whereby the individual goes about his normal everyday business without failing to keep appointments or carry out other planned activities. This goal may be achieved by scrupulously writing down the most minor pieces of information for later reference and by using a watch with an alarm which can alert him to the need to consult his list for the next thing that needs to be done.Alternatively 'recovery' may refer to an improvement in the means (i.e. verbal memory) by which the person used to be able to order his life in these respects with only minimal use of external aids like diaries or lists. In general terms recovery of means implies recovery of the ability to achieve the goals. However the reverse is not true since the person may learn to achieve the same goals but by different means as in the use of lists or notebooks to prop up an inadequate memory.

In the remainder of this book it will often be quite clear from the context whether means or goals are being referred to. In fact the later chapters dealing with possible means of enhancing recovery are essentially concerned with the recovery of goals. Sometimes what is intended may not be quite so obvious. In these circumstances a special effort will be made to indicate which sense of the terms 'recovery' or 'function' is intended.

Another important logical distinction is that between 'recovery' and 'sparing'. In studying the effects of lesions in very young subjects it sometimes appears that they do not show the same deficits that are revealed by similar lesions in adults. For example, infant monkeys with certain types of frontal lesion do not show the impairments on so-called delayed response tasks that can be so readily demonstrated in adult animals who have suffered similar lesions (Goldman, 1974). There thus seems to be complete sparing of a function (whether considered as goal or means) rather than a deficit that is followed by recovery. This latter situation of an impairment followed by recovery os of course found in many other situations.

Conceptually there is quite a clear differentiation between recovery and sparing. Despite this the accounts given in the rest of this book, and especially the discussion of age effects in the next chapter, will not be over-punctilious in maintaining the distinction. Partly this is because more detailed investigations of apparent sparing in young subjects could reveal some subtle but transient impairment and it can be the case that deficits subsequently appear when the subjects are followed up into adult life. More importantly the postulated mechanisms used to explain sparing can also be invoked to explain some aspects of recovery. In any case sparing can be seen as the limiting condition of a mild deficit followed by rapid recovery. It thus happens that what appears on the surface to be a clear distinction tends to blur and result in a considerable degree of overlap when subjected to close scrutiny.

A final point about recovery relates to the fact that it is a time-dependent process in that it requires the passage of time in order to become manifest. Despite the point being fairly obvious once attention is drawn to it, it is sometimes all too easy to fall into the trap of regarding time as a causal variable as in statements like 'the patient's speech has improved because several months have elapsed since he had his stroke'. In fact the mere passage of time cannot of itself cause anything to happen. Time is significant solely because it gives other processes an opportunity to act, and it is these other processes that are the causal agents. Any full explanation of a time-related process needs to be couched in terms of the true causal factors.

PROBLEMS IN METHODOLOGY

In addition to the general methodological problems surrounding research in neuropsychology (e.g. Finger, 1978a; Gregory, 1961; Miller, 1972; Teuber, 1955; Weiskrantz, 1968) the study of recovery presents further difficulties. In many investigations it is necessary to assess subjects on the same measures on two or more occasions after the brain injury has taken place. This presents problems, especially with human subjects where the dependent variable is some measure of cognitive functioning. Prominent amongst these is the well-attested fact that a subject's score on a test may change solely as a function of previous exposure to the test. The most obvious factor here is the practice effect which could lead to a spuriously high impression of recovery from one test session to the next. It is virtually impossible to devise measures for every function of interest that are not subject to such contamination with repeated testing. The obvious means of getting round this difficulty is to have a control group, not expected to show any real change on the variable in question, which is tested and retested on the same measures as the experimental group and over the same intervals of time.

There are potential disadvantages with a control group of this kind. It is sometimes tempting to use normal subjects as controls. If this is the case it would be expected that the controls would score higher than the experimental group on the first testing. There might then be an interaction between the initial level on the measure and the extent of the practice effect when tested on a subsequent occasion. It is conceivable that controls might be obtained from another handicapped group at about the same initial level on the dependent variable but who would be unlikely to show any real change (e.g. neurological patients with similar deficits in whom spontaneous recovery is presumed to have ceased). The trouble is that such a control group would necessarily differ from the experimental group in some ways and this might also affect the extent of the practice effect.

One way of getting round such problems is to have several experimental groups each of which is only tested once on the dependent variables but after different intervals of time. This kind of design requires a large number of fairly homogeneous subjects and this is usually only possible in animal experiments. A form of mixed design was used in a series of studies concerned with the recovery of IQ after severe head injury (Mandelberg, 1975, 1976; Mandelberg and Brooks, 1975). Head-injured subjects were tested on four possible occasions at different intervals after sustaining a severe head injury. A control group was only tested once. Within the experimental group some subjects were only tested on one occasion, others on two, etc. The authors then argued that their data could not be contaminated by practice effects because there was no correlation within the experimental group between the obtained IQ and the number of times the subjects had been previously tested. The disadvantages of this procedure are that such a correlation is a very weak way of detecting practice effects and the data would be very difficult to interpret if the correlations did turn out to be significant. In other words the design offers a possible test for the presence of practice effects and not a means of partialling them out of they are present.

It is possible to plot recovery curves for functions after cerebral insult. One way of doing this (e.g. Roberts, 1976) involves averaging data from a large number of subjects. Whilst averaging is a useful device for smoothing out the random, idiosyncratic variations that may occur in individual subjects it can also seriously mislead if used blindly. An instructive example is provided by Zeaman and House (1963) who plotted learning curves for severely mentally retarded children learning a discrimination problem. When a learning curve was plotted which averaged data across subjects in the most common and straightforward way it showed a long, slow and gradual improvement. As Zeaman and House subsequently demonstrated this picture was not typical of any individual subject. Subjects all responded randomly at first and the random responding went on for variable lengths of time. Once they started to show some learning they learned very rapidly indeed. Averaging these individual curves gave a resultant combined curve that was quite atypical of any individual unless the averaging was done in a slightly unconventional way. Similar things could happen with recovery curves. The solution is to plot curves for individuals as Newcombe *et al.* (1975) have done. If averaging is essential then individual data should be examined to see if they suggest patterns somewhat different from the average curve.

When studying recovery it is easy to concentrate on one dependent variable at a time to the exclusion of others. In practice studies tend to rely on a single measure or, where more than one measure is used, they all relate to the same general function (e.g. speech). Although this simplifies matters it may well oversimplify. For example, the pattern of recovery of a function such as memory may be affected by the presence of other impairments such as dysphasia. Unfortunately there is insufficient empirical evidence to draw any satisfactory conclusions about how different kinds of deficit might interact in recovery. This point needs to be kept in mind when evaluating reports concerned with only one variable, since lesions rarely have just one behavioural effect. It also appears unlikely on *a priori* grounds that the presence of one functional deficit would enhance the recovery of another, except possibly under rather unusual and circumscribed circumstances. On the other hand, it is quite easy to envisage ways in which one deficit might hinder the recovery of another.

A further complication relating to dependent variables has been raised by LeVere *et al.* (1979). Performance on any task may be impaired for more than one reason. The instance cited by LeVere *et al.* (1979) is that of learned brightness discriminations in rats following posterior brain lesions. This task may be adversely affected by the loss of preoperative memories, a reduction in motivation, or a failure to utilize available neural mechanisms. The extent and pattern of recovery may well differ according to which of these mechanisms underlies the deficit. This point has been largely ignored in both human and animal research.

This is by no means an exhaustive account of the methodological problems surrounding research into recovery after brain damage. What it does do is to demonstrate that this is a field which throws up a number of methodological problems in addition to those normally involved in neuropsychological research. Judged by these criteria most of the work to be described later, and especially that using human subjects, does suffer from important methodological inadequacies. This inevitably raises additional qualifications with regard to any conclusions that are drawn.

CONCLUDING COMMENTS

The rest of this book sets out to examine a number of aspects of the problem of recovery in some detail. The next three chapters consider the general pattern of recovery and the factors that influence it. In doing so findings derived from research on both man and animals will be examined. This is then followed by a discussion of the various mechanisms that have been proposed as explanations of recovery. Up to this point the emphasis is mainly on fundamental research although the prominence given to particular aspects is to some degree determined by their potential clinical relevance.

From Chapter 6 onwards the emphasis becomes much more overtly clinical. Chapter 6 is used to draw out the clinical implications of the material already covered. It also sets the scene for the following chapters which look at the recovery of a number of different neuropsychological impairments and at the various techniques that have been suggested as a means of enhancing recovery. Some attention will be given to the evaluation of these techniques although well-conducted clinical trials are generally lacking. The final chapter will then attempt to derive some general conclusions and consider how further progress might best be made. To anticipate a little, it will be argued that as far as the management of neuropsychological impairments is concerned we are very much at the stage of defining the problems and tentatively trying to develop possible solutions. Those looking for a range of well-established methods of intervention of proven clinical value, and which can confidently be used in everyday clinical practice, will be sadly disappointed. There is the promise of better things for the future but very little real fulfilment so far.

A few other comments on the general approach adopted seem called for. Since this book concentrates on recovery it could be seen as playing down the importance of the more traditional concerns of neuropsychology which are the nature of the functional impairment and the anatomical locus of the lesion. These factors are important and may well interact with the pattern of recovery. To this extent the presentation is inevitably one-sided. Nevertheless it is no more so than a book which concentrates on amnesia or the consequences of lesions to the frontal lobes but which completely ignores the fact that the observed impairments are not static but can change both in extent and quality with time. This latter form of bias is usually considered acceptable (covertly if not overtly). In practice, the functional consequences of brain damage are so complex that it becomes necessary to subdivide it into facets and just consider one of these at a time. It is therefore just as legitimate to focus on the process of recovery as to concentrate on any other facet.

A feature of some of the earlier chapters is that data from animal research are fairly closely intermingled with evidence gained from studies of human clinical material. The question arises as to what credence can be placed on findings obtained from animals when the ultimate concern is with man? It is readily conceded that it is difficult, if not impossible, to make a straightforward extrapolation of detailed neuropsychological findings from animal to man and that the relevance of animal research is limited (see Drewe *et al.*, 1970; Rosenzweig, 1980). This is unfortunate because certain kinds of investigation can be much more readily carried out using animals, and animals can also be used for experiments that would be impossible with man for ethical reasons.

For present purposes the findings of animal research are used to fill gaps where information based solely on the study of humans is unavailable, inadequate, or impossible to obtain. The kind of conclusion that is drawn from animal evidence is also restricted. It is nowhere being claimed that the detailed results obtained from experiments with animals give an exact indication as to what might be the case with man. The animal work is used to indicate general principles and possibilities. For example, reference is made in the next chapter to a report by Kimble (1976) dealing with activity levels in rats after hippocampal lesions. The fact that the recovery pattern exhibited by Kimble's rats showed some oscillation between under and overactivity is used to suggest that the smooth recovery curve that some have assumed is characteristic of recovery after brain injury in man need not always be the case. It is certainly not intended to argue that corresponding lesions in humans would similarly cause an initial decline in activity level followed by a period of hyperactivity before returning to normal. Similarly, animal evidence will be cited to the effect that recovery from damage sustained early in life is not inevitably better than that associated with comparable lesions in adulthood. If animal evidence does not always follow the widely accepted assumption of better outcome after early injury then similar qualifications might also be necessary for humans under some circumstances. No one-to-one relationship between specific behavioural deficits and particular lesions across species needs to be impaired.

In the absence of evidence to the contrary it also appears reasonable to assume that the mechanisms underlying recovery are not likely to differ drastically from species to species. If recovery is multiply determined then the extent of reliance on a particular mechanism may vary from species to species but a mechanism that is important for one species ought to be of some relevance to others. Thus a hypothetical process like diaschisis claimed to underlie recovery in man (see Chapter 5) should be demonstrable in animals. Conversely if it cannot be found in animals then its status as an explanation of recovery in man is at best highly dubious.

Having dealt with these preliminary issues attention can now be directed to the major concerns, beginning with some of the factors that are related to recovery.

CHAPTER TWO

Factors influencing recovery: the shape of the recovery curve and age

Having dealt with many of the background issues and problems in the previous chapter it is now possible to turn to one of the major questions. This is the pattern of recovery and the factors that influence it. As with other highly complex areas there are difficulties in deciding just how best to organize the material so as to get to grips with it in the most effective way. Since it is ultimately intended to lead discussion in the direction of clinical practice it is hardly inappropriate to begin by looking at the assumptions that appear to be held, either explicitly or implicitly, by many professionals who work with brain-damaged patients.

There is no single source that sets out these assumptions gleaned from such diverse groups as neurosurgeons, occupational and speech therapists, and psychologists. In fact many of them give the impression of being passed down rather more as folklore instead of being systematically organized principles underlying clinical practice. The same, or at least very similar, notions have guided animal research and it is in the animal literature that the basic notions and assumptions are most clearly set out (e.g. Finger, 1978a; LeVere *et al.*, 1979). The underlying assumptions are:

(1) There is a consistent and regular recovery curve.
(2) Given comparable lesions younger subjects will show less behavioural disruption and will display better recovery.
(3) Heavily overlearned skills are less likely to be disrupted by brain lesions and will give better recovery.
(4) Older skills will be less affected and recover more quickly than recently acquired skills.
(5) More severe lesions will have bigger effects on behaviour and result in slower and more restricted recovery.
(6) Slowly progressive lesions result in less severe deficits and give better recovery.
(7) Experience after the injury can influence recovery.
(8) Any interventions that influence the extent and rate of recovery will be more effective the closer they are applied to the time of injury.

If true many of these assumptions do have some fairly obvious implications for clinical practice even though this may be marginal in some cases. This chapter and the two that follow will explore these assumptions in some detail. It will soon become evident that most of these, if not all, can only be accepted if subject to some qualification. The simple picture that the above statements give with regard to the factors that influence recovery can be rather misleading. There are also some other possible influences that do not fall within the scope of these assumptions, and these will be dealt with later in Chapter 4.

THE RECOVERY CURVE

Some discussions have assumed that the rate of recovery shows a regular relationship with time since the injury or damage. One of the nicest demonstrations of this comes from the work of Newcombe and her associates (Newcombe *et al.*, 1974, 1976) who examined the recovery of reading in a number of cases of acquired dyslexia. Figure 1 shows the improvement over time in the number of errors made whilst reading a standard test list of 60 words in one of Newcombe *et al.*'s cases (M.B.). The data in Figure 1 are quite typical of the recovery curves from all their subjects with a single exception (G.P.) where the picture is nothing like so neat. There were complicating factors in relation to this subject in that it was later established that he had probably never been a fully

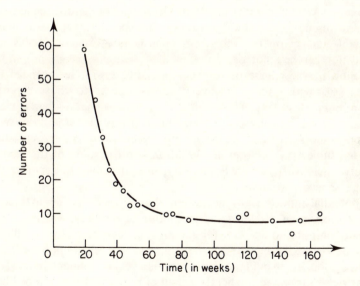

Figure 1. Errors made in reading a standard word list at different times following a left occipatal lesion (from Newcombe *et al.*, 1975. Reproduced by permission of Elsevier Biomedical Press B.V.)

competent reader and had received remedial teaching in reading at school. Unless further anomalous data appear from comparable studies of recovery after acquired dyslexia it is not necessary to regard the slightly disparate findings derived from this single subject as being other than the result of an artifact.

The one serious methodological problem which induces reservations about Newcombe *et al.*'s findings is that it was not established what role practice effects may have had on the repeated administration of the test. It is well established that a commonly used reading test in educational settings with children which similarly involves presenting a list of unrelated words to be read (the Schonell Graded Word Reading Test) does give appreciable practice effects (Curr and Gourlay, 1960). It is just conceivable, although unlikely, that all of the improvement shown by Newcombe *et al.*'s subjects could be attributable to practice effects. What is much more likely is that the degree and rate of recovery is exaggerated by such effects.

Newcombe and her associates have carried out the most elegant studies of the time course of recovery to be reported so far. There are other investigations which have also led to results consistent with the notion that recovery proceeds rapidly at first and then tails off. One of the most convincing of these is that reported by Kertesz and McCabe (1977) who examined the recovery of language in patients with aphasia of different types. Their subjects were not tested as frequently as the dyslexic patients in the reports of Newcombe and her colleagues and so similarly smooth curves could not be expected. Nevertheless the majority of Kertesz and McCabe's subjects produced the same kind of picture. Kertesz and McCabe's subjects were frequently receiving speech therapy for part of the time that they were under investigation. The impact of therapy seems negligible and in the absence of convincing evidence that speech therapy usually has any appreciable impact on recovery from aphasia (see Chapter 7) this possible complication can be ignored.

In following the course of recovery in patients with severe head injuries Roberts (1976) also found recovery curves similar to those reported by Newcombe *et al.* (1974). The qualification here is that Roberts was more concerned with physical recovery, and his recovery curves are derived from averaged data which could then mask very different recovery curves produced by individual subjects. Bricolo *et al.* (1980), in another study of the recovery of physical capacities after severe head injury, give further weak support to the idea of a regular recovery curve.

The potential importance of the shape of the recovery curve lies in three things. Firstly it specifies in greater detail the nature of recovery, which is what any theories attempting to account for the phenomenon of recovery will have to explain. Secondly, if a regular recovery curve can be relied upon for individual cases (as demonstrated in Figure 1) then this is a very convenient finding from the point of view of trying to predict the extent of recovery that might be likely in a given case. Two independent measures of the relevant variable taken at different times could allow the rate, and possibly the extent, of recovery to be predicted. Finally, the presence of a well-defined recovery curve should assist in establishing a baseline against which attempts to influence recovery can be judged. Assessing the effects of intervention is a major problem, and this could be done either by looking for changes in the recovery curve or by using the established curve to estimate that point in time after which no further spontaneous recovery should occur. An intervention resulting in significant changes after this time could then be assumed to be effective.

Unfortunately the data do not exist to allow any reasonable judgement of just how typical the kind of recovery curve published by Newcombe *et al.* (1975, 1976) really is. Extensive investigations would be required to look at all the possible functions that might be subjected to spontaneous recovery following impairment and the different sorts of damage that might produce these impairments. Only a tiny sample of the possible recovery situations has been examined so far. Despite this there is evidence that this simple picture of the recovery curve may not be universally applicable. For example, long-term follow-up studies of some of the earlier series of patients subjected to psychosurgical procedures in the frontal lobes for the relief of psychiatric disorder have shown complications. The depression in intelligence test scores and related measures that was present shortly after surgery had recovered by a year later (e.g. Mettler, 1952; Petrie, 1949). When examined 7–14 years later those subjects who could be traced had shown a further long-term deterioration (Hamlin, 1970; Smith, 1960, 1964). In such circumstances the early recovery may have shown the kind of curve described by Newcombe *et al.* (1975, 1976) and the deviation from this may only be in relation to long-term outcome. It is also possible that this long-term decline might be attributable to other factors. Most of the subjects who could be traced and tested after the long-term follow-up intervals were still resident in institutions. The further decline might be a product of institutionalization or, if the subjects were schizophrenic, to the intellectual decline that can apparently occur in chronic schozophrenia (Miller, 1983).

The long-term follow-up study reported by Blakemore and Falconer (1967) is possibly of greater interest. These authors were concerned with subjects who had undergone anterior temporal lobectomy for the relief of epileptic fits. Left-sided cases with post-operative verbal learning and memory impairments, showed little or no change after a year. Several years after the operation these subjects were found to have some improvement on the tests used. There is no question here of the pattern of recovery showing much correspondence to the curve depicted in Figure 1. Corkin (1979) presents some data which imply that the recovery curve may well vary with age. This is possibly due to an artifact but the study will be discussed in greater detail in the next section.

There have been very few studies in animals which would allow the generation of recovery curves in a comparable way. Nevertheless there are some findings of interest. Finger *et al.* (1982) got a picture very similar to that of Blakemore and Falconer (1967) in that rats with lesions of the sensorimotor cortex did uniformly badly in learning tactile discriminations for weeks and months after the operation. Delayed improvement then became evident 1–2 years afterwards.

Kimble (1976) studied activity levels in rats after hippocampal lesions using the open field test. Activity was reduced immediately after surgery but had returned to normal levels within 3–4 days. Following this there was a longer swing in the direction of overactivity before activity levels finally returned to pre-operative levels on a permanent basis. The significance of the findings of this experiment for recovery in humans is obscure. What it does show is a more complex pattern of recovery than that encountered in the work discussed so far, and it further cautions against the uncritical acceptance of the idea of a regular and invariant recovery curve following brain damage.

It would be convenient if regular curves like that for the recovery of acquired dyslexia, and shown in Figure 1, were the general rule. So far there are inadequate data on which to base a reasonable judgement as to the reliability of this regular curve. On *a priori* grounds it is not unreasonable to expect that the shape of the recovery curve may be influenced by the nature of the impairment in which recovery is taking place and the measure of recovery that is used. It may be that simpler measures which largely reflect a single impaired function (especially in the sense of functions as means) will be more likely to reveal the regular curve. More complex measures that are determined by a number of cerebral functions may show less regular curves because the different functions that are impaired may recover to differing degrees and at differing rates.

AGE AND RECOVERY

It is generally considered that, given comparable lesions, the young will recover more quickly and show less severe impairments than the old. It is also a very common clinical observation that left hemisphere lesions that would be expected to be followed by severe and permanent aphasic difficulties in an adult may be consistent with normal, or near-normal, speech development when produced congenitally or in very young children. It is worth noting in passing that this apparent capacity for adaptation found in very young brains is somewhat paradoxical when viewed against another type of influence on brain development. Malnutrition has a particularly deleterious effect on brain development and later functioning when experienced in early life (e.g. Dobbing, 1974). The resolution of what seems like a paradox could lie in the fact that the period of greatest physical development of the brain in humans occurs shortly after birth. It is not inconceivable that this period of rapid development should confer both an enhanced capacity to adapt to certain types of adverse influence and a greater susceptibility to the effects of others.

When considered initially the idea of comparing young and old (i.e. mature in this context) with respect to the effects of brain injury appears relatively straightforward. Unfortunately this is not so and a little further thought reveals a number of methodological pitfalls. In human patients it is difficult to be sure that truly comparable damage has occurred in both young and older subjects, and this is the most obvious precondition for looking at the effects of age on recovery. In fact lack of such comparability is an important contaminating factor which can effect the interpretation placed upon the results of evidence from human subjects

(St James-Roberts, 1981). Since the types of pathology found in the brains of children and adults show quite considerable differences it means that groups of young and adult subjects with well-matched lesions are almost impossible to find. This particular problem would not necessarily be too serious on its own since it can be more nearly overcome in experimental work with animals. However the situation is further complicated by other methodological difficulties which are equally applicable to humans and animals.

As Johnson and Albi (1978) point out, a number of other contaminating factors need to be taken into account when comparing the effects of lesions at different ages. These boil down to the fundamental point that young and old subjects are going to differ with respect to a number of other variables besides age. For example, the pre-existing experience and behavioural repertoires of young and old subjects will not be the same. The very young child who develops fairly normal language in the presence of a large left hemisphere lesion has either not yet learned, or only just started to learn, to speak immediately prior to the injury. The adult sustains a similar lesion against the background of a well-developed and elaborated language system. The different behavioural repertoires may act to help or hinder recovery. To follow the example of aphasia a little further it might be argued that a well-developed background of language usage and language-related activities might help recovery in the adult. On the other hand, the adult may also have more extensively developed communication systems of a non-verbal type (e.g. the use of gestures). When the main or verbal communication system is disrupted the adult may then be more drawn to switching to means of communication other than speech, if these remain relatively intact.

Another factor of potential importance is that the brains of young and adult subjects can differ in ways other than their capacity to adapt to the effects of lesions. A good example of this is provided by the work of Goldman and her associates on the effects of frontal lesions in monkeys of different ages (e.g. Goldman, 1974). This work will be discussed more fully later. The point of interest at this juncture is that these investigations indicate that the neural mechanisms underlying the behaviour of interest are not always the same in the young animal as in its more mature counterpart. This again makes the question of the relative rates of recovery rather difficult to disentangle.

From a purely clinical point of view it can be argued that it is sufficient to know for some purposes that, say, a 15-year-old with a particular type and severity of memory disorder following a severe head injury will recover much more completely than a 55-year-old with a similar head injury and memory impairment. Whether or not this difference really reflects greater powers of adaptation and recovery in the younger person, or is the result of some artifact of the kind mentioned above, is purely academic if the concern is solely with predicting outcome. If it is desired to go beyond this and try to understand the mechanisms responsible for greater improvement in the younger patient then it becomes necessary to take the possible complicating factors into account. It could also prove to be the case that understanding what is going on will give the best chance to influence recovery to the benefit of those who are afflicted with neuropsychological impairments.

The classical studies of the effect of age on recovery are those of Margaret Kennard (1936, 1940, 1942). This has led to the general notion of better recovery in younger subjects being referred to in some quarters as the 'Kennard principle' (e.g. Schneider, 1979). In her experments Kennard looked at the effect of extirpation of motor cortex in infant and adult monkeys on motor functioning. She concluded from a number of different experiments that damage in early life did not produce the same drastic effects as similar lesions inflicted on adult monkeys. Similar findings have been obtained in other animal laboratories. They involve lesions in other parts of the brain as well as other psychological processes such as roughness discrimination (e.g. Benjamin and Thompson, 1959). The general finding can then be claimed to have some generality across different types of lesion and forms of behaviour.

In humans there is also quite an array of evidence that could be interpreted as being consistent with the Kennard principle. In fact Kennard herself (Kennard, 1940) reviewed the then available literature on motor impairments following both early and later brain damage in human patients and concluded that, for the most part, it fitted in very well with what might have been expected from her interpretation of the animal experiments. Other human examples that could be cited include outcome data on those who have suffered severe head injuries and the work on 'split brain' subjects, as well as the effects of left hemisphere lesions on language.

The question of left hemisphere lesions in relation to age will be examined in greater detail in a later section. In the case of head injury many of the studies of long-term outcome reviewed by Miller (1979a) give indications of better recovery in younger subjects. In most the comparison is between younger and older adults but one of the reports did suggest very much better recovery in children (Carlsson et al., 1968). With regard to 'split brain' subjects, adults who have had the corpus callosum sectioned (for the relief of certain forms of epilepsy) show a number of impairments when specialized testing techniques are used. These often make use of the very brief tachistoscopic presentation of visual stimuli to either the right or left visual fields. These impairments can be related to the disruption of the subject's ability to transfer information from one cerebral hemisphere to the other (e.g. Sperry, 1968). In contrast, subjects with the congenital abnormality of agenesis of the corpus callosum may show some subtle impairments but certainly do not demonstrate the clear-cut disconnection phenomena that can be readily found in adult patients with a sectioned corpus callosum (Ettlinger et al., 1972; Gott and Saul, 1978). One possible explanation that could be advanced is that agenesis of the corpus callosum is often not complete. This might be a partial explanation of why agenesis patients fail to show the 'split brain' effects associated with the adult surgical cases but it is far from being convincing as the whole explanation.

Further studies relating to the effects of early as opposed to later brain lesions in humans are reviewed by Chelune and Edwards (1981). These do not really advance the argument much further and objections can be raised to all the human evidence along the lines indicated in the methodological discussion earlier in this section. The basic problem is of course that it is extremely difficult to find situations involving human patients in which age is the only variable that might plausibly be considered to be determining the differences in outcome. For example, in comparing agenesis of the corpus callosum with surgical sectioning of the same structure it must be remembered that there are other anatomical abnormalities present which differentiate between the two classes of subject. Despite the name, agenesis of the corpus callosum is not the only way in which the brains of such patients differ from the normal (Loeser and Alvord, 1968a,b). Similarly the surgical cases are epileptics and this implies that there is something wrong with the brain to produce the epilepsy in the first case. With the head injuries, where quite pronounced age effects have been found in relation to long-term outcome, the dependent variable is typically some measure of occupational and/or social readjustment (see Miller, 1979a). Measures of this kind can easily be contaminated by external factors. It is possible that an employer may consider it more worthwhile to persevere with a younger worker who has suffered a head injury than with an older individual who has suffered comparable impairments. Finally, St James-Roberts (1981) has shown that in a number of studies comparing younger and older subjects with brain lesions there are appreciable differences in the underlying pathology. The older subjects contain a higher proportion with progressive as opposed to static pathology and this could artifically inflate any beneficial effect of youth.

Even if we return to Kennard's originl work with monkeys Teuber (1974) has pointed out that there are strong hints in her reports that the picture might not be quite as simple as she implied. This is especially true of some of her comments relating to longer-term observations on some of her animals operated on in infancy. The crucial point that emerges at this stage is that, despite its rather obvious attractiveness, it is difficult to find compelling proof of the Kennard principle. A more detailed examination is therefore called for.

A more detailed analysis—animal research

The relationship between age and the consequences of brain injury turns out to be nothing like as simple as the Kennard principle would suggest. In fact the closer the problem is examined the more complicated the relationship appears. Work with animals has started to unravel some of the complexities and two major lines of research using animal subjects will now be described. These are, firstly, the work of Goldman and her associates who have examined the effects of age on the consequences of frontal lesions in monkeys. Secondly, Schneider and his colleagues have reported an interesting and significant set of experiments on the visual system in hamsters following lesions at different ages. These two sets of work by no means exhaust the potentially relevant animal literature and a more extensive review is provided by Johnson and Albi (1978). As a preliminary point it can be noted that at least one example exists in the literature where older rats showed less behavioural disruption following frontal lesions than young adults (Stein and Firl, 1976).

What the work to be described does manage to bring out is a number of important variables that may well need to be taken into account in any comprehensive description of the relationship between age and recovery in any species, including man. Once these selected areas of research on animals have been dealt with the discussion will then return to the more detailed investigations of age effects in man.

It is very well established that a number of behavioural disturbances can follow lesions within the frontal lobes of adult monkeys, especially the dorsolateral aspects (see Miller, 1972; Warren and Akert, 1964). The behavioural impairments reported include a disruption in performance on tasks such as 'delayed response' and 'delayed alternation'. A feature of such tasks is that some time before the crucial response is called for there is a cue of some kind which indicates what the correct response is. The exact nature of the impairment underlying the performance breakdown has not yet been clearly established but the obvious possibility of a disruption in memory has been ruled out, largely on the basis that frontal monkeys generally do well on a range of other tasks which clearly involve memory (e.g. Miller, 1972). It has also been shown that there is a marked age effect in the relationship between disturbances on these tasks and the appropriate frontal lesions (Harlow *et al.*, 1968). Goldman has then taken this work much further, and convenient reviews of her work can be found in Goldman (1974) and Goldman and Lewis (1978).

Goldman *et al.* (1970) placed dorsolateral lesions in the prefrontal cortex of monkeys and confirmed that for infant subjects this did not result in the disruption of delayed response that is so readily demonstrable in adults. However, complete frontal ablations did produce the impairment even in infants. In pursuing this it was found that prefrontal lobectomy in infants spares performance on one commonly affected task (conditional positional responses) but not on another (object reversal). Both types of deficit occur in adults with similar lesions. Thus it can already be seen that even with lesions in the same part of the brain the operation of the Kennard principle is dependent upon the size and/or exact location of the lesion and the specific nature of the task involved.

Further data imply even more serious qualifications to the Kennard principle. In the case of unoperated subjects young animals can carry out delayed response tasks but not with the same efficiency as more mature animals (over 2 years old). Dorsolateral frontal lesions only disrupt delayed response performance in the older subjects but Goldman (1971) showed that the subjects operated on in infancy did have some impairment when they reached 2 years of age. The performance of these younger subjects did not deteriorate with age; it was just that after undergoing the operation in infancy they failed to show the improvement with maturation that occurs in unoperated controls. The most obvious hypothesis to be drawn from this is that the dorsolateral frontal cortex does not mature until the monkey is about 2 years old and therefore cannot mediate performance on delayed response and related tasks until that age is reached.

The findings in the previous paragraph, and the interpretations placed upon them, prompt the further question as to what mediates performance on the relevant tasks before the age of 2 years. It was suggested on the basis of anatomical and other information that the caudate nucleus (or parts of it) might fulfil this role. Goldman and Rosvold (1972) then showed that caudate lesions in very young monkeys produced behavioural impairments when the subjects were about a year old which were as severe as those found following prefrontal lesions in adults of over 2 years of age. It also appears that at 1 year of age bilateral caudate lesions can cause greater deficits than cortical lesions, but the reverse is true when the animal has exceeded the age of 2 years.

Another experiment by Goldman's group (E. A. Miller *et al.*, 1973) looked at the effects of orbital prefrontal lesions on delayed alternation performance. Such lesions in infancy revealed the same deficits as those associated with subjects operated upon as adults once the group receiving the lesions in infancy had reached the age of a year. When tested after a further year this infant-operated group demonstrated considerable recovery. This raises the speculation that the dorsolateral frontal cortex, or another late-maturing part of the brain, might be able to mediate the recovery of this initially profound and fairly long-standing deficit following orbital lesions in infant monkeys.

Goldman's group has also been interested in the effects that experience may have upon recovery after early frontal lesions in experimental animals (see Goldman and Lewis, 1978). Evaluation of this work will be deferred until a later chapter, where the impact of experience on recovery in general will be discussed.

In discussing her work Goldman (1974) draws out some general conclusions. One of these is that age is a relevant variable, not only with respect to the time of the operation but also with regard to the time of testing. To this it might be added that the locus and extent of the lesion and the type of behavioural test used are also important. In other words, as in many other aspects of psychology, the findings obtained can be influenced by changes in any aspect of the experiment. Goldman also appeals to the concept of 'functional maturity'. The notion behind this concept is that during the early stages of development not all structures within the brain may be fully mature in the sense that they can carry out the functions required of them in the fully developed adult. Different structures may gain functional maturity at different ages. Thus Goldman postulates that the caudate nucleus in the rhesus monkey is functionally mature before 1 year of age. As the monkey gets older so the dorsolateral prefrontal cortex matures and becomes more and more involved in mediating such things as delayed response performance which was originally dependent upon the caudate nucleus.

This concept of functional maturity can then be used to explain most of the findings described above. In the infant monkey dorsolateral lesions of the prefrontal cortex should not disrupt those aspects of behaviour commonly affected by such lesions in adults. This is because dorsolateral tissue is not yet mature enough to have taken over its adult roles. As the operated subject matures so a gap in performance between operated and unoperated subjects should emerge. In the younger subjects caudate lesions should produce the deficit. These findings did emerge in the experiments that were described above. In the case of studies of the effects of orbitofrontal lesions it may be that the infant-operated subjects are able to show recovery at around 2 years because the maturing dorsolateral cortex becomes capable of taking over the same role. There should then be no recovery from the deficits associated with orbitofrontal lesions if the operation occurs after the dorsolateral cortex has reached functional maturity since the role of the latter will already have been determined.

The idea that different parts of the brain may not all mature at the same rate could well be useful in explaining other age effects. This is illustrated by the work of Schneider and his colleagues who have looked in detail, and from a more anatomical point of view, at the mechanisms underlying the effects of age on recovery. This involves a long and complicated series of experments on the visual system of Syrian hamsters. In this account it would not be appropriate to give a detailed description of all the stages in an intricate argument, especially with regard to the anatomical details. Fortunately Schneider (1979) has provided a meticulous review of this work and this is recommended to the reader who wishes to see a more rigorous statement.

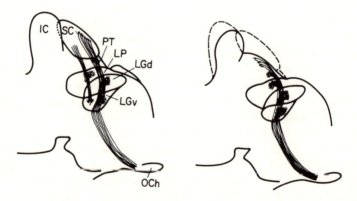

Figure 2. Diagrammatic representation of rostral brainstem of an adult hamster showing axons of the optic tract and tectothalamic pathway. Normal animal is on the left, with similar view after undergoing destruction of superficial layers of the superior colliculus on the day of birth on the right. IC is inferior colliculus; LGd, dorsal nucleus of the lateral geniculate body; LGv, ventral nucleus of the lateral geniculate body; LP, nucleus lateralis posterior; OCh, optic chiasm; PT, pretectal area; and SC, superior colliculus (from Sweet *et al.*, 1977)

At birth most of the terminal projections of the optic tract have yet to be formed in the hamster. Figure 2 shows a diagrammatic representation of these tracts in the normal adult hamster and in an animal that has suffered a lesion in the superficial layers of the superior colliculus (SC) shortly after birth. It can readily be seen that the operated subject shows appreciable differences when compared with the normal control. Amongst other things the operated subject has an abnormally dense terminal projection in the ventral nucleus of the lateral geniculate body (LGv) and, unlike the normal hamster, there is a prominent cluster of terminations in the posterior part of the lateral nucleus (LP). The projection from the superior colliculus to the lateral nucleus is also lost after surgery.

If the early lesion is made unilaterally the abnormal projections described above develop on the same side as the lesion. In addition there is another abnormality. The axons that reach the area of early tectal damage recross the midline and terminate within the superficial grey layer of the unoperated colliculus. It has been suggested that the retinofugal axons compete to occupy the tectal terminal space that remains (Schneider, 1973). It has also proved possible to demonstrate an age effect in the number of axons recrossing. If the right superior colliculus lesion is made at birth, and the right eye is enucleated at different ages, then the extent of the recrossed projection declines with increasing age at the time of enucleation.

In the present context it is, of course, the behavioural correlates of these lesions that are of most interest. The response that Schneider and his colleagues have studied in detail is that of head-turning in response to the visual presentation of food-related stimuli (sunflower seeds) in the left or right visual fields. This response is lost after lesions in the superior colliculus in adult animals but complete bilateral ablation of the superior collicular layers in newborn subjects gives considerable sparing of this response (Schneider, 1970). If the early lesions are unilateral there is some sparing when stimuli are presented to the affected visual field (Schneider, 1973). So far these results could be considered to be manifestations of the Kennard principle. Schneider (1979) argues that the sparing is made possible by anomalous connections to the deeper layers of the colliculus which are left intact by the lesion.

Further findings with unilateral lesions are less clear-cut. If the early lesion in the superficial layers of the superior colliculus is confined to the right side of the brain and the right eye is enucleated then the presentation of food to the left visual field will result in the head turning to the left (the normal response) on most occasions. From time to time head-turning in the 'wrong' direction (i.e. to the right) can also be elicited (Schneider, 1977). In such cases it has already been explained that the left eye develops connections through an abnormal midbrain decussation with the left superior colliculus as well as those with the remaining deeper layers of the same structure on the right side. Schneider (1979) describes how in two animals these wrong responses were nearly or totally abolished by cutting the anomalous decussation after the animals had reached maturity. This implies that turning in the wrong direction is mediated by the anomalous retinal projections which recross to the ipsilateral side of the brain in animals undergoing unilateral operations in infancy.

Schneider (1979) gives some preliminary accounts of further investigations. In the case of subjects showing turning in the wrong direction in response to peripheral visual stimulation it is possible to further reduce their tendency to turn to the appropriate side by operating yet again to produce more extensive undercutting of the superior colliculus on the side of the original operation. Of more direct psychological relevance is the apparent demonstration that the direction of turning can be affected by reinforcement contingencies. Failure to reward turning in either the appropriate or inappropriate directions can lead to the extinction of turning towards the non-reinforced side.

When the animal research is considered as a whole a number of general conclusions are suggested. In the absence of better evidence it seems reasonable to expect that these conclusions might generalize to humans. The most fundamental of these is that the Kennard principle, which suggests that the earlier the lesion the better the outcome, needs some considerable qualification. Some data do fit the Kennard principle quite well but other findings deviate from it. There are also some experimental results which are almost impossible to reconcile with the Kennard principle. A number of factors seem to be important in determining the exact relationship between age and outcome. These include the locus and extent of the lesion as well as the particular measure of performance that is used. Time is also important and not just only in terms of the age of the subject at the time that the lesion was acquired. The age of the subject at the time of testing can also be of significance since long follow-up periods may give a picture that is different from that derived by using shorter periods.

A more detailed analysis—human evidence

Human subjects obviously cannot be studied experimentally in the kinds of way that are possible by using monkeys and hamsters as outlined in the previous section. Because of this less clear-cut conclusions can be expected. Despite this it is still possible to examine the effect of age on outcome after brain damage in human patients in greater detail and with much more rigour than has been described so far. The phenomenon subjected to the closest analysis has been that of language impairments following early damage to the left hemisphere. It is widely agreed that younger subjects show much less severe and long-lasting language impairments than those who are older (Basser, 1962; Lenneberg, 1967). This is especially so if the lesion occurs very early in life where the common belief is that it may be impossible to detect any long-term effects on language at all.

Earlier writers on this topic, such as Basser (1962) and Lenneberg (1967) have suggested some more specific conclusions about the effects of brain lesions in children on later language. Any language impairments were considered to be of short duration and to show complete recovery if the damage occurred before a certain age threshold. Where they did occur these language impairments would most probably be expressive in nature. They are also rather more likely to be encountered in cases with right hemisphere lesions than would be typical in adults.

Woods and Teuber (1978) presented data derived from 64 cases of childhood aphasia that they had been able to study personally. They also considered the published information relating to several hundred other cases. This careful investigation results in Woods and Teuber reaching conclusions that modified or even contradicted the views that had been held previously. They disputed the notion that aphasic disorders in childhood were commonly expressive in nature, and drew attention to cases with apparent jargon dysphasia. Recovery in aphasic children, and even in those that were quite young, was not always as rapid as had been supposed. They also called into question the previously expressed belief that aphasia was rather more likely to result from right hemisphere lesions in children than was the case in adults.

The one common idea relating to childhood aphasia that was not challenged in any way by Woods and Teuber (1978) is that of an age threshold below which complete recovery can be expected. In their study no child sustaining a lesion prior to attaining the age of 8 years was considered to be clinically aphasic. Nevertheless, as Woods and Carey (1979) have argued, failure to refute the age threshold notion does not guarantee that it is correct. In particular the assumption of an age threshold raises two sources of difficulty. The first lies in the wide range of estimates for the threshold which vary from as early as 5 years to as late as the onset of adolescence. Secondly, the failure to demonstrate features of clinical aphasia in subjects who have suffered early brain lesions is not the same as showing that their verbal capabilities are identical with normal subjects. In other words, some verbal peculiarities may remain but not be of the type classically associated with aphasia.

With regard to the second point, Dennis and Whitaker (1976) described three subjects who had undergone surgical removal of one hemisphere within the first few weeks after birth. In the two with left hemisphere removals speech as assessed around 10 years of age appeared quite normal with regard to phonemic or semantic aspects. However there did appear to be some impairment of syntactical competence. This study is limited by the small number of subjects but is interesting in that it suggests that very early left hemisphere damage may leave some fairly subtle but permanent effects on language functioning.

Woods and Carey (1979) reported a more extensive investigation based on the detailed analysis of 27 subjects who had sustained early left hemisphere lesions and who were examined 10 or more years after the injury. The total subject group was split into those who had sustained the lesion before they were a year old and those who had suffered left hemisphere damage at a rather later age (at a mean of around 6 years). In addition to a clinical examination of language and related functions an intelligence test and special tests of language functioning were administered. The clinical examination revealed dysphasia in only two subjects and both of these were in the group with later lesions. As compared to normal control subjects, the early lesion group were significantly impaired on only one of the eight special language tests which dealt with spelling. The later injury group showed deficits on six of these tests which included sentence completion, picture naming and the Token test. Woods and Carey are of the opinion that left hemisphere lesions after the age of 1 year may leave some demonstrable language impairment. They further argue that it may not be sensible to think in terms of any particular age threshold after which full recovery fails to occur.

Whilst the results of Woods and Carey's (1979) investigation, and the conclusions that they draw from them, do not appear to be at all unreasonable the way that their investigation was carried out raises methodological difficulties. There was no attempt to match the subjects with childhood lesions and those normal subjects used as controls on the language tests on a number of potentially relevant variables. The indications are that the experimental subjects were possibly of lower general intellectual level. It could thus be queried whether the poorer language performance of the experimental group was merely a reflection of their lower IQs. Slightly against this possibility, and in favour of Woods and Carey's interpretation, is the fact that the very early lesion group with their minimal language impairment, showed a similar mean verbal IQ to the later lesion group despite the latter's more positive signs of impairment.

Another finding of some possible relevance was reported by Netley (1972) and derived from an experiment using a task that bears some relationship to language. Netley studied a number of subjects who had suffered very early brain damage prior to the age of 1 year and who later underwent hemispherectomy of the affected side. The subjects were then tested at around 10 years of age on a dichotic listening task whereby two different short strings of digits are presented simultaneously to each ear through specially adapted earphones. Those subjects who had suffered their original brain damage in early infancy showed an impairment in recalling the digits presented to the ear contralateral to the hemisphere that was removed. This was not the case in those whose initial hemispheric damage was congenital. Dichotic listening performance is open to interpretation in a number of ways. Regardless of what is the detailed mechanism underlying the contralateral ear effect there is still the suggestion that long-term changes can result from very early brain damage.

There are thus reasons to doubt whether the sparing of language and related functions is ever complete even after very early damage to the appropriate parts of the brain. There are also some other previously expressed conclusions concerning the effects of early brain lesions on language for which more detailed evidence is not yet available. It could be that these will also need to be considerably modified. Despite this there is still no doubt that the extent of recovery and further development of language after left hemisphere lesions in children is certainly impressive when considered against the severe and long-lasting aphasic disturbances that can follow similar lesions in adults. Two further questions now arise. How is it that such extensive sparing or recovery is possible and are there any consequences for non-language functions?

Any discussion of the mechanisms underlying sparing will involve appreciable overlap with explanations of recovery. It is the general intention to leave the presentation and evaluation of the various theories of recovery until Chapter 5. The present comments on the possible mechanisms underlying sparing will therefore be brief and will not pre-empt the later general and more detailed discussion of theories of recovery. However, it does assist the flow of the argument to introduce a small incursion into mechanisms of sparing at this point.

The usual explanation offered for sparing in young children is that the plasticity of the brain, which is at its greatest level during the early stages of development, permits other parts of the brain to take over functions that would otherwise have been subserved by the damaged structures. This interprtation is particularly reinforced by reports of the use of the Wada technique for establishing speech lateralization (Milner, 1974b; Milner *et al.*, 1966). Sodium amytal is injected into the carotid arteries with each side being done separately. Loss of speech immediately following left-sided injection but not immediately after injection on the other side would indicate left hemisphere dominance for speech. In the reports of Milner and her colleagues left-handed or ambidextrous subjects without early brain damage are left hemisphere dominant for speech in 69 per cent of cases. Of the rest 18 per cent are right dominant whilst the rest have bilateral representation of speech. Subjects known to have early left hemisphere damage show different results with only 35 per cent having speech represented in the left hemisphere as opposed to 54 per cent on the right (the rest again having bilateral speech representation). These differences in the proportions having right hemisphere representation are highly significant and strongly suggest that in many cases with early left hemisphere damage there is a transfer of speech to the other side of the brain.

One caveat may need to be entered. It is also possible that the extent to which younger subjects show better recovery may be exaggerated and therefore the degree of extra recovery or sparing that has to be explained may be less than is often imagined. St James-Roberts (1981) has looked at the kinds of pathology that occur at different ages and finds that progressive lesions, such as neoplasms, tend to be more common in samples of older subjects. Because most brain tumours are malignant and recur, cases with neoplastic pathology would show poorer recovery for this reason.

If speech is transferred to the right hemisphere in cases of early damage to the left side of the brain this raises further problems. Either there is surplus capacity within the right hemisphere which can be used to support the development of language or the other functions, which would normally have been the prerogative of the right hemisphere, must suffer in some way. On *a priori* grounds it could be considered unlikely that the normal brain contains large amounts of redundant tissue just waiting to be brought into use should damage occur in other parts of the brain. This is a hypothesis that could only be seriously entertained in the absence of credible alternatives. Milner (1974a,b) has suggested that her data from examination of subjects with early brain damage indicate that the transfer of speech to the right hemisphere only occurs at the expense of a reduced development of other cognitive functions. These other functions are those usually associated with the right hemisphere. Other authorities can be cited in support of this view (e.g. Basser, 1962; Teuber, 1974). That reorganization within the brain is only bought at the price of impairments in other functions is also argued by Jeeves (1981) on the basis of a careful analysis of the effects of total agenesis of the corpus callosum as opposed to later sectioning of this structure.

Goldman's (1974) concept of functional maturity, as discussed in a previous section, might also apply here. Possibly the visuospatial and other functions that are usually associated with the right hemisphere develop later than speech. Thus early in life the right hemisphere is free to take over speech at the expense of a reduced capacity to take on the more typical right hemisphere functions later. Given an initially intact brain then the longer the time that visuospatial and related functions have to become established in the right hemisphere the less that hemisphere is able to take over speech after left hemisphere damage. In consequence the language impairments resulting from left hemisphere damage become more and more permanent as age at injury increases.

Aspects of behaviour other than speech and language have not been so closely studied with regard to the influence of age on recovery. If the evidence on language can be generalized to other functions it would be expected that recovery from early lesions could be impressive but might not be either as rapid or complete as some have imagined. Furthermore this relatively good early recovery would be bought at the price of mildly deleterious effects on the development of other functions. Again, if Goldman's concept of functional maturity holds then the relative order in which the different functions develop would affect their potential rate of recovery. Functions normally developing later would be expected to show the most extensive and permanent deficits. The evidence from animal research also suggests that a mild degree of impairment shortly following an early lesion could possibly be followed by a more serious deficit at maturity.

Woods and Tueber (1978) looked at mirror movements. These can occur in children but are rather rare in adults. They involve a tendency to move one side of the body in a corresponding way in association with voluntary movements of the same parts of the other side. They are usually more apparent in movements of the distal portions of the upper limb. For example, tapping with the index finger of one hand will induce similar, if attenuated, tapping movements in the index finger of the other hand. Mirror movements can occur in hemiparetics, and Woods and Teuber (1978) state their impression that they are more common in adults who suffered from infantile hemiplegia than in those who became hemiplegic as adults. They then studied subjects who had suffered unilateral brain damage in childhood. In the subgroup that had sustained the lesion prior to being 1 year old there was greater evidence of mirror movements than in those who were injured later (at an average age of around 6 years). As far as this single and, it must be admitted, relatively insignificant form of maladaptive behaviour is concerned there is evidence that very early lesions can give a less satisfactory outcome than those sustained later.

Even within the adult age range there is reason to claim that young adults may have a better outcome given similar degrees of brain injury. A number of studies of long-term outcome after severe head injury reviewed by Humphrey and Oddy (1980) and Miller (1979a) have shown this. Particularly clear examples are Carlsson et al. (1968) and Heiskanen and Sipponen (1970). A major qualification in interpreting these clinical investigations is that the measures of outcome used may well have been contaminated by other factors. The measures of outcome were based on such things as return to work and social readjustment. It could be that employers, family members, and social acquaintances may have a greater tolerance for changed behaviour in younger subjects and this might be at least a partial explanation of the age effect.

Such problems have been ruled out in Corkin's (1979) investigation of the effects of bilateral cingulotomy on the ability to detect hidden figures using Thurstone's (1944) test. In general, subjects showed a transient impairment with later recovery. When subjects less than 30 years old at the time of the operation were compared with those who were older, it was found that the latter showed a much bigger deficit. This is in accordance with the notion that age can be an influential factor in determining the consequences of brain damage even within the adult age range. (In fact Corkin interpreted her results as showing that subjects under 30 years of age had no impairment at all because they had mean gain in raw score of only 3.7 after the operation. Since normal control subjects show an average gain of 7.4 on retesting, presumably due to practice effects, it could be that the under-30s suffered a small deficit which wiped out some of the expected gain in score that occurs solely as a result of previous exposure to the test.)

Not all investigations yield this age effect with adult subjects. Sarno (1980) looked at the recovery from aphasia in patients receiving speech therapy and who had become aphasic at ages varying from middle age upwards. Although the age range involved was appreciable it did not exert a significant effect on outcome. Amongst other things this study challenges the practices of those speech therapists who are reluctant to treat aphasic patients over a certain age because they believe that the outcome is poor compared to younger subjects. It could also be suggested that since Sarno's (1980) subjects were treated this might distort the relationship between age and recovery. In the absence of convincing evidence as to the effectiveness of most forms of aphasia therapy (see Chapter 7) this point loses most of its potency.

It is difficult to summarize what is known about the relationship between age at injury and recovery succinctly. What is clear is that the relationship is certainly much more complex than the simple statement that early lesions give smaller deficits with faster and more complete recovery. As a rough-and-ready rule of thumb this notion may be of some validity in a number of situations. There are important exceptions and a number of other factors are likely to interact with the effect of age on recovery. These include such things as the nature of the particular function involved and the state of development of the brain as it relates to that particular function. It is also likely to be the case that whatever happens to the person after the injury will influence the effect of age on recovery.

CHAPTER THREE

Factors influencing recovery: extent of the lesion, degree of overlearning, and time since acquisition of the skill

The conventional view, as well as any *a priori* expectations, would suggest that the more extensive the lesion the greater the resultant deficit and the less complete any recovery is likely to be. It has also been suggested that more heavily overlearned skills are better preserved after brain damage. When they are impaired they will show more rapid recovery. Skills acquired shortly before the lesion are usually considered more vulnerable to disruption and less susceptible to recovery than those acquired some considerable time beforehand. This last relationship is sometimes referred to as Ribot's law. Ribot (1883) posited this after gaining the general impression that more recently acquired information was more susceptible to the effects of amnesia-inducing agents.

The greater disruption of skills that have had less opportunity to become overlearned has appeared in discussions of aphasia under the title of Pitres' rule (Pitres, 1895). According to Pitres polyglot aphasics are likely to show the greatest recovery in the language that they had used most, regardless of whether it was the one that had been learned first.

Again these generalizations seem to be reasonable enough. As the discussion of age effects in relation to recovery in the previous chapter demonstrated, such simple and straightforward rules usually turn out to require at least some qualification when examined more closely. In fact laws like those associated with Robot and Pitres are based on general clinical impressions rather than systematically collected data. In the words of Hecaen and Albert (1978) they 'have been honoured as much by being broken as by being followed'.

One complication is immediately apparent. The degree to which a skill or piece of information has been overlearned, and the length of time elapsed from its acquisition to the occurrence of the brain damage, may represent logically distinct variables. In practice they are likely to be highly contaminated. Skills acquired some considerable time ago are likely to have had a much greater opportunity for practice than those acquired more recently. In the case of human patients skills and information of real practical importance will be likely to have been acquired early and been subject to frequent use. Thus time since acquisition and degree of overlearning will be very difficult to disentangle. In the context of research using experimental animals it is possible to devise investigations that can look at these variables independently but research workers have generally not attempted to manipulate both variables in the same experiment. It will also be seen in the next section that the severity of cerebral insult is far from being a simple variable.

SEVERITY OF INSULT

In order to relate severity to the size of the deficit and the degree of recovery in a meaningful way it is necessary to arrive at a satisfactory way of quantifying severity. One of the most tempting ways to define severity in many contexts is in terms of its functional consequences. Thus one patient's encephalitic illness may be judged more severe than another in retrospect because it left that person with greater functional impairments. From the present point of view such a definition is obviously circular and makes the generalization under consideration a logical consequence of the way that severity is defined.

Severity of insult must therefore be defined independently of its consequences, or at least consequences very directly related to the functions of interest. In some instances, such as closed head injury, this is not too much of a problem and severity can be measured in terms of such things as depth of coma, duration of unconsciousness or, most commonly, length of post-traumatic amnesia. (The use of this latter index of severity assumes that there is some qualitative difference between the psychological changes manifest during the period of post-traumatic amnesia and those present on a more permanent basis. Mandelberg (1975) provides evidence in support of this assumption.) Other types of pathology typically do not lend themselves to such easy measures of the severity of the insult.

Focal lesions raise other problems. The more extensive the lesion, the more severe it may be considered to be. But if severity of insult then correlates with functional outcome the reason for the relationship may not be clear. The example may be taken of a case of a right parietal lesion producing an impairment on some measure of visuospatial ability. A larger lesion may give an even greater initial deficit and less extensive recovery. This could be because the larger lesion has resulted in more extensive damage to the structures responsible for mediating visuospatial abilities. An alternative possibility is that the apparent relationship between size of the lesion and the degree of deficit and its recovery could be due to an artifact. The more extensive lesion may have resulted in no greater impact on visuospatial functioning itself (regarding the function as means rather than a goal). Instead it may have interfered more widely with other functions associated with that general part of the brain and some of these other functions could also play some role in carrying out the task used to measure visuospatial ability. If it is correct to suggest, as will be done in Chapter 5, that at least some long-term recovery is achieved because the subject is able to learn to use alternative strategies to arrive at the same goal, then the more extensive lesion may also affect recovery because it reduces the alternative strategies that are potentially open to the subject.

The consequence of this argument is that it then becomes very difficult to talk sensibly about the relationship between the size of the insult and the degree of deficit or rate of recovery for focal lesions, particularly if the functions concerned are regarded as means. The only potential way of getting round the difficulties is to use very complex investigations which take into account not only the particular function of interest but other possibly related functions as well. If the concern is just with functions as goals, regardless of how the goal is achieved, then investigating the relationship is somewhat more straightforward.

An example of these complexities can be found in Lashley's work on 'mass action'. As the result of a series of experiments in which the performance of rats on tasks such as acquired lightness discriminations and maze running was studied as a function of brain lesions, Lashley (1929) concluded that 'the efficiency of performance of an entire complex function may be reduced in proportion to the extent of the brain injury'. In other words he claimed to have demonstrated a direct correlation between the extent of damage and the size of the impairment. This was then referred to as the principle of 'mass action'.

The notion of mass action inspired much further work and a number of significant experiments (e.g. Hunter, 1940; Pickett, 1952). Whilst the accuracy of Lashley's basic observations has not been questioned it now appears that his interpretations ignored alternative, and in hindsight, better explanations. In the case of maze learning, for example, rats probably make use of a wide range of different sense including touch and smell as well as vision. Given that the primary sensory areas are widely distributed within the brain, then larger lesions are likely to affect more sensory systems and so produce increasing impairment. It therefore follows that what appears to be a mass action effect need not reflect a simple incremental relationship between the extent of the lesion and the degree of impairment in a single function (where the function is defined in terms of means rather than goals). This particular interpretation of Lashley's results is strongly supported by findings such as those of Pickett (1952) who failed to find the same mass action effect in association with brain lesions in animals that had previously suffered peripheral damage to their sensory systems. The peripheral damage would act to reduce the number of sensory systems that the rat could use in learning to run the maze.

It is not intended to pursue the animal literature much further on this point. The only additional comment is to note that the size of the lesion does not necessarily correlate with the degree of deficit. The well-known 'delayed response deficit' has been extensively studied since its first discovery by Jacobsen (1936). This term is used to describe the situation in which monkeys with frontal lesions have an excessive difficulty with tasks in which the cue for the correct response is given some time before the actual response is permitted. More recent work (e.g. Gross and Weiskrantz, 1962; Rosvold and Szwarcbart, 1964) indicates that the delayed response deficit can be fully manifest by much more restrictive lesions involving the dorsolateral frontal cortex or even just the region of the sulcus principalis. In fact it is clear that for localized lesions a close correlation between lesion size and extent of deficit can only hold over a wide range of lesion sizes if the brain is considered to be equipotential for the function in question. Although Lashley (1929) was certainly strongly drawn to the idea of equipotentiality it is only fair to indicate that he later modified his own position to accept some degree of localization of functions.

With humans there is considerable evidence in cases of head injury that both the extent of resultant psychological impairments and the long-term outcome are related to the length of post-traumatic amnesia (PTA) which is the most commonly used index of severity of injury. Much of the relevant work has been reviewed by Humphrey and Oddy (1980), Miller (1979a) and by Schacter and Crovitz (1977). Only the salient features will be outlined here. Mandelberg (1976) found that the IQ level a few months after a severe head injury was related to the length of PTA. This correlation disappeared when IQ was assessed rather later after the injury. This disappearance is not surprising given the general tendency for IQs to eventually return to their pre-injury levels (Mandelberg and Brooks, 1975). These authors did not report their data in such a way as to relate PTA to speed of recovery.

Some investigators have also found a relationship between memory impairment and various indices of severity of head injury, including PTA (Brooks, 1972; Levin et al., 1976). On the other hand, it ought to be noted that other studies have failed to show any correlation between PTA and later memory impairment (e.g. Brooks, 1975). Those studies finding no relationship between PTA and later memory performance, where such a correlation has been looked for, are in the minority and involve the use of samples of severe head injuries where the range of PTAs is curtailed. This will reduce the opportunity to demonstrate significant correlations. Investigators who have used both large sample sizes and a wide range of severity in their head-injured subjects have usually found a definite relationship (Russell, 1971).

As far as longer-term outcome or adjustment is concerned it emerges that a substantial proportion of those who survive severe head injuries fail to return to a level of employment or social adjustment that is commensurate with their pre-injury status (Humphrey and Oddy, 1980; Miller, 1979a). The data reported by Oddy and Humphrey (1980) also indicate that those with the more severe injuries (PTA > 7 days) are slower to return to work where such a return occurs, and more likely to suffer very long-term unemployment, than those whose PTAs were shorter (1–7 days). In Oddy and Humphrey's series recovery of other aspects of social functioning (e.g. resumption of leisure activities) was also slower in those with the longer PTAs. These findings are entirely reasonable and not at variance with what might have been expected on a priori grounds. The trouble is that the dependent variables could be contaminated. There is a tendency for older subjects to have longer PTAs (Russell and Smith, 1961) and it could be that employers might be more willing to tolerate impaired functioning from the younger handicapped worker. Thus it is possible that the relationships could be at least partly spurious.

Despite this minor caveat there does seem to be a very definite relationship between the length of PTA as a result of head injury and the extent of any impairment. Speed of recovery may also relate to PTA. The relationships found are almost without exception in the direction expected. The one set of data that runs against the general rule is that appertaining to the so-called 'post-concussional syndrome' in which the patient presents with vague complaints of dizziness, loss of memory and concentration, headache, etc. In the majority of instances no unequivocal organic foundation can be established for this 'syndrome'. Here a relationship with severity of head injury has been claimed but in the reverse direction. The most dramatic of the data are provided by H. Miller (1961) who reported a large series of head injuries seen by himself for medico-legal purposes (presumably because they were involved in compensation claims). Being medico-legal cases they were certainly not a random sample. According to Miller about a quarter showed 'indubitably psychoneurotic complaints' and the incidence of these was inversely related to the severity of the head injury. In fact about 40 per cent of those cases who had never even lost consciousness were alleged to show what Miller described as 'accident neurosis' (this is virtually identical with what others have more commonly referred to as the post-concussional syndrome). There is good reason to be unhappy with H. Miller's interpretation of his data on a number of counts and a fuller discussion is provided by E. Miller (1979a). For present purposes two things should be noted. One is the fact, already referred to, that the sample contained only medico-legal cases and thus was almost certainly biased. Secondly, the minor symptoms usually considered to be part of the post-concussional syndrome (lack of concentration, dizziness, etc.) may well be masked in those with more prominent handicaps arising out of severe head injuries. H. Miller's (1961) paper thus needs to be treated with some caution although this has not prevented the views expressed from becoming quite influential when compensation claims are being considered.

H. Miller (1961) also indicates that, in his view, recovery from the post-concussional syndrome (or 'accident neurosis') is associated with the final resolution of the legal action for compensation. Later and more systematic observations do not support this. Merskey and Woodforde (1972) looked at cases of minor head injury both with and without possible compensation claims. Although the results were not without some ambiguity there was certainly no marked tendency for the symptoms of the post-concussional syndrome to be encountered more commonly in those with possible compensation claims. Unfortunately recovery from the symptoms does not appear to have been examined in ways of particular interest in this context, but Mersey and Woodforde did indicate that recovery was not directly linked to the resolution of the claim where this was made. Gronwall and Wrightson (1974) have suggested that recovery parallels that exhibited by an information-processing task.

Although there may be some regions of localized contusion in closed head injury the observed pathological changes are spread throughout the brain (Oppenheimer, 1968; Strich, 1961). These consist of such things as microscopic tearing of nerve fibres and the occurrence of small haemorrhages. Despite the fact that the blow occurs to one part of the head the damage to the brain that results from significant head injury is certainly not primarily focal in nature. Another condition that results in diffuse pathology spread throughout the brain is dementia of the Alzheimer's type. The extent of the pathology can be assessed in different ways, either neuropathologically (e.g. counts of plaques or neurofibrillary tangles) or radiologically (by air encephalography or the use of computerized tomography). The topic has been reviewed in some detail by Miller (1977) but it does emerge that the extent of cognitive impairment in dementia is related to plaque counts (e.g. Blessed *et al.*, 1968) and the degree of cerebral atrophy (e.g. de Leon *et al.*, 1979; Willanger, 1970). There are also a number of negative findings but Miller (1977) sets out arguments indicating that the negative results can be readily explained in terms of the poor methodology used. The experimental designs simply were not powerful enough to detect any correlation that might be there because of the small number of subjects involved and the extreme unreliability of the measures used. Because dementia of this kind is progressive it is not possible to look for any relationship between the severity of the pathology and the rate or extent of recovery.

Correlating the size of focal lesions with the level of the initial deficit and amount of subsequent recovery is likely to raise much the same methodological problems in human patients as were outlined in the earlier discussion of animal research. Nevertheless for lesions within a particular circumscribed region of the brain there may be some relationship between size of lesion and outcome, at least as assessed in terms of functions as goals.

A few examples can be cited. It has been claimed that the degree of verbal memory disturbance resulting from anterior temporal lobectomy (carried out to relieve intractable temporal lobe epilepsy) is correlated with the amount of hippocampus that has been removed (Milner, 1966). Lashley (1938) surveyed the then existing reports of cases of motor aphasia resulting from left frontal lesions where it was possible to estimate the size of the lesion. He then claimed that there was a substantial inverse correlation between the size of the lesion and the degree of recovery. Size of the lesion responsible may well relate to language recovery in aphasia in general. Larger lesions tend to produce more extensive and severe dysphasias and the milder dysphasias give the impression of yielding more extensive recovery (Darley, 1975).

Contrary examples also occur. For example, Miller (1972) reviewed the evidence relating to changes in intelligence test scores after frontal lesions in man. Some reports indicate intellectual loss, often with later recovery, after a variety of psychosurgical procedures (e.g. Mettler, 1952; Rylander, 1951). On the other hand cases have been described in which even quite massive frontal ablations failed to produce any change in intelligence test scores (e.g. Hebb, 1945). As Miller (1972) comments, the discrepancies are not explicable on the basis of simple and obvious variables such as the size of the lesion.

The establishing and interpretation of relationships between the size or severity of the lesion on the one hand, and the amount of deficit or the rate and extent of its recovery on the other, is a complex business. It is undoubtedly safest to look at this type of correlation in the case of generalized pathology such as is found in patients with closed head injuries. There is evidence consistent with the expectation that more extensive pathology will produce greater impairments although there are a few possible exceptions (e.g. that of the post-concussional syndrome). The finding that malfunctioning tissue can sometimes give even greater impairments than the total ablation of the same tissue (see Miller, 1972) also raises complications. Evidence relating to the rate and extent of recovery is rather sparse but what there is generally runs in the expected direction. As might be anticipated in view of the methodological difficulties outlined at the beginning of this section, the situation is rather more confused in the case of focal lesions.

OVERLEARNING

As already indicated it has been considered that overlearning can provide some protection against the disruptive consequences of brain damage. There have been several relevant experiments with animals and a good proportion of these have produced positive results. A not untypical experiment is that of Thatcher and Kimble (1966). These authors were concerned by the fact that reports of amygdaloid lesions in rats sometimes claimed disruption of learned avoidance responses but sometimes did not. They hypothesized that the inconsistency in the findings might be related to the differing amounts of pre-operative training used in the various experiments. Thatcher and Kimble (1966) gave rats avoidance training in a shuttle box. One group was trained to the usual type of criterion whilst the other received an additional 120 training trials after the same criterion had been reached. After bilateral electrolytic lesions of the amygdala had been induced subjects were again retested on the same avoidance task. The group just trained to criterion showed some impairment post-operatively but there was no loss in the subjects given the overtraining.

Findings of this nature have been shown to have some generality with regard to the type of task used and lesion location. For example, it has been found that pre-operative overtraining helps to preserve retention of acquired visual discriminations after ablations of the temporal neocortex (Chow and Survis, 1958; Orbach and Fantz, 1958); visual pattern discriminations after pretectal lesions (Thompson et al., 1967); and learned tactile discriminations after lesions of the somatosensory cortex (Weese et al., 1973). The report of Weese et al. (1973) is of additional interest because these workers also introduced a second post-operative tactile discrimination which had not been experienced by the subjects given training or overtraining prior to the operation. Overtraining significantly enhanced post-operative relearning of the pre-operatively learned task. It also showed a definite tendency, although not to a statistically significant degree, to similarly assist post-operative acquisition of the new task.

Unfortunately the situation gets more complex. Other experiments, apparently equally well conducted, have failed to find any overtraining effect at all. Glendenning (1972) was unable to find any protective effect of overtraining in preventing the loss of a simple visual discrimination after posterior lesions in rats. However, pre-operative training, whether to simple criterion or with overtraining, did assist in the post-operative acquisition of the same habit as compared with animals which experienced no pre-operative training at all. Similarly, Raab and Ades (1946) found that the amount of pre-operative experience with an auditory intensity discrimination did not affect retention after brain lesions of different kinds. A more recent experiment with negative results is that of Gabriel *et al.* (1979). This was built on the 'overlearning reversal effect' originally shown by Reid (1953) whereby overtrained (but cerebrally intact) subjects were quicker to learn the reverse of the discrimination that they had originally been trained on. Others have supported this finding (e.g. Mackintosh, 1974). Gabriel *et al.* (1979) trained and overtrained rats on a tactile discrimination and then got them to learn the reverse of this discrimination after various types of lesion had been induced or after sham operations. Rats with lesions were slower to learn the reverse habit than the sham-operated controls but there was no overlearning reversal effect in that both trained and overtrained subjects took equally long to learn the reversal. The impact of this experiment is weakened by the fact that the expected straightforward overlearning reversal effect failed to emerge in the sham-operated controls. The authors suggest that this might be because the effect obtained by Reid (1953) and others was most commonly demonstrated using some form of visual or spatial stimuli.

It is possible that the discrepancies between the various experimental results relating to the effects of overlearning on the extent of impairments resulting from brain lesions might be resolved if the initial learning parameter had been explored more fully. It does seem to be the case (except in the rather unusual circumstances of the experiment by Gabriel *et al.*, 1979) that pre-operative training does improve post-operative relearning of a habit as compared with similarly operated animals starting to learn the task with no prior exposure. If this is the case it would not be surprising if the amount of pre-operative training required to have an optimal effect on post-operative retention or reacquisition varied considerably as a result of alterations in other experimental parameters. These might include such things as the nature of the task, the kind of lesion, and the species involved. In some situations this optimum might be reached, or very nearly reached, if the subject is trained to the kind of learning criterion often adopted in such studies (e.g. 95 per cent correct responses over 20 consecutive trials). Under other conditions, achievement of this sort of criterion might leave the subject well below the maximum protective power of pre-operative experience. Only in the latter case would the design of experiments published so far permit the obtaining of an appreciable overtraining effect. Another possible contaminating factor is the length of time elapsed between the initial learning, or overlearning, and the occurrence of the lesion. It remains to be seen if these factors are adequate to explain the differences between the reported findings.

In human patients the one more-or-less comparable situation that has attracted some attention is that of the recovery of speech in polyglot aphasics. As was indicated at the beginning of this chapter Pitres (1895) suggested that when aphasia occurred in polyglots recovery was likely to be most extensive in the language that had been used most, regardless of whether it was the one that had actually been learned first. It would be unwise to relate this statement too closely to the animal overlearning situation since languages are much more complex than simple discrimination tasks and can be learned at different levels. Most true polyglots will also have learned even their least-used language beyond the comparable level of the 95 per cent criterion used as the index of basic learning in animal experiments. Thus in polyglots the comparison is likely to be between two overlearned skills of which one may be more overlearned than the other.

Evidence on polyglots has come almost entirely from clinical reports and these have been discussed in some detail by Albert and Obler (1978), Benson (1979b) and Hecaen and Albert (1978). Before considering the findings it ought to be noted that there are appreciable difficulties in trying to study polyglot aphasia. Prominent amongst these is the need to have an examiner, or examiners, who have a fairly sophisticated knowledge of the languages concerned. It is not acceptable for a patient thought to have been bilingual in French and English to be examined by an English-speaking examiner whose acquaintance with French is confined to a few years of instruction whilst at secondary school and the occasional few weeks holiday on a French campsite. It may also not be easy to establish which language the patient has used most extensively. For example, a man now in later middle age may have come to an English-speaking country from Poland at 18 years of age. He may then have learned and used English very efficiently and extensively in some contexts but always spoken Polish at home, initially with his parents but also after having married another exile. In such circumstances it is very difficult to establish which has been the most practised language.

The general question of aphasia in those who are adept in more than one language has many interesting facets. Those particularly interested in this area are referred to Albert and Obler (1978) since the present account is confined to only one aspect. Paradis (1977) surveyed over 100 polyglot aphasics and came to the conclusion that the most common pattern of recovery was for the different languages to recover in parallel within the individual subject. There were several instances where this did not happen. In fact the literature as a whole may overemphasize the exceptions because of the natural tendency to publish case reports detailing new or unexpected features. Lambert and Fillenbaum (1959) described 14 cases who were bilingual French Canadians. In general these tended to give some support to both Pitres' and Ribot's laws. Another important factor that emerged in this study was the environment in which recovery took place. Although Montreal, the city in which the investigations were carried out, tends to be bilingual the individual hospitals will generally use one language rather than the other. Not surprisingly patients recovering in hospital were biased towards the language in common usage around them.

Albert and Obler (1978) extracted details of 105 cases recorded in the literature and added information concerning a further three unpublished cases of their own. Each subject was coded for 29 variables although full data were not available for all subjects. It was possible to assess recovery patterns in 47 of these subjects. In almost half of this subgroup of 47 the recovery in both or all the languages followed a parallel course. About twice as many were apparently consistent with Pitres' law in their recovery as were clearly in contradiction with it. Ribot's law, predicting that the language learned first would recover best, was contradicted slightly more often than it was confirmed. Age emerged as a factor in determining whether Pitres' law was followed in that younger subjects were rather more likely to follow Pitres. Whilst this analysis provides a nice quantitative picture it is based upon cases published by a large number of different authors and the sample may be far from representative of bilingual or polyglot aphasics. Given the already mentioned likelihood that cases with unusual or unexpected features are more likely to be the subject of published case reports it would be foolish not to treat Albert and Obler's analysis with some caution.

It is difficult to draw conclusions about the effects of overlearning on recovery, or about its analogue in aphasia, Pitres' law. The overlearning effect does seem to emerge more often than not in animal research. It could also be, as argued above, that the exceptions typically result from a failure to explore a sufficient range of levels of pre-operative training. In human patients many bilingual and polyglot aphasics do follow Pitres' law but well-attested exceptions have occurred. Just how frequent the exceptions are is impossible to estimate from the data available so far.

TIME ELAPSED SINCE ACQUISITION

The last issue to be dealt with in this chapter involves the notion that the longer the time elapsed from the acquisition of a skill or memory to the time of brain damage the less likely it is to be disrupted and, if disrupted, the better that it will recover. This is the principle commonly referred to as Ribot's law (Ribot, 1883). As was explained in the early parts of the chapter, the time elapsed since acquisition is likely to be related to the degree of overlearning in any practical situation. This is despite the fact that the two variables are logically distinct. Animal research offers the most obvious way round this dilemma. Unfortunately there is very little systematic work of any relevance in the literature. Because of this there will be no preliminary evaluation of animal studies and the few bits of pertinent animal research will simply be introduced to expand and extend the evidence derived from humans.

A common observation is that the many conditions that can produce a severe disruption of memory have both anterograde and retrograde effects. In the case of severe head injury, to take but one example, there is likely to be an amnesia for events which occurred shortly before the injury was sustained. This retrograde amnesia (RA) most commonly extends for a period of seconds or minutes but can sometimes be much longer (Lishman, 1978). There is, of course, also a much longer period of confusion after consciousness is regained, which is usually described as post-traumatic amnesia (PTA). Even after PTA is resolved the severely head-injured patient will be left with some permanent anterograde amnesic difficulties (Schacter and Crovitz, 1977).

It is RA that is of particular interest here. It is a phenomenon that is not confined to head injuries and it can be observed after many relatively sudden cerebral insults (e.g. surgical removal of the mesial portions of the temporal lobes and electroconvulsive therapy). Analogous RA effects can also be demonstrated in animals. Using avoidance learning Chorover and Schiller (1966) showed impairment of retention if a single electroconvulsive shock occurred shortly after a single learning trial. Not only was there a definite RA but the extent to which retention was affected was inversely related to the time passed between the learning trial and the electroconvulsive shock. Similar RA effects can be found in many other situations with animals (Deutsch and Deutsch, 1973).

The marked vulnerability of the most recent events to RA effects is clearly consistent with Ribot's law. The further implication is that recovery will be more probable and extensive for events affected by RA but which occurred earlier in time. It is a common observation in head-injured patients that RA shows some spontaneous reduction or shrinkage with time. Similarly H.M., the well-known Montreal case with extremely severe amnesia resulting from bilateral temporal lobe lesions, exhibited an RA of about 3 years shortly after the operation. Follow-up several years later showed that this had shrunk to about 2 years (Milner, 1966). Zangwill (1964) reports some detailed observations of shrinkage of RA in patients with head injuries. These were not entirely as might be predicted from Ribot's law. Often memories did not return in chronological sequence but events within the period of RA would emerge and slowly become linked to material that had never been lost, and to one another.

Although the fit is certainly not perfect Ribot's law gives the impression of holding reasonably well for the type of RA phenomena that have just been discussed. There is now the question of more distant effects. Many patients with marked memory problems, such as those with dementia or the Korsakoff syndrome, give the appearance of having retained very little since the onset of their condition. In contrast the recollection of events from the remote past seems relatively good and can leave the examiner feeling that this is normal or near normal. However, it may be that in conditions like the amnesic syndrome this impression is misleading and that there is some appreciable RA for distant events. Is this the case and, if so, does the pattern of loss follow Ribot's law?

The first attempt to systematically study remote memory in patients with the amnesic syndrome was reported by Sanders and Warrington (1971). Briefly the technique involved identifying news items of major concern at different times between 1930 and 1968. These were turned into questions requiring a straightforward recall of the event and others with a forced-choice recognition format. Faces commonly shown in the newspapers over the same period were also identified and again used in recall and forced-choice versions. The resulting questions were given to five amnesic subjects of mixed aetiology and a number of matched normal controls. The overwhelming impact of the results is that recall or recognition of information from the past is very poor in amnesic subjects. In Sanders and Warrington's experiment there was also no indication of the gradient that would be expected on the basis of Ribot's law whereby the more distant information is relatively better retained in the abnormal group.

A number of similar studies have been carried out in Boston using groups of alcoholic Korsakoff patients (Albert *et al.*, 1979; Marslen-Wilson and Teuber, 1975; Seltzer and Benson, 1974). Figure 3 shows a typical plot of the data from one of these studies and clearly shows the expected gradient. The investigation of Albert *et al.* (1979) used three questionnaires which were again applied by Butters *et al.* (1979) to eight subjects with Huntington's chorea. This latter group performed poorly but showed no temporal gradient. In yet another series of studies based on a similar methodology Squire *et al.* (1976, 1981) found some evidence in favour of Ribot's law in looking at the RA effects of electroconvulsive therapy.

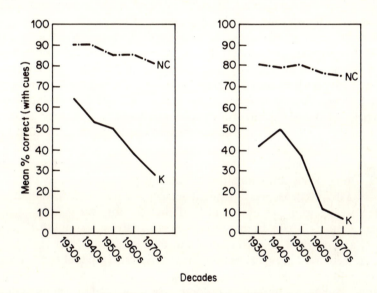

Figure 3. Percentage of items correct in Korsakoff patients (K) and normal controls (NC) on easy (left) and hard (right) items of recall questionnaire dealing with information related to different decades (from A. Albert *et al.*, (1979) *Arch. Neurol.*, **36**, 211–216. Copyright 1979, American Medical Association)

Whilst it is conceivable that Huntington's chorea might give rather different results which could be contaminated by the generalized dementia that occurs in that condition, the discrepancy between Sanders and Warrington (1971, 1975) and the Boston studies using Korsakoff cases (e.g. Albert *et al.*, 1979) gives greater cause for concern. The Albert *et al.* (1979) experiment was designed to show that differences in questionnaire design were not responsible for the anomalies. Butters and Cermak (1980) point to differences in the subjects used.

The Boston workers used only alcoholic Korsakoff cases whilst Sanders and Warrington's experimental group was more heterogeneous, containing cases with amnesia following coal-gas poisoning and resulting from temporal lobe lesions as well as those with the Korsakoff syndrome. Zangwill (1977) suggests that more careful clinical studies are needed to resolve the issue with attention being given to personal and impersonal memory.

In this writer's opinion the most likely reason for Sanders and Warrington's anomalous result lies in a methodological point. In their investigation the amnesic group did extremely badly on all questions. Performance was never more than barely above chance levels for the questions with the forced-choice format. It is questionable whether an appropriate statistical test would have shown there to be any recognition effect at all at the usually accepted significance levels. In the recall version the average amnesic subject was very close to getting no score at all. In order to test for a temporal gradient it is necessary to have at least one time point at which the subjects can recall an appreciable amount of information. If they retain virtually nothing at all at the longest interval their performance cannot deteriorate at later points on the graph.

This is not to claim that the Boston results are above question. Their alcoholic Korsakoff cases were presumably heavy drinkers for some prolonged period prior to the onset of the Korsakoff state. During their period of heavy drinking they might have been less likely to acquire information about events in the news, television programmes, and other things tested for in the experiments. For this reason recall of material from further back in time, and before drinking got out of control, would be expected to be better, thus producing a gradient similar to that predicted from Ribot's law. This argument could be partially countered by the electroconvulsive therapy (ETC) studies where it would be much less plausible to postulate comparable contaminating factors that could operate over the kinds of time period involved. Depression might account for poor registration of events for a few weeks prior to a course of ECT, but not for years.

Finally, attention can be redirected to the analysis of published cases of bilingual and polyglot aphasia carried out by Albert and Obler (1978). These were described in the previous section. From this it emerged that Ribot's law was at least as likely to be broken as followed in language recovery. However, recovery of language is undoubtedly going to be influenced by a number of other factors. It is also appropriate to reiterate the point that the samples of subjects on which the Albert and Obler analysis is based are unlikely to be random. There may well be a bias towards overrepresenting atypical cases. All that Albert and Obler's analysis can show is that Ribot's law is not always followed in recovery from aphasia but it is impossible to say just how often exceptions are likely to be encountered.

When considered overall, much of the available data does show at least a rough fit with Ribot's law. By the same token it also has to be admitted that there is an appreciable amount of data that does not fit. In evaluating the latter it is unfortunate that there is almost no information as to how Ribot's law might interact with other factors influencing recovery.

CHAPTER FOUR

Factors influencing recovery: the remaining issues

A number of other factors which can exert some influence on recovery remain to be discussed. The possible influence of environmental manipulations on recovery is of considerable relevance to later considerations of possible therapeutic interventions. Other factors to be discussed include the allegedly beneficial effects of multi-stage as compared to single-stage lesions, the contribution of individual differences, and the timing of interventions. Some of these points will be covered more extensively than others. Those receiving the most superficial treatment are where the issue has largely arisen in animal research and has only minor relevance to the kinds of clinical problems that are encountered with human patients.

ENVIRONMENTAL INFLUENCES

There is evidence that environmental manipulations can have an effect on recovery. This is of particular interest in the present context since it gives considerable encouragement to the idea that psychological interventions may be of value in the rehabilitation of brain-injured patients. Quite a substantial chunk of the work that might be of potential importance in this section arises out of attempts to design therapeutic interventions for patients with neuropsychological impairments. Therapeutically oriented interventions are the major concern of later chapters and therefore will not be covered here.

Manipulations prior to injury

Parts of the previous chapter dealing with Ribot's law and Pitres' rule examined aspects of the general question of pre-injury experiences on later recovery. There are other aspects which still need to be described. This work, which has arisen only in animal research, has been reviewed by both Finger (1978b) and Greenough *et al.* (1976). It concerns environmental manipulations not involving training or overtraining on the dependent variable.

An experiment of this type yielding reasonably straightforward results is that of Hughes (1965). He reared rats between the ages of 33 and 66 days in environments which either consisted of standard laboratory conditions or were altered in some way. The altered environments could be impoverished or enriched as compared to the standard situation. Experimental subjects then received postero-ventral or antero-dorsal hippocampal lesions whilst controls underwent a sham operation. All subjects were then tested post-operatively on the Hebb–Williams mazes. The pre-operative environment had no effect on the sham-operated controls but a marked effect on those with lesions. The picture was that of the more enriched environment offering some protection against later deficits.

Other findings similar to those of Hughes (1965) could be cited (e.g. Smith, 1959). There are also instances where pre-operative environmental manipulations have failed to exert any influence at all on post-lesion behaviour. Finger (1978c) used enucleated rats reared in either barren cages or cages containing a variety of objects that could be explored tactually. After lesions of the somatosensory region there was no difference between the groups when it came to learning a somatosensory discrimination.

So far there is no clear picture as to the protective powers of enriched pre-operative environments to ameliorate the consequences of later lesions. One obvious contaminating factor that might possibly explain the varied results is that of the severity of the deficit that is produced. In the Finger (1978c) experiment it could be that a lesion producing a less severe somatosensory defect might have proved more sensitive to pre-operative differences. Another point is that, in the extreme case, the environmental management could get closer and closer to pre-operative practice on the test used post-operatively. This then brings discussion back to the question of pre-operative learning and overlearning as discussed in the previous chapter.

The effects of pre-operative environmental manipulations will not be taken any further. This is because it is a question that has so far produced very little that might even remotely be applied to the human situation.

Environmental manipulations after the lesion

As already indicated, attempts to manipulate the environment of experimental animals after the lesion has been placed constitute the closest analogy with therapeutic manipulations in human patients. Using rats both Schwartz (1964) and Will et al. (1976) have placed posterior cortex lesions very early in life and then studied the effects of subsequent environments on maze learning at maturity. These different environments involved such things as giving increased opportunity for the animals to gain perceptual and motor experiences as opposed to being reared in bare cages, either in groups or alone. In both of these experiments environmental enrichment was found to give better performance on the outcome measure.

Inevitably there are other investigations that have not produced such positive findings. For example, Bland and Cooper (1969) described three separate experiments in which rats received posterior lesions at either 1 day or 3 months after birth. The post-operative environment was then manipulated but this had no effect on later visual discrimination learning. In discussing research of this nature Goldman and Lewis (1978) suggest that the critical factor could be the dependent variable. They believe that post-lesion experience may be able to influence later maze learning but not such things as visual discrimination learning.

Goldman and Lewis's (1978) emphasis on the nature of the dependent variable makes considerable sense. The sensory modality most affected by a posterior lesion will be vision. If the visual system suffers considerable damage then the ability to carry out tasks that can only be done by purely visual means may not be modifiable. However, a problem such as maze learning, for which other sensory modalities can be used, might respond to extra experience which somehow helps the animal to make more extensive use of these other sensory modalities. An alternative, but not mutually incompatible, hypothesis is that the effect of post-lesion experience is a function of how closely this experience corresponds to the particular task used as the outcome measure and the severity of the deficit. It could be that in Bland and Cooper's (1969) experiments the obtained deficit was too severe or the experience provided not relevant enough.

Goldman herself has found that rhesus monkeys with lesions of the orbital prefrontal cortex in infancy can perform almost as well as normal animals when tested at about 2 years of age if they had also had extensive experience of cognitive tests. Subjects not given this experience, although otherwise treated in exactly the same way, showed very marked impairments (Goldman, 1976). Further experiments in this series showed that the beneficial effects of added experience are confined to those subjects given lesions in early life and not those operated on at the age of 18 months.

In a further study Goldman and Mendelson (1977) looked in more detail at the nature of the experience offered in the post-operative period. Monkeys were given early orbital prefrontal lesions and some were given training on a non-spatial task. The critical later testing involved both a spatial and a non-spatial task with the latter similar to the situation used in post-lesion training. Despite this the post-operative training had a beneficial effect on the spatial task only. This implies that whatever is contributed by the additional experience given between lesion and later test it is not just a straightforward learning effect. This is an intriguing finding which warrants replication and, if still upheld, further investigation.

The work so far has largely concentrated on lesions given in very early life. Where the lesions have been placed in mature animals it has been rather more common to find that enhanced experience has no beneficial effects (e.g. Bland and Cooper, 1969; Goldman, 1976). However, this is certainly not always the case. In Will and Rosenzweig's (1976) experiment rats were given lesions at 4 months of age. Subjects were then reared in groups in large cages with a range of stimulus objects or reared individually in relatively bare cages. Later learning with the Hebb–Williams mazes showed that the enriched environment did have an appreciable effect. Although not directed at the particular question under discussion at present, the experiment of Black *et al.* (1975), which will be described more fully in the next section, also gave positive effects of this kind.

It is not unreasonable to expect that the kind of experience given between lesion and any test or relearning of the pre-operatively acquired skill would be a potent factor. Some evidence for this expectation comes from an experiment reported by Guic-Robles *et al.* (1982). Rats subjected to simultaneous bilateral ablations of the visual cortex can relearn a pre-operatively trained black *vs.* white brightness discrimination but not one based on horizontal *vs.* vertical black-and-white stripes. Guic-Robles *et al.* also trained some of their rats post-operatively on a black/white brightness discrimination followed by training in situations where the conditions fell in between those in the black/white discrimination and the horizontal and vertical stripes situation (i.e. a white surface with thin horizontal black lines and a black surface with thin vertical white lines). After this experience, which gradually approximated to the crucial task, all of the critical group were able to learn the otherwise impossible horizontal *vs.* vertical stripes discrimination.

In trying to summarize these findings it does appear that, under some circumstances at least, environmental manipulations can influence the extent of a behavioural impairment. In this context both pre- and post-operative experience can be of significance. These findings give support to the notion that behavioural interventions could be of some value in ameliorating neuropsychological impairments in human patients. The effects observed are possibly more readily demonstrated in subjects given lesions in early life where the experience is given post-operatively. Similar findings have been reported in adults, but it is probably correct to state that the main thrust of the work on post-operative experience has been concerned with the effects of early lesions. In rats at least, some impairments appear easier to ameliorate by experience than others, but the mechanisms involved have yet to be explored in detail. Goldman and Mendelson's (1977) work implies that whatever mechanisms are involved are not a simple learning effect whereby additional experience on the same or a similar task just transfers to the later and crucial test situation. This is an intriguing result and needs confirmation. On the other hand, Guic-Robles *et al.*'s (1982) findings would fit into a learning framework.

Timing of the intervention

At the beginning of Chapter 2 attention was drawn to the common clinical impression that the sooner after any brain lesion any intervention is instituted the more effective it is likely to be. A tendency to this effect was noted in Basso *et al.*'s (1979) trial of the effects of speech therapy on aphasia. Other experts on the treatment of aphasia have also suggested that early treatment is best and this is discussed in an extensive review of aphasia treatment by Darley (1975). Since the evidence for the efficacy of interventions such as speech therapy in aphasia is rather weak (see Chapter 7) it could be that these impressions are the result of an artifact. Spontaneous remission typically occurs at a much faster rate in the period shortly after the lesion has occurred and this could lead to the impression of greater therapeutic gain in the early stages if therapists mistakenly regard spontaneous improvement as a response to treatment.

Cope and Hall (1982) carried out an investigation intended to provide an experimental test of the effects of early intervention. They had two similar groups of patients who had sustained severe head injuries. The patients in one group entered an active rehabilitation programme before 35 days post-injury and the other more than 35 days after injury. Using the Glasgow scale both groups had a similar long-term outcome. When time spent in the active rehabilitation programme was examined the late-entry group needed about twice as long before being considered fit for discharge. The difficulty is that this particular dependent variable may have been contaminated by other factors. It is not known whether those taking the decision about when to discharge from rehabilitation were blind to the experiment and its significance. It could also be that patients were, in effect, discharged after having made a certain amount of progress. Given that the maximum rate of spontaneous recovery occurs in the earliest stages it would take the later-entry group longer to show the same amount of recovery.

It is difficult to investigate this question with the desirable degree of rigour using clinical situations but comparable experimental situations can be produced in animals. In Goldman's (1976) experiments on the role of experience on recovery from early prefrontal lesions it was found that better behavioural recovery occurred if the enhanced experience was given soon after the lesion. The snag with this is that it confounds the possible effects of early intervention with developmental factors because the lesions were placed early in life. It could just be that younger subjects were better able to benefit from post-operative experience.

An experiment that avoids this pitfall is that of Black et al. (1975). They placed lesions in the region of the motor cortex in adult monkeys. Both groups of subjects in the experiment received similar lesions and underwent the same post-operative training programme designed to facilitate movements in the affected limbs. The difference between the groups was that the special post-operative intervention was applied shortly after the lesion in one group and several weeks after in the other. On a later test given at the same post-operative interval for both groups, the group with early intervention performed significantly better.

There is little methodologically sound information on this point. Clinical opinion runs strongly in the direction of believing that early therapeutic interventions are the most efficacious. Given the usual pattern of spontaneous recovery it is easy to see how this impression could be gained without the basic assertion being necessarily true. On the other hand, the one adequately designed experiment to be reported so far, that of Black et al. (1975), does clearly support clinical opinion. In view of the many inconsistencies which emerge when most other factors relating to recovery are examined it would be prudent not to place too much confidence in this one experiment until the results have been repeatedly confirmed using subjects with other behavioural deficits and different types of intervention. In the next chapter the processes that might underlie recovery are examined, and the evidence could be interpreted as showing that early recovery is mediated by different mechanisms from those underlying later recovery. If this is so then different kinds of intervention might have maximal effectiveness when applied at different stages of recovery.

DEVELOPING AND MULTIPLE LESIONS

Brain lesions do not necessarily occur all at once. A space-occupying lesion such as a meningioma may develop very slowly and then be removed surgically. It might be anticipated that a slowly developing lesion would result in less severe disruption and give better recovery than a lesion damaging similar tissue which occurs much more rapidly, or even almost instantly. Finger (1978d) draws attention to a paper apparently written by a French physician Marc Dax in 1836 and thus antedating Broca's famous papers by almost 30 years. Unfortunately Dax's paper was only brought to wider notice after his death and after Broca's publications but Drax did draw attention to the association between left hemisphere lesions and aphasia. Furthermore Dax clearly outlined the view that a slowly developing lesion in the left hemisphere might not produce the expected dysphasic disturbances. Thus the notion that slowly developing lesions have less serious effects has a long pedigree.

This question can be explored in animals using serial lesions whereby the effects of producing the total lesion in one stage can be compared with those of making a lesion of similar extent but in two or more stages. This leads to another problem that is occasionally encountered in clinical practice. This is the patient who has substained two separate lesions in different places. In fact the interactive effects of two separate and unrelated lesions can be very different from what might be anticipated by simply adding the expected consequences of the two lesions when considered alone.

Serial lesions

Finger (1978d) has provided a detailed review of the animal evidence relating to the effects of staged or serial lesions. This has emerged as a rather complex issue. There are a number of factors than can influence the consequences of serial lesions and these include such things as the time lag between the different operations (always only two operations in the evidence to be considered here) and the experiences allowed the subject during the inter-operative interval. In addition there is, as usual, a fair quota of conflicting reports in which factors found to be of some potency in other studies fail to emerge to a significant degree.

The importance of the topic of serial lesions for the overall concerns of this book is not sufficient to justify the space for a thorough analysis. The aim of this section is therefore much more limited. This is just to illustrate the kind of findings that have been obtained, and the complexities that they give rise to.

Those wishing to have a more definitive account are referred to Finger (1978d) and Finger *et al.* (1981).

It is also important to note a significant feature of serial learning experiments in animals which makes them less of a close analogue for the human situation than is desirable for those whose major concern is with clinical issues. The typical animal experiment compares a single-stage bilateral lesion with a two-stage procedure in which one side is extirpated first followed by the other at a later date. Slowly progressive lesions in human patients very rarely involve just one hemisphere and then the other.

The standard experimental paradigm in this research is that animals are initially trained on a task; they then undergo a standard lesion administered in one or two stages, and are then retested on the same task. Sometimes when the lesions are given serially there is also a period of interpolated training between the two operations. The final, post-lesion exposure to the task often involves relearning to criterion, to examine the rate of recovery with appropriate experience. Taken as a whole the results of these experiments are very variable. There are a number of findings indicating a better outcome after serial lesions (e.g. Braun, 1975; Gentile *et al.*, 1978; Stewart and Ades, 1951). These are at least partially counterbalanced by other studies which show no effects at all (e.g. Kircher *et al.*, 1970; LeVere and Weiss, 1973). There are a number of other variables which might determine when and where serial effects are found and these are discussed in some detail by Finger (1978d).

An obvious variable is the time interval between the two operations in the subject receiving serial lesions. Probably the first to look at this variable systematically were Stewart and Ades (1951). Monkeys were trained on a single auditory avoidance task and then received bilateral removal of the superior temporal gyri either in a single stage or serially. Various inter-operative intervals were used for the subjects with serial lesions. Simultaneous bilateral operations resulted in a loss of the trained response and a failure to relearn it even with quite extensive retraining. If the serial lesions were given 6 days or less apart they also produced a loss of the habit. There was some retention if the inter-operative interval was longer than this.

A major difficulty with the Stewart and Ades (1951) experiment is that the number of subjects used was rather small in comparison with the number of different experimental conditions. Fortunately other investigators have confirmed the importance of the inter-lesion interval (e.g. Glick and Zimmerberg, 1972; Patrissi and Stein, 1975) although the critical interval for the retention of some effect of the original training appears to be longer than was reported by Stewart and Ades (1951). In the case of Patrissi and Stein (1975) the effect of frontal lesions on spatial alternation in rats was under examination. The critical inter-operative interval required to give near-normal retention in the serial lesion groups appeared to be of the order of 20 days. The differences in critical inter-operative interval in the various studies could well reflect differences between the types of subject, task involved and the location of the lesion.

Another feature of some potential significance is what happens to subjects with serial lesions between the operations. Kircher *et al.* (1970) suggested that inter-operative training could be critical after their failure to observe any beneficial effect of serial lesions on the retention of a black–white discrimination in rats. Amongst others Glendenning (1972) produced evidence in support of this viewpoint in that he found that inter-operative training did have an appreciable effect in a serial lesion experiment. On the other hand, LeVere and Weiss (1973) got no serial lesion effect despite a good interval between operations and the introduction of inter-operative training. Similarly Stewart and Ades (1951) failed to show any contribution attributable to inter-operative training regardless of whether the inter-operative interval was short or long.

A number of other variables have been implicated in serial lesion effects (see Finger, 1978d). It has been suggested, for example, that whether the lesion is cortical or subcortical could be important. Some have also argued that serial lesions are only likely to result in a sparing from deficits associated with single-stage lesions where the task involved is simple (LeVere and Weiss, 1973). Echoing the findings of Guic-Robles *et al.* (1982) described in a previous section, Finger *et al.* (1981) showed that the nature of the retraining procedure used at the end of the experiment could determine whether a serial lesion effect was found. In this experiment a serial lesion effect was only obtained for a difficult tactile discrimination if the post-lesion training progressed from a simpler, but related, discrimination to the difficult one.

Taking the literature on serial lesions as a whole there is much variability in the findings and no simple general conclusions can be given. It is possible that the confusion is more apparent than real in that it arises because not all the possibly relevant variables and their mutual interactions have been explored.

Lesion interaction

The serial lesion situation is but one possibility within the whole question of the effects of multiple lesions. In the serial lesion paradigm each step is considered as contributing to a total lesion. Experimental subjects or human patients may suffer two or more lesions which are not linked in this way and which may involve rather different parts of the brain.

Under these circumstances it would be wrong to assume that the consequences of two lesions are simply the sum of the effects of each when considered separately. Synergistic effects certainly do occur. It is well established that unilateral temporal lobe lesions in man produce memory impairments. Yet estimating the impact on memory of bilateral lesions by simply additively combining the effects of right and left temporal lesions would not give any indication of the extremely severe amnesic disorder produced in a patient like the famous Montreal case of H.M. who underwent bilateral mesial temporal lobe excisions (e.g. Milner, 1966; Iverson, 1977).

The animal literature contains a number of examples of experiments other than those following the serial lesion paradigm in which the subjects received more than one lesion. Ettlinger *et al.* (1968) studied the visual discrimination impairment that follows inferotemporal lesions in monkeys. This is usually not complete and there is recovery in that operated subjects can slowly relearn this type of discrimination. In this particular experiment Ettlinger *et al.* (1968) paired inferotemporal lesions with lesions in either the preoccipital region or in the superior parts of the temporal lobe. Neither of these two additional lesions, when administered alone, will normally affect visual discrimination although the areas involved are adjacent to the inferior temporal region. The preoccipital region has strong reciprocal connections with the inferotemporal region but this is not the case for the superior portions of the temporal lobe. Regardless of the order in which the lesions were placed the combination of inferotemporal and preoccipital lesions resulted in very severe visual discrimination impairments with no sign at all of relearning in many subjects. The addition of superior temporal to inferotemporal lesions did not result in any exacerbation of the impairment in visual discrimination learning.

In a similar type of experiment, also using monkeys, Mohler and Wurtz (1977) looked at the effects of partial striate and partial superior collicular lesions on saccadic eye movements occurring when the subject identified a spot of light presented within the scotoma formed by the lesions. Considered separately the two lesions had different, but by no means drastic, effects on the identification of the spot of light and the saccadic eye movements that occurred. A combination of these two lesions gave a permanent and complete impairment in the ability to identify stimuli presented within the affected parts of the animals' visual fields.

Both the above experiments are alike in showing the combined effects of two lesions to be much more than the simple addition of the consequences of each when considered separately. Other comparable examples could be described (e.g. Baumann and Spear, 1977). Despite this it should not be assumed that the severity of a functional deficit resulting from one lesion can only be enhanced by another lesion. Instances of the reverse can be found in both the human and animal literature.

Using rats it is very well established that lesions of the lateral hypothalamus can produce aphagia. If such subjects are kept alive artificially they often begin to eat spontaneously after a few days. Glick and Greenstein (1972) examined this phenomenon in subjects with prior ablations of the frontal cortex. Those receiving the additional lesion first recovered eating behaviour much more rapidly than controls which only received the hypothalamic lesion.

A situation that could be considered reasonably comparable was reported by Welch and Penfield (1950). They had five cases of infantile hemiplegia who were later operated on in adolescence or early adult life. Excision of motor cortex on the side contralateral to the hemiplegia was found to result in decreased spasticity and an improvement in functioning in the affected limbs. This might be viewed as the possible interacting effects of two lesions but there is another possible mechanism. This finding could also be just another example of the general principle that removal of malfunctioning tissue can give a better outcome than leaving this tissue in place (see Miller, 1972). Stereotactic surgery for the relief of

Parkinsonism (e.g. Calne, 1970) is another example in humans where the addition of another lesion results in a reduced impairment.

Multiple lesions obviously interact in complex ways. The outcome after two lesions can be both much more and much less than what might be expected from simply adding the typical effects of each of the lesions when occurring individually. Although explanations of the interactions have been offered in individual cases there is no work leading towards general rules for predicting lesion interactions. Under some circumstances the interactive effects of two lesions can have implications for understanding the mechanisms underlying recovery and so certain aspects of this topic of lesion interaction will arise in the next chapter.

WITHIN-SUBJECT VARIABLES

The size of any behavioural deficit and the extent and rate of recovery may well be influenced by intra-subject variables. The most obvious of these, and possibly one of the most potent, is age. The influence of age on recovery has already been dealt with in some detail in Chapter 2 and it would be unnecessarily repetitious to go over the same ground again. It will be remembered that there is some justification for the commonly held view that younger subjects will sustain less severe impairments and show better recovery after comparable lesions. However, this is at best only a crude rule of thumb. In the case of younger children the greater plasticity and adaptability of the brain is bought at a price. Examples exist in the animal literature of lesions in early life resulting in behavioural impairments not encountered after similar lesions in mature subjects. There are also hints of this in some clinical research with human subjects. Within the adult age range the general impression is that younger subjects do have a better outcome but this is not always so. Studies in which an age relationship does occur are often in a position where age could have been confounded by other factors.

Another important subject variable is handedness. It has been demonstrated that patients with aphasia after left hemisphere lesions generally show better recovery of speech if they are left-handed (Smith, 1971; Subirana, 1958, 1969). There is little reason to doubt this finding although the question as to why this should be so is open to dispute. The commonly offered explanation is that left-handers, or those with left-handed tendencies, are better able to transfer speech functions to the right hemisphere after left-sided damage. An alternative explanation can be argued along the following lines. The human split-brain research strongly suggests that even right-handers possess some elementary speech processing capacity in the right hemisphere (e.g. Gazzaniga and Sperry, 1967). It is not unreasonable to expect that right hemisphere speech is even better developed in left-handers, even in the majority of left-handers that would normally be considered to be left dominant for speech (Milner, 1974a). Thus the better apparent recovery in left-handers after left hemisphere lesions may be a reflection of the fact that they have a greater pre-existing speech capacity in the right hemisphere to fall back on.

There is another laterality effect evident in recovery. Even when looking at non-speech functions, such as mobility and the ability to redevelop the basic activities of daily living, it has been found that stroke patients with left hemisphere lesions generally do better than those with lesions in the right hemisphere (Langton-Hewer, 1982; Marquardsen, 1969).

A large number of other variables might also relate to recovery after brain damage. However, it is often difficult to be sure if these are independent of the effects of the brain lesion itself. For example, it might be argued that the extent of recovery is at least partly a function of the patient's motivation and determination to improve. It is then not at all easy in most instances to decide whether a lack of motivation to overcome handicaps in a given individual is a manifestation of the patient's personality that was there prior to the injury, or if it is a consequence of that injury. Another possibility is that the lesion has exacerbated a tendency that was already present. From the practical point of view the important thing is the influence of the particular factor on recovery and the reason why it is so is of more secondary importance.

Golden (1978) indicates a large number of variables that might relate to recovery. These include such things as IQ level, motivation, presence of emotional problems, etc. These will not be discussed in any detail because the evidence advanced for most of these factors is rather weak, coming from such sources as general clinical impressions rather than objectively gathered data. It is all too easy for clinicians to look back at their failures and attribute these to poor motivation, aggressive response towards staff, unsuitable personality, and related factors. This is not to claim that a feature like motivation may not be of any importance, but it is necessary to draw attention to the unsatisfactory nature of the evidence.

A number of more objective studies have found that IQ and/or premorbid educational level (which tend to be correlated to an appreciable degree) do relate to outcome after brain damage (e.g. Ben-Yishay et al., 1970a; Humphrey and Oddy, 1980; Smith, 1971). Unfortunately in some studies, and especially those relating to outcome after head injury (Humphrey and Oddy, 1980), the criterion of recovery has been return to work. It is possible that the more intelligent and better-educated work in occupational settings where there is more tolerance of handicap. Such artifacts are less likely to be in operation in the other two studies cited.

From the descriptions given it is difficult to separate out motivation and personality variables. Bond (1975), in discussing outcome after severe head injury, particularly identifies the personality changes that often occur as impeding recovery and rehabilitation. In a similar vein Evans (1982) draws attention to the head-injured patient's tendency to become aggressive. Again in relation to the rehabilitation of head injury Holland and Whalley (1981) stress the victim's difficulties in adjusting to his injury and handicaps.

Such features have also commonly been noted in patients with aphasia. Benson (1979b) discusses emotional reactions in aphasics, and Robinson and Benson (1981) showed that there was a relationship between aphasia and depression. Robinson and Benson were unable to disentangle the cause of the depression but it was more common in those with non-fluent aphasias and was not related to lesion size as measured by the CT scan. Darley (1975), in his extensive review of the treatment of aphasia, cites a number of authorities who strongly believe that motivation and level of aspiration are potent variables in determining response to aphasia therapy.

It does seem clear that age, handedness, and side of lesion do bear some relationship to recovery, although handedness has so far only been shown to be relevant to the recovery of speech in aphasia. There is wide agreement that other intra-subject variables such as intelligence, personality, motivation, and emotional state can affect outcome but objective data are lacking. Nevertheless it is certainly quite plausible that these factors should relate to the ability to regain functional goals.

DRUGS

Since this book is mainly concerned with the behavioural effects of brain lesions and with the influence of environmental or behavioural manipulations on recovery, pharmacological interventions will not be considered in any detail. Nevertheless it should be noted that the consequences of brain lesions can be either enhanced or reduced by pharmacological agents. The relevant work on humans has obvious therapeutic implications and will be dealt with in later chapters in the context of therapeutic issues in general.

There is an extensive literature dealing with the interaction between brain lesions and drugs in animals. This has been covered in a fairly recent review by Glick and Zimmerberg (1978). This paper demonstrates that the effects of drugs on recovery from the effects of brain lesions are rarely simple. The effect of a drug on a lesion-induced deficit typically depends upon a number of other factors such as the size of the lesion and the experience of the subject prior to the administration of the drug. It can also depend upon the details of the particular test situation used. If similar complexities occur in humans it would then be naive to expect to find a single drug that would help to, say, alleviate organically induced memory impairments of all types and under all circumstances. Effects are likely to be very much more selective than this.

COMMENT

Chapter 2 began by setting out a series of generalizations about recovery after brain damage. These were of the order that younger subjects would show quicker and more extensive recovery than older subjects. These generalizations have now been considered in some detail. In every instance it has been found on closer examination that the generalizations do have some degree of support but that there are also important exceptions or qualifications that need to be taken into account. In other words these generalizations must be regarded as nothing better than rough-and-ready approximations to what most commonly occurs.

In order to deal with the possible influences on recovery in a reasonably manageable way it has been necessary to consider each one separately. In the real-life clinical situation these variables will, of course, interrelate and interact. It is also possible that some of the inconsistencies noted in discussing a particular variable might have been eliminated if all other factors that might contribute to or influence recovery were held constant. On the other hand, it could well be the case that examining the interactions between the different factors would lead to a picture that is even more complex and difficult to understand. It is difficult to comment further until investigators have actually started to explore possible interactions in a systematic way.

Whatever the outcome of this kind of investigation it can hardly be disputed that the recovery of function after brain injury is a complex process influenced by many factors. There is still a considerable way to go before the clinician is likely to achieve a useful level of prediction of outcome in the individual patient who has suffered damage or disease of the brain.

CHAPTER FIVE

Explanations of recovery

The previous chapters have dealt in some detail with the course of recovery and the factors that influence it. It is now time to take a fairly close look at the various mechanisms that have been postulated to explain the recovery process. In effect what the explanations of recovery have to account for are findings of the kind presented in the three preceding chapters. In fact some of the more detailed discussions of topics such as the 'Kennard principle' (see Chapter 2) have already introduced mechanisms that might be of value in accounting for recovery in general.

Quite a large number of possible mechanisms of recovery have been suggested. In very broad terms these can be classified into three major groups. These are here designated as 'artifact theories', 'anatomical reorganization', and 'functional adaptation'. An immediate point of some importance is that these different types of explanation are not necessarily mutually exclusive. Thus it is possible in a given instance that recovery might be brought about by a range of different mechanisms which fall into all three of these categories. This makes evaluation of individual theories a little difficult since evidence for one type of explanation does not automatically make the others less plausible in the usual way of theoretical controversies where the alternative hypotheses are in direct competition with one another. Despite this information relating to one theory can have some bearing on the others in a rather weaker sense. If it is demonstrated that recovery in a given instance is largely due to one particular mechanism then this limits the potential scope of the rest despite the fact that it cannot prove that other mechanisms are not involved at all.

Since evidence relating to one kind of explanation does have some bearing on how the others can be viewed it is probably best to separate the discussion of theories into two parts. In the section that immediately follows an attempt will be made to describe the various mechanisms that have been proposed in a relatively neutral and non-evaluative way. The theories can then be critically examined in the following section, which will concentrate on their logical and empirical status and range of applicability as this appears in the light of present knowledge. The following chapter will then take up the implications of these theoretical issues for clinical practice.

OUTLINE OF THEORIES

The various explanations of recovery that have been put forward form a very mixed bag both in terms of the kinds of mechanism that they impute and in their level of development as theories. Some of the explanatory notions that have been suggested do qualify to be described as 'theories', in that it is possible to derive testable hypotheses from them. Others are just vague and general ideas which require much further development before they ought to be dignified with the accolade of 'theory'.

As has already been indicated the following description will split the suggested explanations into three groups. It is almost inevitable with classifications of complex ideas that the bases on which the classifications are made appear to be less clear-cut the closer they are examined. This is certainly true here, but the classification used below is justified in that it draws attention to potentially significant aspects of the recovery process.

Artifact theories

What these theories have in common is the general assumption that there are two components in the initially observed impairment after brain damage. The lesion will destroy certain tissue with the loss of those aspects of behaviour for which the intact functioning of the destroyed area is essential. This can be described as the primary deficit. The primary deficit is permanent or, if it does show some recovery, its recovery is not explained by theories in this group.

In addition the insult will produce temporary, or largely temporary, disturbances in the physiological functioning of other parts of the brain not involved in the primary deficit. These in turn will result in secondary behavioural impairments. As this additional and temporary disruption is resolved so the secondary deficits will recover. It is not unreasonable to regard the functions underlying these secondary deficits as being suppressed or inactivated rather than being lost. Hence the recovery is an 'artifact' in the sense that the notion of recovery implies that what has been recovered must have been truly lost rather than inhibited or suppressed.

The main issue which the 'artifact theories' attempt to explain is the occurrence and resolution of these secondary deficits. There are a number of physiological changes which follow any brain insult (Schoenfeld and Hamilton, 1977) and many of these could give some additional temporary disruption of functioning with a consequent appearance of recovery. One very obvious candidate is the phenomenon of oedema. Oedema is likely to occur in tissue surrounding that directly affected by the lesion. In oedema there is an increase in tissue water content, mainly in the form of extracellular fluid, and this results in an increase of overall tissue volume (Fishman, 1978). Oedema will resolve spontaneously with time and in clinical practice can be reduced by the administration of certain drugs, especially the steroid dexamethasone. It also impairs the functioning of affected tissue in that there is ample clinical evidence that the active treatment of oedema can produce remarkable and rapid behavioural improvements in patients with lesions known to be surrounded by oedematous tissue. Oedema can also produce more generalized effects if it is severe in that it significantly raises intracranial pressure. In extreme cases it can be life-threatening for this reason. The resolution of oedema surrounding a lesion is therefore one mechanism that might explain some recovery.

The major explanation in the artifact group, and possibly the most frequently referred to of all theories of recovery, is von Monakow's (1914) notion of diaschisis. von Monakow's book is not readily available and is by no means the easiest document to understand for those whose German is less than fluent. Fortunately an English translation of the key portion of this book has been provided by Pribram (1969). The present account is based largely on this translation but it ought to be noted that it has proved difficult to give an exact rendering of von Monakow's ideas in English. Almost inevitably the accuracy of this translation has been disputed (Markowitsch and Pritzel, 1978). For the present the minutiae can be ignored since all that is required is a general understanding of the theory. Detailed points will emerge in a later section when the available empirical evidence is discussed and the theory is evaluated.

The basic principle underlying von Monakow's ideas is that when a lesion occurs in a particular part of the brain a form of shock can occur elsewhere. The parts of the brain susceptible to this shock effect can be adjacent to the site of the primary insult or in quite distant parts that are linked in some way to the area of primary disturbance. This transmitted shock von Monakow chose to call 'diaschisis'. The exact nature of diaschisis was never adequately specified but von Monakow was clear that it is a process quite distinct from that of oedema. Since it is most commonly only a temporary phenomenon there is a subsequent recovery. The original formulation even postulated a form of permanent diaschisis to account for deficits apparently not attributable to the primary lesion and which failed to show any recovery. This extension of the theory to cover any deficit no matter how transient or permanent makes the theory more complex, less testable, and therefore less attractive from a scientific point of view. Nevertheless Teuber (1974) has suggested that the idea of permanent diaschisis may have some value in explaining deficits on such tasks as those requiring the identification of hidden figures, which seem to be present on a long-term basis after focal lesions in many different parts of the brain.

Russian workers (see Luria, 1963) have used the notion of inhibition in a rather similar way to von Monakow's diaschisis. The basic proposition is that the primary injury causes inhibition of activity in other parts of the brain, possibly by a reduction of acetylcholine activity at the synapse. The concept of inhibition differs from that of diaschisis in that the latter is considered to spread along specific pathways linked to the site of injury whilst the spread of inhibition is much more amorphous. An immediate advantage of this Russian model over most of the others that will be discussed is that it has led directly to therapeutic intervention. The nature of the therapy and its possible effectiveness will be discussed later.

A final theory within this artifact group has recently been proposed by LeVere (1980). Unlike those described already it is based directly upon experimental work with animals. LeVere suggests that an early consequence of damage is to cause the subject to shift control of behaviour to undamaged neural systems. The initial behavioural deficit therefore represents the gap between what these other systems can achieve on their own and what the subject could achieve with the damaged system prior to the insult. Where recovery occurs this is because there is a return to the original neural system that was affected by the injury and the utilization of whatever aspects of this system have been spared. This theory belongs in the artifact group because whatever is recovered was never really lost.

The main artifact theories have been described above but these by no means exhaust the possible mechanisms that could be invoked under this general heading. For example, Lashley (1950) postulated that amnesia might be produced not by the loss of tissue actively involved in mediating memory but by disturbances in attentional mechanisms. If this were so then an improvement in attention, produced by whatever means, would also result in an apparent improvement in memory. Today the idea that amnesic disturbances might be a by-product of attentional deficits does not seem very plausible except under certain limited conditions. The importance of Lashley's suggestion in this context is that it draws attention to the fact that a disturbance in one function may have effects on others. This could then have implications for apparent recovery.

Anatomical reorganization

The idea of anatomical reorganization carries the implication that when damage occurs to one part of the brain recovery can take place by means of other parts of the brain taking over the functions originally subserved by the damaged parts. An immediate corollary of this theory is that it assumes some degree of localization of function. In fact, as Rosner (1974) has indicated, recovery presents no real problem for anyone who believes that the brain is undifferentiated with respect to function. The remaining mass of brain tissue will contiue to operate in the same way. Because the available mass is reduced there will be some loss of overall efficiency but all functions will be picked up again as the initial period of generalized shock after the injury starts to dissipate. As was argued in the introductory chapter it is very difficult to avoid the conclusion that there is some degree of localization of function. This is by no means as perfect as some of the extreme advocates of localization would have liked it to be, but this is no problem since the principle of anatomical reorganization as an explanation of recovery merely assumes that there is some degree of localization.

As described so far the idea of anatomical reorganization is no more than a vague and general principle. According to Rosner (1974) the first person to use this principle in a more explicit theory of recovery was the British neurologist John Hughlings Jackson towards the end of the nineteenth century (see Taylor, 1931). Jackson regarded the nervous system as being organized at different levels. He argued that the higher levels came later in evolution, are more easily excited, can inhibit lower levels, and control a given function in a more sophisticated way. The different functions are nevertheless represented at each level. If part of the higher level, i.e. part of the cortex, is damaged then control of any function that is disturbed can be taken over at a lower, subcortical level. This subcortical level is also specialized for the function concerned but its efforts will hitherto have been inhibited by the appropriate section at the higher level. Although this hypothesized mechanism might explain recovery a consequence would be that the extent or quality of recovery could never be perfect. This is because the responsible part at the lower level is not as sophisticated as the higher level prior to damage.

Another early view is that of Munk (1878). Munk considered that regions of the brain not originally connected in any way with the lost function might take it over. In addition to making no reference to levels of organization this differs from Jackson's position in that for the latter the lower-level structure that deals with the affected function was already linked to that function. It was just that its earlier potential contribution had been suppressed. For the kind of substitution espoused by Munk there need to be, within the brain, regions that are either free from other demands (i.e. which are otherwise redundant) or which can completely or partially reject an existing role in order to take over that associated with the part of the brain that has been damaged.

Views of the kind put forward by Munk are often appealed to in order to explain recovery. A common assumption is that recovery from aphasia is cases with left-sided lesions is made possible by the right hemisphere taking over at least some of the verbal functions normally subserved by the left. Some have even based attempts at remediation of aphasic disturbances on the assumption that this is the crucial mechanism underlying recovery (Buffery, 1976).

Functional adaptation

Again the idea behind functional adaptation is no more than a general principle. Unlike the artifact and anatomical reorganization models no more specific mechanisms have as yet been postulated. This approach to explaining recovery really deals with the subject's reattainment of functions as goals rather than the recovery of the means by which the goals are achieved.

The general idea is that an afflicted individual might be able to relearn the ability to achieve a certain goal affected by neural damage by means other than those originally employed. For example, the writer usually ties a tie with minimal reference to visual feedback either by looking in a mirror or by looking down at what he is doing. A small amount of visual feedback is used but control of the activity is exerted mainly through tactile and proprioceptive feedback. Should he suffer a lesion that selectively impairs tactile and proprioceptive feedback whilst leaving the ability to initiate movements in the upper limbs relatively intact, then it might be possible for him to relearn to tie a tie by relying much more extensively on visual feedback obtained through a mirror.

The most detailed statement and elaboration of the principle of functional reorganization has been provided by Luria *et al.* (1969) who discuss its application to remedial work with a number of different types of clinical problem. A significant implication of this principle is that it implies that appropriately directed training may be of considerable value in enhancing adaptation following brain damage.

EVALUATION

As already indicated, an important point affecting the evaluation of the various possible mechanisms that might underlie recovery is that they are not mutually exclusive. This is certainly the case when considered at the level of general principles such as anatomical reorganization, functional adaptation, or artifact explanations. Even within these general categories of explanation the more specific theories are often not competitive in the sense that to hold one automatically implies the rejection of the others. This means that in evaluating the different explanations the problem is much more complex than if it were just the case of trying to identify the most plausible from within a set of mutually exclusive alternatives. For each possible mechanism it is necessary to ask two questions. These concern the likelihood that the postulated mechanism actually plays a part in overall recovery and, if so, its significance in relation to all the other processes that might also underlie recovery. These questions are further complicated by the possibility that the relative importance of the different mechanisms may vary from situation to situation. Ideally the factors underlying variations of this kind need to be described and explained.

One variable that could have an appreciable effect in determining the kinds of mechanism that are important in recovery might be age. For example, it will be suggested later that there is evidence that anatomical reorganization, by whatever means, is more likely to be a significant determinant of recovery in children than it is in adults. Since the main concern of this book is with brain damage in adults the question of recovery in children will not be pursued very far.

Artifact theories

There can be no real doubt that some recovery is the consequence of artifactual processes of the kind described earlier. Oedema is a well-established phenomenon (e.g. Fishman, 1978) which certainly can exaggerate deficits observed in the acute phase. Other short-term physiological reactions will also occur after brain lesions and will take time to resolve (Schoenfeld and Hamilton, 1977). Whilst not in dispute such phenomena are not of great interest in this context because they are transient and measured in days, or weeks, at most. The real concern is with recovery that extends over longer periods of time.

Despite the frequency with which it arises in discussions of recovery and its long history, von Monakow's (1914) theory of diaschisis has not been subjected to much careful scrutiny. In general the tendency has been to report findings which might fit nicely within the diaschisis framework but which cannot be regarded as an adequate test of the theory. One example is Russell (1981), who reports a single case with involvement of the left temporo-parietal lesion as a result of encephalitis. Initially the patient showed a wide range of neuropsychological impairments but these reduced over a period of many months until he was left with what appeared to be a permanent acquired dyslexia which matched the site of the original focus of infection.

There have been a few attempts at experimental tests of the idea of diaschisis. The first of these were reported by Kempinsky (1954, 1958). In one of these experiments he looked for negative steady potential shifts over the surface of cats' brains following middle cerebral artery occlusion. Such changes were observed only in the territory directly served by the occluded artery and there was no spread of electrical disturbance to other parts of the brain surface, as might be expected on the basis of the theory of diaschisis or even the inhibition theory described by Luria (1963). In the later paper Kempinsky (1958) reported data obtained by the electrical recording of activity in the optic cortex after stimulation of the more distal parts of the optic pathways. Lesions in parts of the brain unconnected with the visual system were found to diminish activity in the optical cortex in response to similar forms of stimulation. Kempinsky was also able to show that this effect was not mediated by vascular changes.

Whilst Kempinsky's (1958) experiment does go a little way towards providing evidence in support of diaschisis a number of problems still remain. Firstly the effects obtained were only transient and apparently lasted for less than an hour. Diaschisis has universally been put forward as a possible explanation of recovery extending over very much longer periods than this. The second difficulty arising out of Kempinsky's work is that diaschisis is usually alleged to occur in parts of the brain that have some link with the damaged area. It is not a general, indiscriminate effect that spreads all over the brain. This point is completely ignored in Kempinsky's work which could almost be better seen as a test of Luria's (1963) inhibition theory.

The most adequate test of the diaschisis theory yet available has been provided by West et al. (1976). In this experiment electrophysiological recordings were taken from the outer layers of the dentate gyrus of the hippocampal formation in rats. A large number of cells in this region receive afferent input from the entorhinal cortex but there are also other inputs. West et al. began by establishing the typical response in the dentate gyrus resulting from stimulation in the different places providing an afferent input. The entorhinal cortex was then ablated. The expectation resulting from the notion of diaschisis is that the ablation of the area producing the major afferent input would produce diaschisis in at least that part of the dentate gyrus under study. This should then give a consequent alteration in the response to stimulation of the other areas providing an afferent input. No evidence of this was obtained.

On the face of it West et al.'s (1976) experiment fails to obtain evidence of diaschisis in just the kind of situation where it ought to be most apparent. Of course it cannot show that diaschisis effects would not be obtained by studying other brain areas and under different experimental conditions. The experiment has also raised a dispute as to the true nature of von Monakow's ideas. As has already been indicated von Monakow's (1914) book is not the easiest work to understand and the accuracy of the translation of the crucial section given in Pribram (1969) has been challenged. Markowitsch and Pritzel (1978) took up this point in discussing West *et al.*'s (1976) negative results. According to Markowitsch and Pritzel the theory as put forward by von Monakow stated that diaschisis occurs suddenly in most cases but by no means all. Their point is presumably that if West *et al.* (1976) had waited long enough then effects consistent with diaschisis might have emerged. Similarly diaschisis most commonly dissipates with time although this is not invariably the case and the effect may be permanent. On some occasions no diaschsis effects may occur at all. Whilst Markowitsch and Pritzel could well be correct in drawing attention to the fact that the original formulation of the theory foresaw situations in which diaschisis did not follow the general rule of rapid onset and subsequent dissipation with time, the introduction of any exceptions presents difficulties. This is especially so where there is no account of the circumstances under which the exceptions are likely to arise. The theory thus becomes less rigorous and more difficult to test experimentally. It would be foolish to imagine that the results of any single experiment could ever completely invalidate a major theoretical position in any field. Nevertheless the failure of the only well-conceived experiment purporting to test the theory, that of West *et al.* (1976), can hardly do otherwise than enhance doubts about the adequacy of the concept of diaschisis.

The Russian use of the concept of inhibition (e.g. Luria, 1963; Luria *et al.*, 1969) implies a more general process than diaschisis. Given the considerable complexity of the brain with its multiple interconnections between the various centres it cannot be considered inherently implausible that damage at one point could have far-reaching effects on other parts of the brain. There are also empirical findings that seem to be best interpreted by a process of inhibition or something akin to it. Luria (1970) examined the frequency with which gunshot wounds in different parts of the left hemisphere produced speech disturbances. If testing was carried out shortly after injury then speech disturbances were surprisingly common for lesions all over the left hemisphere. These were certainly not confined to damage within those regions of the left hemisphere traditionally associated with aphasic disorders (see Figure 4). Follow-up several weeks later showed that the incidence of aphasia had considerably decreased, but especially so for lesions in places outside the classical speech areas. The obvious interpretation is that aphasia initially resulted from lesions outside the speech areas because of inhibitory effects emanating from the site of the primary injury which affected the speech areas. As this inhibition dissipated so speech recovered.

Some of the evidence described when evaluating the notion of diaschisis is also of potential relevance here (e.g. Russell, 1981). As already pointed out Kempinsky's (1958) attempt to get experimental evidence for diaschisis would be far better construed as an attempt to demonstrate generalized effects of lesions that might be equated with some form of inhibitory process. It will be recalled that Kempinsky did find changes in negative steady potential shifts in areas not

64

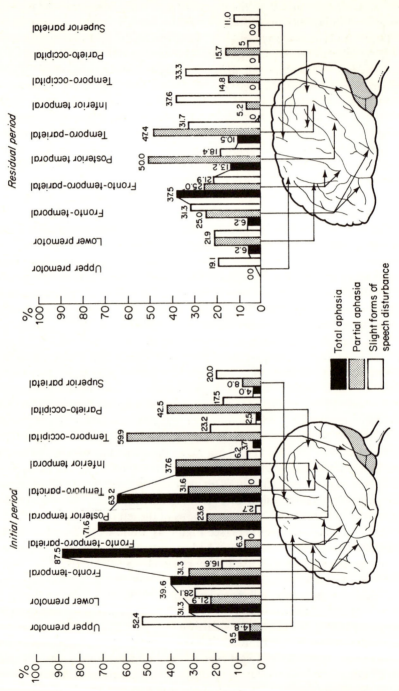

Figure 4. Severity of aphasic symptoms arising from injury at different sites shortly after injury (left) and when subjects were seen some time later (right) (from Luria, 1970)

directly involved with the lesion. The snag is that the effects were transitory in that they only lasted for less than an hour.

In order to put a theory based on the concept of inhibition into a form capable of direct test it is necessary to specify just how the inhibitory effect is mediated and how it can be detected. The Russian workers (Luria, 1963; Luria *et al.*, 1969) have postulated that insults to the brain can increase cholinesterase concentration in surrounding parts of the brain and possibly also in parts of the brain far removed from the site of injury if they form part of the same or a related functional system. Cholinesterase levels influence acetylcholine levels and hence synaptic conduction. This is then the mechanism that is alleged to underlie inhibition. An important prediction from this model is that drugs which block the action of cholinesterase should enhance recovery.

Luria (1963) and Luria *et al.* (1969) have described a number of investigations suggesting that recovery can be enhanced by the administration of drugs such as neostigmine and galanthamine as an anti-cholinesterase therapy. It is claimed that these drugs can produce very rapid responses in some cases (within an hour or so after a single injection) and it sometimes happens that beneficial results can be obtained even years after the injury. From the accounts given, this work seems most encouraging but difficult to evaluate properly because the Russian workers do not give detailed accounts with the results of careful evaluation of the subjects in quantitative terms, let alone carrying out the kind of drug trials expected in the West.

As far as this writer is aware there has been no attempt reported by Western investigators to replicate the Russian findings with regard to the effects of cholinergic agents on recovery from CNS lesions. Brailowsky (1980), in his review of neuropharmacology and brain plasticity, is similarly unable to locate any Western studies. However, he does draw attention to two animal experiments by Ward and Kennard (1942) and Watson and Kennard (1945) which claimed some increase in the rate of recovery of motor functions as a result of the administration of cholinergic agents after decortication in monkeys. For rather unrelated reasons there has also been considerable interest in the possible use of cholinergic agents in the treatment of dementia but the results of these endeavours have been, at best, variable (e.g. Drachman and Sahakian, 1980).

LeVere's (1980) position, developed from experiments on rats, involves mechanisms at a behavioural rather than a physiological or biochemical level. The chain of argument used by LeVere (1980) is quite complex and only the outline can be described here. Those particularly interested are advised to consult the original papers.

A series of experiments in LeVere's laboratory has looked at the disruption and apparent recovery of learned brightness discriminations after visual cortex lesions in rats. It is possible that the loss of a learned discrimination after such lesions is due to the disruption of the relevant memory trace but alternative possibilities do exist. In particular it could be argued that what has happened is not the loss of the ability to make brightness discriminations or the capacity to retain such discriminations once learned, but that something has happened which makes the animal unable to utilize what it has learned pre-operatively.

It seems unlikely that retention of the pre-operatively learned discrimination has been lost because strong proactive effects of pre-operative learning on the post-operative learning of the reverse discrimination can be demonstrated (LeVere and Morlock, 1974). A further experiment by LeVere *et al.* (1979) indicated that the loss of the original learned discrimination was probably not due to motivational changes. In this same paper LeVere *et al.* report another experiment in which a transfer paradigm was used. Subjects were first given lesions and then trained on an initial brightness discrimination. They were then able to make use of this training in learning a second discrimination.

LeVere (1980) concludes from these and other experiments that the apparent loss and later recovery of brightness discriminations with post-operative training cannot be due to the loss of the ability to make such discriminations. There is thus no lost ability which then recovers. Something must then interfere with the post-operative expression of the skill acquired pre-operatively which does not involve the excluded mechanisms. LeVere (1980) opts for the possibility that after the visual cortex lesion, which must be presumed to have some effect on visual processing, the animal then attempts to solve the problem by other means (i.e. by using information not affected in any way by striate lesions). In the present context this is likely to fail and because it fails the animal then learns to fall back on whatever visual capacity is left in order to make brightness discriminations. (There is evidence that the ability to make more complex kinds of visual discrimination may be really lost.) LeVere (1980) then goes on to review evidence that can be interpreted as showing two things. These are, firstly, that the neural insult will cause a shift towards the utilization of neural systems not directly involved in the injury and, secondly, that the animal compensates by trying to learn to achieve the same goal by different means.

One of the more critical studies in support of LeVere's hypotheses is that of Davis and LeVere (1979), who confirmed and then built upon some previous research by LeVere and Fontaine (1978). This showed that a drug (8-axaguanine) interfered with the acquisition of new brightness discriminations in rats with posterior lesions but did not affect performance based upon such discriminations once they had been learned. In rats given pre-operative training on a brightness discrimination, administration of this same drug prior to post-operative retraining actually enhanced recovery of the discrimination. According to the theory this is because it did not interfere with the expression of pre-operative learning but would have a deleterious effect on the learning of inappropriate compensatory behaviour based upon the use of other sensory systems. A further set of experiments (LeVere and LeVere, 1982) also purports to show that after visual decortication rats will ignore visual cues and respond to non-visual cues in trying to escape or avoid foot shock. By using a series of transfer experiments the authors also showed that this compensatory mechanism retarded the recovery of visual functions (or, more accurately, the emergence of whatever visual functioning remained after the lesion).

LeVere's work is of considerable interest and gives the most penetrating attempt so far to provide a detailed analysis of the mechanisms underlying the apparent loss and subsequent recovery of a function after brain injury. Whilst falling into the artifact group of theories LeVere's ideas also provide a link with the notion of functional adaptation which will be considered in detail later.

Anatomical reorganization

There is no doubt that anatomical reorganization in some form or other is a commonly accepted explanation of recovery and sparing (e.g. Bach-y-Rita, 1981a,b). The commonly reported finding that young children with even quite extensive lesions of the left hemisphere may develop language abilities that are at least very close to those of their normal peers (e.g. Woods and Carey, 1979) makes the idea of the right hemisphere taking over speech functions difficult to resist. As indicated in Chapter 2, one expected corollary of this is that the spatial functions normally subserved by the right hemisphere would tend to suffer if this hemisphere takes over the speech role. Evidence consistent with this has been found (Milner, 1974a,b).

Even more compelling evidence of the abnormal development of speech in the right hemisphere comes from the use of the Wada technique, whereby sodium amytal is injected into the carotid artery on one side. This has clearly revealed a markedly increased incidence of right hemisphere dominance for speech in subjects with early left hemisphere damage (Milner *et al.*, 1966). Goldman's work on the differential effects of frontal lesions in infant and adult monkeys also implies the capacity for some degree of anatomical reorganization (see Goldman, 1974 and the account given in Chapter 2). However, it would be a logical extension of her concept of functional maturity to expect that the ability to undergo anatomical reorganization would be confined to subjects who have yet to reach full maturity.

It appears quite likely that anatomical reorganization in some form can and does occur in the very young. The status of this principle as an explanation of recovery in mature subjects is much more open to question. It is particularly tempting to appeal to findings like those of Subirana (1958) which indicate better recovery from aphasia after stroke in subjects with left hemisphere lesions who also happen to be left-handed. The assumption is then made that left-handers are better able to redevelop speech in the right hemisphere and it is this that results in their better recovery from aphasia.

Such arguments go way beyond the evidence, and equally plausible alternative hypotheses can be advanced. For example, there is evidence from research on split-brain subjects that the right hemisphere can process and use speech in a limited way even in right-handers (e.g. Sperry, 1968). This happens without any left hemisphere lesion to produce aphasia and it would not be entirely unreasonable to expect that this right hemisphere ability to process speech is more fully developed in left-handers. The apparent recovery from aphasia could merely be the consequence of the patient starting to make full use of a capacity for language already present in the right hemisphere, but which has been dormant up to the time of the lesion which produced the aphasia.

There have been a number of more searching experiments directed at examining the capacity of the right hemisphere to take over speech functions. Pettit and Noll (1979) tested 25 aphasic subjects and a similar number of matched normal controls on tests of dichotic listening. The subjects were tested on two occasions with the severity of the aphasia also being examined in the aphasic group. The results indicated that the aphasic subjects did improve between the two testings. The pattern of improvement was such that the aphasic subjects became relatively more able to detect and report dichotic stimuli presented to the left ear. This was assumed to reflect increasing right hemisphere dominance for speech. Although the improvement between the two tests shown by the left ear in the aphasic subjects was statistically significant the magnitude of the change was small. It is also possible that the change reflects an alteration in strategy whereby the subjects learn with practice to rely more on the intact, if less well-developed, inherent capacity for speech in the right hemisphere by giving greater attention to stimuli presented to the left ear. It is not necessary to assume any development of speech capacity in the right hemisphere subsequent to the lesion that produced the aphasia in order to explain this finding.

In most studies purporting to show development of speech in the right hemisphere after aphasia the time at which this right hemisphere speech capacity was acquired is crucial. Since there is some pre-existing right hemisphere speech capacity in all subjects it then becomes necessary to show that any shift in control of speech functions to the right hemisphere after a left hemisphere lesion producing aphasia really is associated with a corresponding increase in right hemisphere speech capacity. Investigations like that of Pettit and Noll (1979) or Meyer et al. (1980), which showed increase in cerebral blood flow to the right hemisphere after aphasia, do not prove that the right hemisphere speech capacity has been enhanced following the acquisition of aphasia. They are equally consistent with the subject having changed strategies in order to make use of a right hemisphere speech capacity that was already present.

In addition to the experiments already cited there are two single-case investigations which merit comment because they might be claimed to get round the particular methodological difficulty described immediately above. The first, and least convincing, is a report by Cummings et al. (1979). They described a middle-aged man who suffered a left middle cerebral artery embolism. This resulted in a global aphasia and the CT scan was said to indicate a total destruction of the classical left hemisphere language areas. Follow-up assessments over 2 years later revealed considerable improvement in the subject's aphasia but no improvement in neurological status. The authors suggest that the recovery of language must be due to the development of language capacity in the intact right hemisphere.

Part of their reason for making this claim is that the CT scan showed complete destruction of the usual left hemisphere speech areas, thus ruling out the possibility of using the left hemisphere to regain speech. This argument does not allow for the fact that the CT scan is still a fairly coarse instrument for determining the exact extent of an infarct and so the claim that all left hemisphere speech areas were destroyed cannot be accepted without reservation. The authors also raise another point in contending that recovery was mediated by the development of right hemisphere speech. In this patient comprehension recovered rather better than expression, and it has been found in split-brain studies that the right hemisphere's limited language capacity is more evident for comprehension than expression (e.g. Sperry, 1968). This is a fairly weak point since it may be just that the nature of the particular left hemisphere damage made recovery of expression more difficult or that the patient switched to using pre-existing comprehension abilities in the right hemisphere.

The second single-case report is that of Gazzaniga *et al.* (1979) who studied a subject who had undergone a complete resection of the corpus callosum at the age of 15 years in order to relieve intractable epilepsy. Initially this subject, like many others with split brains, gave some signs of language comprehension in the right hemisphere. Tachistoscopic studies were carried out several times post-operatively. Words or pictures were presented to the left or right visual fields under appropriate experimental conditions (i.e. with exposure times too short to allow eye movements to influence where the stimulus appeared in the visual field). At 18 months post-operatively the subject could only verbally identify words or pictures presented to the right visual field. Later test periods (2–3 years post-operatively) showed the development of the ability to give verbal reports on material presented to the left visual field (and hence right hemisphere).

In this writer's opinion this is one of the most convincing pieces of evidence from human research in favour of anatomical reorganization in the adult. Unfortunately it is still open to question. One possibility is that in the later testings the verbal responses to left field presentations might still have been controlled by the left hemisphere. This could be possible because the subject learned to transfer information from the right to left hemispheres via the anterior commissure. This seems unlikely, for reasons given by the authors and which will be taken up in the discussion of the next point.

A well-described characteristic of many split-brain subjects is their ability to develop sophisticated 'cross-cueing' strategies (Gazzaniga, 1978). For example, if a stimulus is presented tachistoscopically to the left visual field and hence the right hemisphere, the subject may still be able to make a yes/no verbal response to an appropriate question about the stimulus with a high degree of accuracy. This can occur by means of the following mechanism. The right hemisphere knows what the stimulus is and can process language well enough to recognize whether 'yes' or 'no' is the correct response. This response can only be initiated vocally by the left hemisphere which has lost its direct link with the right hemisphere by sectioning the corpus callosum. The information can then be transmitted indirectly. The left hemisphere is aware of the possible response alternatives and the slightest nod or shake of the head initiated by the right hemisphere is then sufficient to cue the correct response under the control of the left.

It is therefore incumbent upon anyone relying on Gazzaniga *et al.*'s (1979) account to look into the possibility that the development of the ability to give verbal reports of stimuli presented to the left visual field might be based upon some form of cross-cueing. Gazzaniga *et al.* (1979) also state that the subject remained unable to make same/different judgements about two stimuli except where both stimuli were presented to the same visual field (this was their reason for rejecting inter-hemispheric transfer via the anterior commissure). This would be surprising if the right hemisphere had really acquired the ability to make verbal reports since both hemispheres would then be able to initiate a response describing the stimulus that each had seen (by speaking aloud or subvocally). One hemisphere could then make the comparison. It is also of significance that Gazzaniga *et al.* report that this same subject was using cross-cueing on a different task.

The description of these few studies by no means exhausts the human evidence that might be cited in relation to the hypothesis that recovery is mediated by anatomical reorganization. Nevertheless the work described is amongst the most convincing and it does illustrate the considerable difficulty in using behavioural data from patients in trying to evaluate this possible means of recovery. Human experimentation usually does not permit the very rigorous experimental control that is required. It is also highly desirable when evaluating hypotheses of this sort to be able to consider what is happening at a physiological as well as a behavioural level.

An important series of animal experiments has been summarized by Meyer and Meyer (1977). As with many of LeVere's studies described above, Meyer and Meyer were very much concerned with Lashley's (1935) finding with regard to learned brightness discriminations in rats. If pre-operatively trained rats are subjected to radical bilateral posterior lesions there is no apparent retention of the learned discrimination. It appears from these findings, which have been replicated many times, that the posterior cortex must have some role in dealing with learned brightness discriminations in the intact animal yet the operated subjects can still use the anterior cortex to mediate the re-acquisition of the same skill. Meyer and Meyer (1977) suggest three possible explanations of this phenomenon. The anterior cortex may have the same original capacity for visual functioning as the posterior cortex but this is only deployed when necessary. Secondly, the anterior cortex may not initially be able to deal with visual information but may take over this function when the posterior cortex is lost (i.e. anatomical reorganization may occur). Finally, it may be that the posterior cortex originally learns the discrimination in one particular way; possibly as a pattern discrimination. The anterior cortex may not be able to assume this specific role but may be able to learn the discrimination by some other means such as the discrimination of flux (i.e. by substitution or functional adaptation).

Meyer and Meyer (1977) give an account of a large series of experiments designed to investigate these possibilities further, but which also do not take into account the kind of hypothesis presented by LeVere (1980) and discussed earlier. As in the description of LeVere's work a detailed and comprehensive account of all the experiments will not be given. The reader with a particular interest in this work is urged to consult Meyer and Meyer's (1977) paper and the work described therein for himself. An important preliminary finding was that the apparent ability of rats with posterior cortex lesions to relearn the brightness discrimination with the same facility as unoperated subjects meeting the task for the first time turns out to be the result of an artifact. Both Lashley and the Meyer group's original experiments trained subjects to choose the lighter of the two stimuli. Normal rats show a marked initial tendency to avoid the lighter of the two stimuli and this tendency is lost in subjects with posterior ablations. Once this tendency has been overcome normal rats learn the discrimination much faster than those with posterior lesions. This disposes of the possibility that the anterior cortex has the same initial facility for learning this type of visual discrimination.

One interesting difference between Meyer's work and that of Lashley (see Lashley, 1921) is that the former found that bilateral anterior ablations also had a deleterious effect on the post-operative retention of a previously learned brightness discrimination. This effect was nothing like as drastic as that of posterior lesions but it was definitely present. Meyer and Meyer (1977) attribute Lashley's failure to get any disruption with anterior lesions as being the consequence of overtraining the animals in the pre-operative learning phase. The implication here is that the anterior cortex must play some part in learning the discrimination even in the intact animal.

Certain predictions follow from any assumption that the relearning of a discrimination in animals with posterior lesions is the consequence of an anatomical reorganization whereby the frontal regions take over the functions of the posterior cortex. If serial ablations are made of posterior and then anterior cortex, with retraining between the two operations, then the effect of the anterior lesion on the habit should be more marked than if the anterior lesion were given alone. This is because the pre-existing posterior lesion will encourage the anterior cortex to take over the functions usually mediated by the posterior cortex. In the experiments carried out by Horel et al. (1966) this prediction was not borne out.

Another relevant series of experiments has been reported by Bauman and Spear (1977) and Spear and Bauman (1979). Removal of the visual cortex in cats (areas 17, 18, and 19) causes severe, long-term impairments in form and pattern discrimination. Recovery after these deficits can occur with extensive retraining. Further removal of the lateral suprasylvian visual area reintroduces these deficits in an even more severe form (Bauman and Spear, 1977). The lateral suprasylvian area thus appears to be involved in the reacquisition of discriminations after visual cortex ablations although the exact mechanism behind this recovery cannot be deduced from this finding alone. Spear and Bauman (1979) suggest that the lateral suprasylvian area may be able to mediate retraining after visual cortex lesions in two possible ways. One is that the animal may be able to relearn the discrimination by using information that would normally reach this area anyway (i.e. a functional adaptation type of mechanism). The second possibility is that the suprasylvian area actually takes over the functions of the visual cortex (anatomical reorganization). If the latter is correct it is not unreasonable to expect that electrophysiological recording from the lateral suprasylvian area would show changes in the properties of neurons following visual cortex lesions and subsequent retraining. As it turned out comparisons of recordings from this region in normal subjects and in subjects with visual cortex lesions both shortly after the operation and after retraining revealed no differences. Again there is no evidence to support the notion of anatomical reorganization although it could be argued that the electrophysiological recording techniques used were not adequate to detect changes that had occurred.

A fair summary of the work described so far would be that the young organism does appear to have some capacity for anatomical reorganization. On the other hand, there is no compelling evidence that this mechanism operates in mature subjects. It must be admitted that failure to prove that this mechanism operates in adult subjects is far from the same as proving that it does not or cannot operate under some circumstances. Nevertheless quite detailed analyses of recovery after certain kinds of lesions in animals, as in the work of Meyer and Meyer or Bauman and Spear described above, do not support the notion of anatomical reorganization. Further similar examples could be cited such as the studies of visual neglect in rat and monkey described by Steel-Russell and Pereira (1981). When put together in this way these negative findings do carry some force.

One further line of evidence can be put forward to support the notion of anatomical reorganization in adult subjects (e.g. Rosner, 1974). Certain physiological changes are known to take place within the damaged central nervous system and these could provide a mechanism by which anatomical reorganization might be mediated. These are described in greater detail by Devor (1982) and Wall (1980). These mechanisms include unmasking (Wall, 1980), denervation supersensitivity, and certain forms of axonal growth that have been shown to follow some lesions.

Denervation supersensitivity refers to a tendency for denervated neurons to acquire an enhanced sensitivity to the transmitters that impinge upon them (Ungerstedt, 1971). Thus any fibres surviving damage in a given area, and which release the same transmitters, will have a larger effect than they did prior to the injury. Such a mechanism could not explain anatomical reorganization in the sense of an entirely different part of the brain assuming the role of a part that was damaged, but it could explain how a damaged subsystem of the brain could regain some of its lost functional capacity.

Nieto-Sampedro et al. (1982) have found enhanced neuronotrophic activity at the site of the lesion which decays away over time. It has also been well established that axonal growth occurs after damage to the mammalian central nervous system (Moore, 1974; Goldberger and Murray, 1978). This can happen in two ways that are illustrated in Figure 5. If an axon is transected the distal part will degenerate. The remaining proximal part may form a growth cone and then regenerate new axons and terminals. Another form of axonal growth, known as collateral sprouting, can also occur. When part of the innervation to a structure is damaged other, and intact, neurons may develop collateral sprouts.

The possible contribution of these physiological mechanisms to an

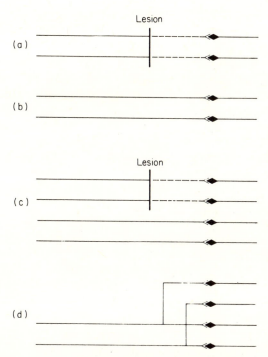

Figure 5. Diagram to show state immediately after a lesion (a and c) and after physiological adaptation by regeneration (b) or collateral sprouting (d)

understanding of recovery of function is discussed in detail by LeVere (1975) and also considered by Cotman (1978) and LeVere (1980). Whilst such things as axonal regeneration and collateral sprouting can result in unusual connections developing between different structures after brain lesions in young subjects (Kawaguchi *et al.*, 1979; Schneider, 1979) this degree of plasticity only seems to be possible in the very young (LeVere, 1975, 1980). The extensive evidence reviewed by LeVere (1975) indicates that the mature nervous system is quite stable. Processes such as regeneration, supersensitivity, and collateral sprouting do occur but are quite specific and restricted to the parts of the brain directly involved in the neural insult.

The significance of this is that physiological processes of the type just mentioned cannot be appealed to as the potential underpinnings of anatomical reorganization in adult subjects, at least in the way that anatomical reorganization is generally conceived. The very restricted region within which these processes occur means that they could not, for example, result in the adult patient with aphasia developing the power for speech in the hitherto non-dominant hemisphere. In a sense these physiological mechanisms do involve a form of anatomical reorganization but at a very local level. In the present state of knowledge they could only be used to explain how a particular subsystem of the brain could itself adapt to damage and thus help recover its functional capacity.

The transfer of the function to an unrelated part of the brain could not be mediated by these mechanisms.

There is a very recent area of research that could have a bearing on understanding of the physiological mechanisms underlying recovery, and possibly even on ideas relating to anatomical reorganization. This is work in which foetal brain tissue is transplanted into the brain of animals that have sustained an experimental lesion (see Zimmer, 1981). In one such experiment Low *et al.* (1982) showed that the transplantation of embryonic septal nuclei could partially reverse the memory impairment in rats that results from septohippocampal lesions. This is particularly so when physostigmine injections are also given.

As yet this work is certainly a very long way away from the possibility of brain grafts as a therapeutic measure in humans. In addition the significance of this work for the understanding of the normal processes of recovery is unclear. This is because it is not yet established how the transplants achieve their effects. It could be that the grafted tissue merely acts to provide an efficient source of additional acetylcholine to the damaged cholinergic neurons in the host. There are precedents implicating this type of mechanism in other brain transplant experiments. Low *et al.* (1982) go beyond this to suggest that the transplanted embryonic tissue in their experiment actually formed functional synaptic connections that played a part in the recovery of test performance. In fact this latter claim is not unequivocally proved by their results.

This work on brain transplants is mentioned because it has some potential for understanding and manipulating recovery. It will not be taken further because its significance for the central concern of this chapter is obscure.

Functional adaptation

As far as the position stands at present neither the artifact theories nor anatomical reorganization emerge as likely total explanations of much of the observed recovery after brain damage in the mature subject. This is so regardless of whether these different types of process are considered as acting singly or together. This therefore suggests that functional adaptation plays an important part in recovery.

There is considerable evidence that functional adaptation of some kind or other does occur, and examples of this will be set out below. Despite this the notion of functional adaptation has a real weakness. This is that it remains, as yet, a vague and general principle. No worthwhile suggestions have been made so far as to the detailed mechanisms involved and the factors that determine its operation.

The evidence in favour of functional adaptation or compensation is not merely of this negative kind. Luria (e.g. Luria *et al.*, 1969) has described the deliberate use of this process in the rehabilitation of various types of functional impairment. It would be somewhat redundant to describe examples here since this work will appear again in later chapters. The crucial point for the present is that whilst this work is suggestive the accounts given are of uncontrolled case studies and the evidence could not be claimed as being convincing proof that functional adaptation takes place. Another limitation is that even if we accept this work as an indication that functional adaptation is possible, the examples given merely imply that subjects can be artificially trained to achieve similar goals by different means. There is no necessary implication that such functional adaptation occurs spontaneously.

In a previous section (p. 69) it has already been described how split-brain subjects can develop sophisticated cross-cueing strategies and this phenomenon seems to be very well established (Gazzaniga, 1978). Although not generally considered in these terms, this cross-cueing is a very nice demonstration of the brain-damaged subject's ability to compensate for deficits by developing alternative strategies. In this case it can operate so efficiently and subtly that very careful observation and experimentation is required to detect it.

Another example is provided by Landis *et al.* (1982). They described a single case with visual impairments due to mercury intoxication. This patient was unable to read many words directly but could use his remaining visual capacity to trace the letters with his finger. This then allowed him to identify the word. Again an alternative strategy had been acquired in order to achieve a given goal.

Holland (1982) has described an interesting descriptive study of a number of aphasic patients living together in a residential unit. It was observed that a number of subjects had devised a wide range of alternative communication strategies to get round their difficulties in speech. Other subjects used very few alternative strategies. The strategies that were used included circumlocution, keeping a paper and pencil handy in order to write, pointing at objects, using gestures, indicating to the listener that he should try to supply the word, and using high-association words as cues (e.g. 'it's not a poster—it's a print').

Demonstrations of functional adaptation can also be found in animal experiments. For example, Gentile *et al.* (1978) looked at manipulatory and motor behaviour in rats after cortical lesions. Medial parietal lesions affected locomotion but subjects with such lesions could relearn to run along an elevated runway with the same speed that they achieved prior to the operation. When their running was filmed and analysed in detail it was shown that these subjects had different movement patterns from the normal controls. This implies that recovery of running speed was at least partly the consequence of some forms of functional adaptation.

It might be argued that the account of recovery of learned brightness discriminations in rats set out by LeVere (1980), and described in the section on artifact theories, runs contrary to functional adaptation as an aid for recovery. In brief LeVere suggested that following posterior lesions the subjects tried to use other neural systems to solve the discrimination problem. It was only by again placing reliance upon those parts of the original system that had survived that it was possible to relearn the discrimination with normal facility. In this instance, and assuming that LeVere's analysis is correct, the attempt at functional adaptation was counterproductive. It was, however, clearly an attempt at functional adaptation.

As LeVere himself points out, the test situation used in brightness discriminations is extremely restrictive and it is difficult to imagine what other intact mechanism available to the rat could be utilized in order to deal with the problem in a different way. There is nothing here to imply that an attempt at functional adaptation would not be helpful in more complex experimental situations where alternative means of solving the same problem are possible. In fact it might be predicted that if functional adaptation were the major mechanism underlying long-term recovery then the degree of recovery in achieving a given goal would vary directly with the availability of potential alternative means of achieving the same goal.

OVERVIEW

To reiterate a point already made, there is no question of trying to settle upon the 'right' explanation of recovery. The various possibilities are, for the most part, not mutually exclusive. In very general terms explanations falling into each of the three major categories can be invoked and backed by some supporting evidence. The meaningful question is therefore what processes operate, under what circumstances, and to what degree? This is a much more difficult question to answer. This is even more so since the answer is likely to vary with the kind of damage, the particular functional deficit that is being considered, and with the various characteristics of the subject who has sustained the damage.

In contrast the conclusions that can be drawn so far are very limited. Oedema and certain other related physiological processes do take place and can affect functioning. Their effects are only short-term but they probably explain at least some recovery in the very early stages. It has yet to be proved that other alleged processes like diaschisis and inhibition that fall within the artifact group are capable of explaining longer-term recovery. LeVere's (1980) model may have some validity as an artifact theory but may well only apply in quite the way that he has proposed it to very restricted tasks where alternative means of achieving the same goal are not possible.

Anatomical reorganization or substitution must probably be regarded as established for young subjects. As the age of the subject at the time of injury increases, and after physical maturity is reached, the potential for anatomical reorganization is likely to be very limited. Physiological mechanisms such as denervation supersensitivity and axonal regeneration or sprouting do operate, but their effect is restricted to the particular anatomical system that is damaged. They cannot be used as a basis for the argument that anatomical reorganization occurs to the extent that a structure previously totally divorced from an impaired function can then take over that particular function.

Of the processes that might be invoked to explain longer-term recovery in mature subjects functional adaptation or compensation is the only one that can be regarded as having definitely been shown to occur under at least some circumstances. This does not mean that all longer-term recovery in adult subjects must necessarily be explained in this way. The concept of 'functional adaptation' is also unsatisfactory in that it is rather vague and begs the question as to what methods of adaptation are employed. On an *a priori* basis it is quite possible that there are a large number of different methods of compensation used depending upon individual circumstances. Nevertheless it would appear that if attempts to enhance longer-term recovery in patients are to be based on a mode of recovery that is known to operate spontaneously then functional adaptation is the mechanism that must be looked to. The clinical implications of this will be taken up in the next chapter.

CHAPTER SIX

From theory to practice

From the point of view of the clinician trying to do something practical to help the individual suffering the adverse consequences of brain damage the issues discussed so far may be interesting but also rather beside the point. The crucial question is what can be done to assist recovery and adaptation. This chapter is designed to act as a bridge between the more theoretical aspects dealt with in the previous chapters and the techniques for clinical intervention to be described in the rest of the book.

It is hoped that this chapter will achieve two objectives. The first is to draw out from the material presented so far a number of implications for clinical work. The theoretical work is not without some relevance to clinical practice since there is good reason to suppose that any attempt to apply psychological principles or techniques to rehabilitation will be considerably affected by the kinds of processes that are thought to underlie spontaneous recovery. The second aim of this chapter is to discuss certain general issues relating to the use and evaluation of the specific techniques to be covered in subsequent chapters.

THE GOAL OF INTERVENTION

In any clinical activity it is useful to have some idea of the goals that can be reasonably attempted. It is obviously impossible to specify detailed goals for all brain-damaged patients and all the kinds of impairments at which psychological interventions might be directed. What can be done, and what is useful at this point, is to set out some general characteristics of what might be considered to be reasonable goals.

In very broad terms it is possible to describe two rather different types of goal. The first can be described as restitution and the second as amelioration (Miller, 1978). Restitution implies the full or partial regaining of lost functional capacities and therefore involves recovery of functions as means. Amelioration is a much more limited goal and is concerned with assisting the afflicted individual to function as well as possible despite his handicaps. An approach based on amelioration is one stressing the regaining of functions as ends and plays down or ignores the recovery of functions as means. An important assumption underlying most of the rest of this book is that amelioration is a much more sensible and potentially attainable goal than restitution for any psychological intervention directed at the management and rehabilitation of brain-injured subjects.

One argument for stressing amelioration rather than restitution comes from the examination of explanations of recovery given in the previous chapter. It is not unreasonable to expect that intervention will be most effective where it attempts to extend and build upon the natural processes of recovery. It was argued that as far as longer-term recovery in adults is concerned the only mechanism that has convincingly been demonstrated to be in operation is that of functional adaptation. In fact the notion of functional adaptation as an explanation of spontaneous recovery implies that brain-damaged subjects themselves relearn to achieve certain goals in different ways. This raises the very real possibility that careful analysis of the situation followed by suitably designed training procedures, as advocated by Luria *et al.* (1969), might be able to enhance the value of this process.

Another reason for directing psychological intervention at amelioration lies in the nature of psychological knowledge. It is very difficult to understand how purely psychological models of such processes as memory and language could lead to the development of any means of directly improving some specific aspect such as the capacity of short-term memory or the retrieval of words from the lexicon. It is much easier to think of ways in which the patient might be able to circumvent the effects of a curtailment of short-term memory. Just how a deficient short-term memory might be brought back closer to its normal capacity is difficult to envisage, except possibly as a result of some form of pharmacological intervention yet to be devised.

Not all authorities would agree with this analysis. Buffery (1976) suggests an approach that is more akin to restitution. He argues that a person with aphasia following a left hemisphere lesion might be helped to develop speech in the right hemisphere. The technique suggested is by the presentation of verbal material to the left visual field and hence initially to the right hemisphere by means of a tachistoscope. Forcing the right hemisphere to be active in processing speech might then assist in getting this hemisphere to develop an enhanced capability for the handling of verbal material.

Buffery presents no real evidence to support his idea, which is based on the assumption that recovery from aphasia is mediated by the hemisphere originally non-dominant for speech. Although this has been a popular notion it was argued in the previous chapter that, with the exception of young children, there is no compelling evidence that recovery is normally achieved by this means. Another problem with Buffery's technique is that normal, left speech dominant people when viewing verbal material in the left visual field presumably pass the information from the right to the left hemisphere for processing. Just why this normal interhemispheric communication should break down in aphasia is not explained. If it does not break down then there is no real advantage in going to the trouble of using a tachistoscope to achieve presentation of stimuli to one hemifield.

However, it is possible that Buffery's technique might help for other reasons. This is because any task requiring the aphasic subject to process verbal material might assist recovery and also force him to develop his own strategies to cope with verbal information.

Implications of amelioration

The favouring of amelioration as the general goal has certain implications. These arise from the fact that it is a much more limited goal than restitution. Restitution raises the hope of a possible complete recovery, whilst amelioration accepts that no matter how extensively the consequences can be circumvented the basic deficits are likely to be permanent.

A more specific way in which the effects of amelioration are likely to be limited lies in the expectation that the benefits of any intervention directed at amelioration are likely to be situation-specific. This can best be enlarged upon by the use of a simple example. A person with a memory deficit resulting in a much-reduced ability to acquire new information may find that this causes problems in a whole range of situations that may emerge in everyday life. He may forget things that friends and colleagues have said to him, fail to remember the names of people introduced to him at social functions, and find that he has arrived at a shop with no recollection of what he set out to purchase. If a treatment could be found to improve or restore memory function (as means) which would improve those aspects of this person's memory processes that have been impaired then this would be expected to result in an improvement in all the practical situations described, together with any other situations affected by the memory impairment.

If amelioration is the goal an attempted intervention will aim at discovering strategies that will help the person to cope with such situations despite his poor memory. Making lists is one possibility. This may be very effective as an aid when shopping but the same strategy may not work very well in other situations. Writing down the names of everyone met at social gatherings whilst they are still fresh in the mind could be socially inappropriate and impractical. Strategies of this nature may therefore be of limited relevance and some of those to be described in later chapters are very specific indeed. On the face of it some amelioration strategies may be capable of generalization to many other situations but the history of work in behaviour therapy and related fields warns that generalization effects can be very small.

If the effects of amelioration are likely to be limited in the ways described a further implication is that attempts at amelioration will need to be directed at carefully selected target problems. In the example given above, of a person with a memory impairment, it would be outside the bounds of practical possibilities to expect to be able to go through every aspect of the patient's behaviour that might have suffered because of the memory impairment and try to find means of dealing with all of them. Successful intervention is likely to depend upon identifying crucial situations and aspects of behaviour which need to be adequately dealt with in order for the patient to achieve a fuller and more independent life.

Real success in the clinical setting is therefore likely to depend not only upon being able to generate effective techniques but also upon being able to identify the appropriate circumstances in which to apply them. For the waiter with a memory impairment being able to recall customers' orders may determine whether occupational readjustment is possible, whilst forgetting the names of casual acquaintances may be nothing more than a minor inconvenience. Putting a considerable amount of therapeutic endeavour into the former could be very worthwhile whilst devising a successful strategy for the latter may have very little impact on the patient's overall level of adjustment and his progress towards a relatively independent life in the community.

Given these limitations the obvious question arises as to whether it is likely to be generally worthwhile putting in the appreciable effort that is probably required in order to enhance the functioning of brain-damaged patients by psychological means. Given the present state of knowledge it is impossible to answer this question without considerable qualification. This is an area of work that is in the early stages of development. As the following chapters will show, there is not an abundance of evidence pointing towards clinical effectiveness arising from well-conducted clinical trials. It is probably fair to say that there are some encouraging signs that intervention might be useful in certain situations. This is consistent with the writer's own clinical experience. This includes a good number of failures but there also appears to be a small proportion of patients for whom effective rehabilitation is blocked by a failure to perform adequately in well-defined situations. In such cases psychological attempts at amelioration can have clinically useful consequences. The fact that the number of people who can be effectively helped at present is small is undoubtedly a major limitation in this field. On the other hand, it would be unfortunate to take an unduly pessimistic view at this stage and anything approaching a confident evaluation must await more extensive attempts to develop new techniques and to apply those already available in more effective ways.

In principle there are two ways in which amelioration of deficits might be achieved. The first is by training the patient in alternative ways of reaching the same goal whilst relying upon his own resources. For example, the case of acalculia described by Saan and Schoonbeek (1973) had a spatial element in his disability. He had difficulty in identifying which side of the paper to start from in writing down multi-digit numbers such that he might write 'sixty-nine' as 69 or 96. Thus a strategy was required to locate the left side of the paper first. If the patient is right-handed he might be asked to remember that he picks up the pen in his right hand and the hand that is left (i.e. remains) is the 'left'. This can then cue in left-hand side of the paper. (In fact this was not the strategy actually used by Saan and Schoonbeek because their patient was Dutch and therefore the particular cue given by the English words was inappropriate.)

The alternative strategy is to adapt the environment to suit the patient's needs. The clerk described very briefly by Miller (1980b) had to deal with telephone queries from customers and had difficulty in later trying to identify and recall all the relevant details. This was dealt with by providing him with a notepad on each sheet of which was duplicated an outline of the information he needed to extract from the customer in order to deal with the query. This could then be written down in the appropriate places. This served as an aide memoire to ensure that all the relevant details were elicited from the customer, including the exact nature of the query. It then acted as a storage device until the clerk could find time to deal with the problem.

In searching for possible techniques that might be of value in amelioration once the problem has been identified there are a number of possible sources of inspiration. One is the literature on normal behaviour. There is some knowledge as to the conditions that might enhance or retard performance on certain tasks. This information could be used to suggest manipulations of potential value to the impaired patient. One instance that has been exploited fairly extensively is the considerable literature on the role of imagery in verbal learning and memory. Under some circumstances at least, normal memory performance can be considerably enhanced by the use of imagery. This has led to a number of attempts to look at the effect of imagery on retention in patients with memory impairments. This has mainly been in an experimental context but attempts to use imagery to ameliorate clinically relevant problems have also been described (see Chapter 8).

Therapeutic strategies may also be derived from studies of the nature of the impairments found in brain-damaged patients. An example that will be described more fully later (p. 124) is provided by Jaffe and Katz (1975). These authors used a particular form of cueing in teaching information to a severely amnesic subject because this type of cueing had been shown to be especially effective in enhancing recall in experimental studies of patients with the amnesic syndrome. In the absence of well-described and proven therapeutic techniques it is certainly of considerable value to have a good knowledge of the more experimental and theoretical literature relating to both normal and abnormal subjects.

The therapist's own ingenuity is also of some importance. The individual case approach as advocated by M. B. Shapiro (1970) and in related publications, whereby the clinician sets out to investigate the particular nature of an individual patient's problems and then to devise interventions based upon this analysis, is of considerable potential value. The case described by Saan and Schoonbeek (1973) contains some elements of this.

PREDICTION OF RESPONSE

A point that has already been made in the discussion of possible goals for intervention is that the gains resulting from any attempt at intervention can realistically be expected to be modest in most circumstances. Spectacular improvements will be rare and it is also the case that even the most enthusiastic of those who have published accounts of attempted therapeutic interventions directed at neuropsychological impairments have refrained from claiming to have produced changes of great magnitude. It is worth reiterating that even modest gains can still be useful and may make an appreciable difference to an individual's overall level of adjustment under some circumstances. In a number of occupations it can be the case that some loss of efficiency can be tolerated, providing that a minimal level of performance is achieved. Where a person's performance is near to this minimum level but definitely below it, then a relatively small improvement following intervention could make all the difference in achieving a satisfactory return to work.

It would be of considerable assistance in this kind of situation if factors likely to predict a good response to intervention could be identified. As yet the problem of trying to predict response has not been tackled. As a starting point it might be imagined that factors relating to good recovery in general might be associated with a good response to intervention. The material reviewed in Chapters 2, 3 and 4 indicated that, in general, such things as age of the subject, the degree to which the skill in question had been overlearned, and the timing of intervention, might relate to recovery. Nevertheless it was also demonstrated that there are important exceptions to most of these generalizations. It would therefore be unwise to rely too heavily upon these things as predictive factors in individual cases. In fact the writer's limited experience is that a much more potent factor than any of these is the abilty to select discrete but clinically significant goals.

The only one of the possible predictors from previous discussions that has emerged unscathed, in the sense of a failure to find contradictory evidence, is that early intervention gives better results than later intervention. In some instances this impression may emerge because spontaneous recovery generally proceeds much faster in the earlier stages, and this could give a spurious indication of a better response to early intervention. Despite this there is at least one experiment that gives better results from early intervention whilst controlling for this factor (Black et al., 1975). The relative effects of early as opposed to later intervention have not been extensively explored and it is possible that further research will reveal some significant exceptions to the general rule.

So far it certainly appears that the ability to tackle a problem early may be an important predictive factor. That this should be so is certainly logical if it is accepted that much recovery is due to functional adaptation. With early intervention the subject is presumably being encouraged to adopt a fairly efficient ameliorative strategy right from the start. With later intervention it may also be necessary to unlearn a maladaptive strategy that has spontaneously developed. Unfortunately there is a practical difficulty in trying to opt for early intervention. Patients will quite typically show a wide range of neuropsychological impairments after a brain insult has occurred. Many of these may prove transient and it may not be until some time afterwards that the picture of likely permanent disabilities becomes clear. It is also likely to be the case that the really crucial problems of living may only emerge after the patient has attempted to return to his former lifestyle. The desirability for early intervention thus needs to be balanced against the need to ensure that the goals selected relate to long-lasting impairments that have a real significance for the patient's readjustment to normal living.

The need to strike a balance in timing intervention is more of a practical difficulty with some kinds of deficit than others. It is often possible to make a shrewd guess very early on as to whether appreciable long-term aphasic disturbances are likely to occur. If this is the case then early attempts to stimulate and encourage basic verbal interactions may be readily justified given the extremely important role that spoken interpersonal communications play in everyday life. In the case of certain memory impairments the situation is much more difficult. Here effective intervention may need to be much more closely directed at specific situations in which the memory impairment results in a major handicap. It may only be when the patient attempts to return to a more normal life in the community that situations can be reliably identified as causing particular difficulties.

Age is a factor that is sometimes used by speech therapists and others as a predictor of outcome. Given a scarcity of resources it is sometimes advocated that aphasic patients over a certain age should not be treated in preference to younger subjects. Whilst age does appear to be related to outcome the demonstrated relationship within the adult age range is not so great as to make it a reliable indicator on its own. There are also investigations, like that of Sarno (1980), which found that recovery from aphasia in elderly people is not necessarily less impressive than that occurring in subjects in middle age.

If it is correct to ascribe much longer-term recovery to functional adaptation and regard any direct intervention to assist recovery as an extension of this process, then the presence of other impairments besides the one of immediate concern may be of predictive value. If the key problem relates to memory then the presence of a number of other functional impairments will considerably reduce the possible scope for amelioration.

Although firm empirical data are difficult to obtain there have been many who have recorded the impression that personality and level of motivation relate quite strongly to outcome (e.g. Adams and Hurwitz, 1963; Bond, 1975; Golden, 1978). The writer's own experience also points to the importance of insight. It is far from uncommon for those who have suffered severe head injuries to fail to appreciate the extent of their cognitive difficulties. This may be just one manifestation of the personality changes that can result from head injury. It is hardly surprising that an individual who does not appreciate the full impact of a problem is also not prepared to put much of an effort into doing something about it. On the other hand, too sudden a realization of the full impact of his cognitive changes may produce a reaction involving depression and despair, which is also not conducive to suitable participation in rehabilitative activities.

The very many factors that might relate to outcome and response to intervention have the practical consequence of making prediction very difficult in respect of individual cases. At best the factors discussed can only act as very general guidelines and many exceptions to the rules can be encountered.

EVALUATION OF RESPONSE

An important issue that arises in connection with any form of intervention or therapy is its effectiveness. As the subsequent chapters will show there has now been an abundance of attempts to relieve or ameliorate the neuropsychological impairments that arise from brain damage. In spite of this very little has been published in the way of properly controlled clinical trials aimed at demonstrating the therapeutic efficiency of the various techniques that have been used. There have even been very few well-designed single-case studies aimed at demonstrating effectiveness. Partly this lack of a serious concern with evaluation arises because this is a fairly new field of endeavour and it is logically necessary to put work into the development of potentially useful techniques before these can be subjected to full-scale evaluation (Miller, 1980b). Although this excuse for the lack of concern with evaluation does have some justification in many instances it is not always applicable. There is now quite a long history of work in the field of aphasia therapy and yet the number of controlled trials of even quite well-established approaches to the treatment of aphasia is quite small.

Other factors may have led to the relatively few attempts at systematic evaluation and the generally poor quality of the evaluative work that has been done. These are the considerable methodological and practical difficulties that arise. The actual findings of the evaluative studies will of course be described in the appropriate chapters dealing with the management of memory disorders, aphasia, etc. The present discussion is a general one and aims to set out the problems that arise in trying to carry out such evaluations. Naturally these do have many features in common with the logic of clinical trials as these emerge in considering the effects of other kinds of therapeutic intervention applied to other types of patient. It is not intended to give a detailed account of these common features yet again, since a number of competent and detailed accounts already exist (e.g. Chassan, 1979; Johnson and Johnson, 1977). Here the focus will be upon those practical and methodological issues that are of particular concern in evaluating the kinds of intervention considered in later chapters.

An important point that is easily overlooked is that the question of the effectiveness of a therapeutic technique is often not susceptible to a simple answer. To take an example, Sarno et al. (1970) examined the effect of programmed instruction and an alternative therapy on patients with severe aphasia. As compared to a no-treatment control group neither form of intervention had any effect. Although this was a relatively well-conducted trial, and there is little reason to dispute the accuracy of the finding, it would be wrong to conclude from this investigation that programmed instruction is of no value in the treatment of aphasia. Programmed instruction might have been useful if carried out in a different way, or for a longer period of time, or if directed at rather different goals, or with a different type of aphasic patient. What follows from this is that it is often misleading to describe a form of therapy as effective or not. It is only possible to make statements about its value under particular sets of circumstances. An unqualified statement about effectiveness is only justified when the technique has been tested extensively throughout the range of situations in which it might conceivably be applied and it has universally been shown to be effective or ineffective.

Any trial can be considered under at least three headings. These are the selection of subjects, the measurement of change, and the therapeutic procedures to be subjected to investigation. With regard to the selection of subjects the earlier chapters have alredy identified a number of variables which may affect outcome and which may therefore need to be taken into account. These include such variables as age, nature of the lesion that produces the deficit, handedness (especially in the treatment of aphasia), and the time elapsed since the onset of the lesion. Severity of the deficit, the presence of other impairments, and a number of 'softer' factors such as motivation, degree of insight, and expectation of improvement could also affect response to treatment.

One problem that can readily be foreseen is that the collection of groups of subjects with the same kinds of neuropsychological impairment leading to the same kinds of difficulty in everyday life will be extremely difficult. Even in subjects with broadly similar lesions the functional consequences can be very variable. A potentially powerful answer to this problem is the use of single-case experimental designs. The logic of these is now well worked out (e.g. Hersen and Barlow, 1976) and Shallice (1979) has discussed the use of single-case research in neuropsychological investigations in general. Saan and Schoonbeek's (1973) account of the treatment of a case of acalculia demonstrates that methodologically sound single-case experimental designs can be used to examine the treatment of neuropsychological impairments.

Although it may be difficult to collect groups of subjects with very similar impairments of such a degree as to cause a significant real-life problem, milder versions of the same difficulties are usually much more common. Thus disturbances of visuospatial ability are frequently encountered but in relatively few instances is this the cause (or at least the only significant cause) of a patient exhibiting significant difficulties in navigating his way around the local town or neighbourhood. If the latter is the real focus of concern then it may be helpful to approach the problem by looking at what manipulations might assist those with relatively mild impairments. This could then give a lead as to the sort of thing that might be of value for those in whom finding their way around has become an important difficulty in everyday life.

The selection of suitable dependent variables is also a cause for concern. Again this is best considered in terms of a more concrete example. It has been suggested that patients with very severe (global) aphasia might benefit from being taught artificial language systems such as 'Vic', which is based upon specially designed visual symbols and described by Gardner et al. (1976). In testing out this system it is not immediately obvious what the appropriate dependent variable might be. If the concern is with whether severely and globally aphasic subjects can actually learn to use the system, and to what level of sophistication, then the thing to look at is their rate of acquisition of the meaning of new symbols together with the increasing complexity of the information that can be understood or expressed when using the system. This is the kind of information reported by Gardner *et al.* 1976). From a more practical point of view it can be argued that the really important questions extend beyond just showing that the patient can learn to use the system with a given degree of proficiency. If it is to be of value to the patient in his normal environment and to those who come into close contact with him, then he must not only be capable of learning the system but he must also actually make effective use of it in everyday situations. It is quite possible that the patient will learn the system in hospital and then never make use of it outside the learning situation. In order to get at this point something like direct observation of the patient's communication in his normal environment, together with some evaluation of its effectiveness, will be required.

The time at which measures are applied can also be important. It is possible that a special remediation procedure may not affect overall level of competence in the long term. On the other hand, the treated subject may achieve an optimal level of performance at a much earlier date. In order to tease out this kind of effect it is necessary to apply the dependent variable both before and after treatment, but also at suitable intervals for some time after the cessation of treatment. This is also one of the aspects of the evaluation of outcome that can only be properly examined by the use of group studies. Time-related effects of this kind cannot be teased out from single-case therapeutic experiments.

It is highly likely that the therapeutic interventions being examined will not be relatively simple procedures like the administration of drugs (although no drug treatment is really simple), but will be quite complex treatment packages. Variations in the components of the package could have a critical effect on outcome. This means that the actual procedures involved will need to be carefully specified. In addition it may not be easy to decide what is the adequate control procedure. Some form of control is likely to be necessary to rule out the so-called 'non-specific' effects of treatment. For example, improvement in a group taught special imagery or coding procedures to help in the learning and retention of certain kinds of information could be the result of such things as extra practice in remembering, greater expectancy of improvement, and better motivation to do well in the treatment group. Demonstrating the critical component in the treatment package may require control conditions which include alternative treatments but without the allegedly effective ingredient.

The problem of determining what are suitable control procedures for testing psychological treatments can be quite complex and has been discussed in some detail by Kazdin (1979) with particular reference to such things as behaviour therapy for neurotic problems. Broadly similar considerations will apply in the present context. In particular the control procedure should involve subjects in the same amount of basic practice, and seem to the subject to be as inherently plausible a means of assisting in the resolution of his difficulties as the procedure under investigation (Shapiro, 1981). Once techniques of proven value have been developed the issue of control procedures then becomes much easier when trying to evaluate new techniques. Then the question of real practical significance becomes whether the new technique is better than the old, and the two procedures can then be compared without the same necessity to include a plausible pseudo-treatment.

Some investigators have tried to get round the need to have a control group other than by the use of such things as single-case designs where the subject acts as his own control. The argument has been advanced (e.g. Sparks *et al.*, 1974) that if subjects in a therapeutic investigation are only treated after the time at which spontaneous recovery can be presumed to have ceased, then a control group becomes superfluous since any improvement must be due to the treatment. This suggestion has some appeal when first encountered, but closer examination reveals serious weaknesses. Since the available evidence indicates that earlier intervention is more likely to be effective the considerable delay between the onset of the problems and the actual therapeutic intervention may strongly attenuate any positive effects. Even if positive effects are obtained the reason for them could still be obscure. The design does not rule out the possibility that any improvement was due to non-specific or 'placebo' effects. A final important consideration arises out of the evidence presented in Chapter 2, which indicated that longer-term changes could occur as the result of no apparent intervention even after the situation has appeared static for some time (Blakemore and Falconer, 1967; Smith, 1964).

Another question that should arise in the evaluation of different forms of therapeutic intervention, and which is typically ignored, is that of cost-effectiveness. It is possible to spend a considerable amount of effort in trying to help brain-injured patients and yet only achieve modest gains. It is therefore pertinent to ask whether the time and effort put in by both therapist and patient are really justified by the benefits produced. This aspect of evaluation raises its own methodological problems, e.g. how do you place a value on a particular behavioural change. However, this does not mean that the question should be ignored by those who advocate particular forms of intervention, whether this be surgery, psychoanalysis or behaviour therapy. In a situation like that at present under consideration, where gains will often be small and hard-won, it is important to keep the questions of cost-effectiveness in mind even though no hard data of any relevance have yet been obtained.

Even when a therapeutic technique can be shown to be of undoubted benefit in trials that meet all the usual criteria for sound experimental design, the reason for change in subjects can still remain ambiguous. In considering the treatment of aphasia it might be shown that a given form of speech therapy enhances the number of objects that aphasic patients can name with accuracy, and even increase the range and extent of their verbal interactions in everyday situations. In such circumstances it could still be misleading to assume that speech therapy had any effect on language *per se*. It could be that the therapy had just increaed the subjects' confidence to use their residual language capacity to its fullest extent rather than avoiding verbal interaction as much as possible, and only naming objects in the test situation when absolutely certain that they were correct.

The evaluation of treatment effects is therefore very complex and no single investigation is going to cover all the possible sources of variation let alone unequivocally establish or reject the value of any form of treatment. Nevertheless this does not excuse sloppy experimental design or the failure to exercise a suitable level of critical judgement in evaluating the results of intervention studies. Possible confounding effects can be checked out in further investigations.

This discussion also emphasizes the very marked methodological inadequacies of most of the work to be described in the following chapters. It would make discussion extremely tedious indeed if the full range of possible criticisms were to be applied to each investigation as it is described. Many of these methodological points will therefore not be reiterated every time that they arise. However, in attempting to draw conclusions about the value of work in any given area the methodological issues will be taken into account even if they are not explicitly stated.

CHAPTER SEVEN

Aphasia and its management

Aphasia is an extremely complex and difficult topic with a number of interlocking themes. This makes it rather difficult to pull out certain aspects, such as those concerning recovery and treatment, without running the risk of seriously distorting the situation. At best there will be some simplification and at worst the discussion is likely to ride roughshod over certain contentious issues. In a single chapter it will also be necessary to assume that the reader has some basic familiarity with current thinking about aphasia. Useful general accounts have been provided by Benson (1979a,b) and by Kertesz (1979a).

This chapter is specifically designed to do three things. The first is to set out what is known about recovery from aphasia. Next the various approaches to the treatment of aphasia will be described. Finally, an attempt will be made to evaluate the effectiveness of the various forms of therapy. This latter exercise will be less than ideal because the evidence just does not exist to permit anything approaching a comprehensive evaluation. In the concluding discussion some suggestions will be made as to how this unsatisfactory state of affairs might best be remedied.

RECOVERY FROM APHASIA

Some information concerning recovery from aphasia has already been presented in the earlier chapters. In order to make the account coherent it will be necessary to go over some of this material again, although the emphasis will be different. Most of the work to be described will not have been referred to before, so the account should not get too repetitive. Since this book is basically concerned with neuropsychological impairments in adults, the question of recovery from language impairments in children will be ignored.

An important limitation in trying to describe the natural course of recovery in aphasia is that there are very few studies of untreated aphasics. Given the lack of convincing evidence that aphasia therapy does have a major impact on recovery (see the later section in this chapter) it seems reasonable to assume that treatment would have had very little influence on the measures that have been used in the study of recovery. This being the case there is probably very little distortion involved in dealing with many studies of treated aphasics as if they had remained untreated.

Patterns of recovery have been specifically examined by Kertesz and McCabe (1977) and also Kertesz (1979a). They, like almost all who have specifically commented upon the point (e.g. Butfield and Zangwill, 1946; Vignolo, 1964), find that spontaneous recovery occurs at the fastest rate during the first few weeks or months after onset. A good example is provided by Kertesz and McCabe (1977) and reproduced in Figure 6. This shows the recovery curves of a number of subjects with Broca's aphasia. The dependent variable is language functioning as measured by the Western Aphasia Battery. As can be seen, some of the subjects had speech therapy but there is no convincing indication that this had any effect. In this study rapid recovery seemed to occur over the first 3 months or so. The rate of recovery then levels off but recovery continues for up to 2–3 years, and even longer in some cases. One possible contaminating factor is that the Western Aphasia Battery might show practice effects and thus give a spurious picture of recovery. Such a factor is unlikely to have accounted for the major part of the earlier and more rapid recovery, but it might go some way to explaining the apparently prolonged period of slow recovery.

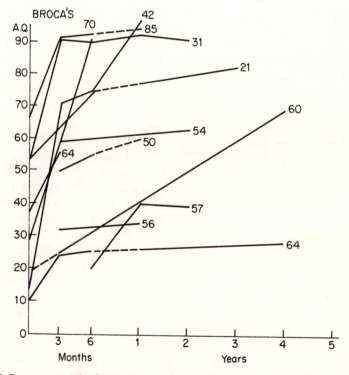

Figure 6. Recovery graph of patients with Broca's aphasia. Interrupted lines show periods of speech therapy and subjects' ages are shown by the numbers at the end of each plot (from Kertesz and McCabe, 1977. Reproduced by permission of Oxford University Press)

Another point on which there is fairly general agreement is that younger aphasic subjects show better recovery. In an influential review Darley (1975) cites several studies supporting this generalization. Kertesz and McCabe (1977) found a general trend towards older subjects doing less well, but this was not statistically significant. These authors also point to certain of their elderly subjects who showed extremely good recovery and to some relatively young subjects with a poor long-term outcome. Darley (1975) cites Schuell, a well-recognized authority on aphasia, as suggesting that age might only be related to recovery in an indirect way. It would also be unwise to make estimates of likely outcome after aphasia largely on the basis of age, because the association, whilst undoubtedly encountered in many studies, is weak and many exceptions do occur. Sarno (1980), for example, found no difference at all in rate of recovery between her younger and older subjects.

To follow up Schuell's suggestion that the influence of age might only be indirect, there is good evidence that age is related to other variables which, in turn, can also influence recovery. The type of aphasia encountered in older patients tends to differ from that found in younger adults (e.g. Basso *et al.*, 1980; de Renzi *et al.*, 1980; Eslinger and Damasio, 1981). Eslinger and Damasio (1981) examined a substantial sample of subjects with aphasia due to stroke and showed that those with Broca's and conduction aphasia were generally younger than those with Wernicke's and global aphasia. Whatever the reasons for this association between age and type of aphasia, and these remain obscure, there is evidence that type of aphasia does have a bearing on recovery, and this will be dealt with later.

Another factor that could act as a link in the apparent relationship between age and recovery is the aetiology of the aphasia. In particular traumatic injury of the brain is more common in younger adults and, where it produces aphasia, shows very good recovery of language. In contrast strokes tend to occur in people who are middle-aged and older. Where recovery has been examined in groups of aphasic subjects of mixed aetiology it has invariably been found that cases of traumatic origin do well, and much better than those where the cause is vascular (e.g. Butfield and Zangwill, 1946; Keenan and Brassell, 1974; Kertesz and McCabe, 1977). Keenan and Brassell (1974) also draw attention to the fact that the younger subjects recovered rather better, but in their series the younger subjects were more likely to be traumatic in origin. In fact a follow-up study of severely head-injured patients has shown that significant long-term aphasic difficulties are fairly uncommon (Heilman *et al.*, 1971). This is a statement that could certainly not be made in relation to strokes.

So far the results of investigations show considerable agreement but this consistency is not maintained. Many authors have come to the conclusion that the different types of aphasic disturbance are not equally liable to recover. Dispute has entered with regard to which particular types show the best recovery. In what is now a classic study Butfield and Zangwill (1946) reported on 70 dysphasic patients seen in the Brain Injuries Unit in Edinburgh. In addition to observing a better outcome in traumatic cases, they concluded that recovery was better in the milder cases and those with predominantly expressive disorders. One limitation of this study is that the sample studied was unusual in containing a large number of younger military subjects with dysphasia produced by trauma. Fortunately a number of subsequent investigations have examined recovery as a function of the type of aphasia. What is clear is that global aphasics have a particularly bad outcome (e.g. Kertesz and McCabe, 1977), but this is hardly surprising since it is the most severe form of aphasia.

Most investigators looking at this aspect of recovery have used either the expressive versus receptive or the fluent versus non-fluent distinctions. These two subclassifications are not entirely equivalent although they do overlap considerably. Given the crude nature of much of the data it is probably not too outrageous or misleading to equate expressive dysphasia with non-fluent, and receptive with fluent, dysphasia in this particular context. A number of investigations have yielded results compatible with Butfield and Zangwill (1946) in finding a better outcome after expressive/non-fluent dysphasia (Culton, 1969; Kertesz and McCabe, 1977; Weisenberg and McBride, 1935; Wepman, 1951). Another series of authors has reported evidence to the contrary, with greater improvement in the receptive/fluent forms of aphasia (Basso *et al.*, 1979; Prins *et al.*, 1978; Vignolo, 1964). It is difficult to reconcile these different findings retrospectively other than by pointing to the large number of additional factors that appear to be able to influence recovery. It is typically the case that the investigations cited have not attempted to control for most of the other variables that could influence outcome apart from those of immediate interest. Unless the difference between expressive/non-fluent and receptive/fluent dysphasia is so great as to completely dwarf the impact of any other variable then the appearance of conflicting results is only to be expected. Culton (1969), for example, offered the opinion that in his study expressive disorders may have shown greater recovery simply because the measures that he used for this aspect of speech started out at a lower level and may thus have had more room for improvement.

It has already been commented upon that global aphasics have the severest form of aphasia and fare extremely badly with regard to subsequent recovery. As a general rule, and despite the observation of Culton (1969) described immediately above, it does seem to be the case that recovery is better following the milder manifestations of aphasia. (In fact Culton's observation is not necessarily inconsistent with this view if his patients had moderate levels of expressive disorder and extremely mild comprehension problems.) Gloning *et al.* (1976) and Kertesz and McCabe (1977) have all found better recovery in mild rather than severe dysphasia. In an experiment to be described in greater detail later, Sarno *et al.* (1970) examined the effects of two different treatments in patients with rather severe global aphasic disturbances, and found no change in her groups. This reinforces the view that those with the more severe manifestations do not do well regardless of whether they are treated or not.

A number of other variables have been thought to exert some influence on recovery from aphasia. It is quite well attested that left-handed patients with aphasia recover better than those who are right-handed (Subirana, 1958a,b;

Gloning *et al.*, 1969). Geschwind (1974) has also claimed that amongst right-handers those with left-handedness in their close relatives are better off than those whose relatives are all right-handed. There is some evidence, although not fully accepted by all, that the degree of functional asymmetry between the two hemispheres differs according to sex. The two cerebral hemispheres are claimed to be less functionally specialized in women (McGlone, 1980). If this is the case it might be expected that women would have a greater capacity for recovery from aphasia than men. In the one study that has specifically tried to examine this point no appreciable sex differences were found (Kertesz and McCabe, 1977).

In his review of the treatment of acquired aphasia Darley (1975) cites a number of authorities in relation to the effect of such variables as premorbid intellectual level and educational status on recovery. The information on which the various opinions are based is less than satisfactory but there are no substantial grounds to believe that previous educational level is important. Darley tends towards the view that higher IQ might be associated with better recovery but there is no convincing evidence on this point and Sarno (1981) remains sceptical. Eisenson (1949) argued that physical state might affect recovery since the less physically handicapped would have greater mobility and hence more varied and extensive environmental stimulation. That associated physical, including sensory, handicaps might relate to recovery would not be surprising but some unpublished work cited by Darley (1975) indicates that this is not always the case.

Emotional and personality changes do occur in patients with aphasia (e.g. Benson, 1979b, 1980; J. Sarno, 1981). According to Benson (1980) the anterior aphasic with the non-fluent type of disorder often becomes depressed. Being aware of his disability he can become very frustrated and possibly even aggressive. Aphasia due to more posterior lesions does not produce such an awareness of communication difficulties in the afflicted individual. These patients may be unconcerned and lack insight. It is entirely logical to expect that these associated problems would not assist recovery but there is a lack of firm evidence.

Finally, there is evidence that neuroradiological findings are associated with recovery (see Sarno, 1981). In one study Yarnell *et al.* (1976) looked at the CT scans of aphasic patients several months after suffering a stroke, and came to the conclusion that the size, location and number of lesions all correlated well with outcome. Bilateral lesions were associated with poor outcomes. Again such conclusions are not unexpected but they are drawn from a fairly small sample of just 14 subjects and it would be advantageous to have them confirmed by data from much larger groups.

Overall it seems that a large number of factors may correlate with recovery and spontaneous recovery occurs most rapidly over the first few weeks after onset. All other things being equal, it emerges that the more severe aphasic disorders, and especially global aphasics, tend to do badly. It is difficult to go very far beyond this because the various influences will no doubt interact with one another and it is difficult to establish which variables are really crucial. Age presents a good example. There are marked age effects in many studies but age is contaminated by other variables like the type of aphasia and aetiology. What is required are further studies that look at a broad range of potentially relevant variables and which then use techniques like partial correlation and different forms of multivariate analysis to tease out the important variables. The problem is that such investigations require large numbers of subjects and good measures of all the variables.

METHODS OF TREATMENT

The literature that could be considered relevant to the treatment of aphasia is surprisingly large. A multitude of therapeutic notions have been put forward and the job of describing them rapidly becomes unmanageable if all the different variations are taken into account. The following survey of treatment methods therefore cannot be considered comprehensive. Fortunately the situation can be simplified without the loss of really crucial information. This is because certain major approaches have tended to dominate thinking. Even though the variations and ramifications of these may be quite extensive the general principles can be described relatively easily. In addition many suggestions as to therapeutic techniques are little more than the expression of vague ideas with nothing more than the authors' own clinical impressions or theoretical hunches to support their use.

This section will first describe the major approaches and then give a brief account of a selection from the rest. In making the selection the general principle has been to give a fairly representative sample of the therapeutic methods that can be found in the literature. It has also been assumed that there is little point in giving detailed accounts of possible techniques in the absence of at least some reason to believe that they might be of some value.

Stimulation therapy

Overall this emerges as being the most influential approach to treatment. The basic notion derives from Wepman (1951). Although differing in some ways from Wepman the frequently cited accounts of aphasia treatment given by Schuell *et al.* (1964) and Taylor (1964) are almost certainly best regarded as falling within this general tradition (Kertesz, 1979a; Sarno, 1981).

The distinctive philosophy or assumption underlying the stimulation approach is not often clearly articulated, and a number of authorities who might be regarded as being part of this general tradition do not always appear to hold absolutely to its central tenet. This is that, in helping patients to recover from aphasia, therapy works because it stimulates the occurrence of speech and not because it re-educates or retrains. Wepman (1951) clearly did not think of aphasic patients as improving because of any process that might be considered as having anything to do with learning or retraining in the use of language. Therapy is effective when it provides the kind of stimulation that will lead to a verbal response by the patient, and which is provided at an appropriate level and in an appropriate way.

Wepman's distinction between stimulation and re-education (or retraining) can be clarified by an example. He describes a patient who was not naming objects but who was stimulated daily with a number of words like 'water', 'nose', and 'radio' in an appropriate context (Wepman, 1951). Nevertheless the first word actually used by the patient was 'ladder'. This happened at home when she was faced with such an object and this occurred despite the fact that the word 'ladder' had only been encountered once in therapy. According to Wepman this kind of occurrence is quite common. He then argues that this shows that it does not matter which words are used as stimulators, as would necessarily be predicted from any retraining model of therapy. The key factor is that there has been stimulation at the proper level.

It should be noted that this is weak evidence on which to base such a conclusion about the role of stimulation. No matter how intensive the therapy it is extremely unlikely that the therapy sessions provided the patient's only contact with language. In fact it could be that she spent more time trying to communicate with nursing staff, her spouse, and others with whom she came into daily contact than she did with the therapist. It could then be that the word 'ladder' had cropped up outside therapy. Another possibility is that the patient's spontaneous recovery had progressed to the crucial point where naming was about to return and that this particular word was produced just because a ladder happened to be there and the focus of her attention at the right time. Someone else in the vicinity could have cued the word by indicating the ladder in some way just beforehand. What the real mechanism was is impossible to determine, and there is no cause to argue the relative merits of the different options. The issue is simply that it is quite easy to think up a whole series of reasonably plausible hypotheses to account for this patient's use of the word 'ladder' at that time, and no evidence that the one favoured by Wepman is the best.

In passing it may be noted that Wepman's categorical distinction between stimulation effects and retraining or re-education is quite weak on logical grounds. It must be presumed that Wepman's language stimulation, when properly applied, leads to some gradual change or improvement in the patient's use of speech. Operationally this is very difficult to distinguish from a training situation. This can only be done if it is shown that the repeated stimulation cannot be linked to the change in speech in any way that could be encompassed by a training process. In this context a training process could extend beyond simple practice (e.g. practice with the word 'house' leading to its more frequent use in a wider range of appropriate situations) to all kinds of generalization effects. Thus practice on the word 'house' could lead to enhanced use of the word 'mansion' by semantic generalization or even enhanced use of the word 'garden' by means of the common link in word association. When viewed in this way it could be quite difficult to make an unequivocal discrimination between stimulation and retraining. This is especially so given the complexity of verbal stimuli and their multiple possible dimensions of generalization.

Wepman (1951) stressed two other features of treatment. One of these is motivation, and here the patient needs to be able to redirect his behaviour towards the goal of regaining language. The second is facilitation. By this Wepman meant the patient's state of readiness to respond. This of course is a necessary counterpart of his emphasis on stimulation and his view as to how it works.

Schuell *et al.* (1955, 1964) and Taylor (1964) set out in a little greater detail different methods or principles to use in determining what kinds of stimulation to use. Schuell's group stress the use of intensive auditory stimulation, varying such features as loudness, length of utterance, frequency of occurrence in the language of words used, etc. according to the level of the patient. Stimulation should be repetitive and not directed at eliciting a particular form of response. The correction of errors in the patient's speech should not be emphasized and the various possible modalities of stimulation ought to be used (e.g. spelling a word aloud to assist the patient in writing). Various detailed activities are described to illustrate these principles in use. Taylor (1964) has some other suggestions such as basing a session around a family of words (e.g. the name of pieces of furniture) but she places greater stress on procedures that may be of use in eliciting particular responses (e.g. by getting the patient to give the response 'table' first as a means of assisting him to say 'chair'). This emphasis on the elicitation of responses takes Taylor (1964) away from the pure version of the stimulation approach.

The rationale for stimulation therapy is not well established. The basic principle of emphasizing stimulation rather than retraining, even assuming that this distinction is really valid, is a very general one and does not lead directly and unambiguously to specific therapeutic interventions. Although subsequent publications have tried to put flesh on Wepman's (1951) bones, and tried to describe what therapists might actually do, many of the more detailed suggestions are almost equally consistent with other approaches, including those quite specifically based on the idea of operant conditioning.

Programmed instruction and the operant approach

In many other contexts it could be naive to lump these two things together. Although some manifestations of programmed instruction are based directly on operant principles this is clearly not true of all (Kay *et al.*, 1968). Similarly not all operant training programmes would justify being labelled as programmed instruction. In the case of aphasia therapy the distinctions between these two separate but overlapping concepts have been blurred. The so-called programmed instruction techniques used in the treatment of aphasia appear to have been largely based upon operant principles, and many do not appear to be programmed instruction within the usual, rather narrow definition of that term. Given this background there are advantages in dealing with programmed instruction and operant techniques together.

Ever since Skinner's (1957) attempt to analyse verbal behaviour in terms of operant conditioning principles derived from the study of simple experimental learning situations in animals, the use of operant principles in the field of language has been highly controversial. It has been strenuously opposed by linguists and a good example is Chomsky's (1959) review of the book *Verbal Behaviour* (Skinner, 1957). As far as aphasia therapy is concerned there is no need to adopt a strong position in relation to the ability of operant principles to explain all aspects of language. All that is required is the very much weaker position that such principles can be used to modify verbal behaviour and that clinically useful means of treating aphasia can be derived from them. It is then accepted that operant principles may not be able to cope with all the different manifestations of language or its breakdowns. It is this weaker position that seems to have been adopted by Sidman (1971) who, as a noted expert in the operant field, became interested in the analysis of language in aphasic patients. It is also the weaker position that is being considered here.

A large number of authors have advocated what is basically an operant approach to aphasia (e.g. Bollinger and Stout, 1976; Costello, 1977; Brookshire, 1967; Goodkin, 1969; Holland, 1969; Sidman, 1971). Not all of these specifically acknowledge this (e.g. Bollinger and Stout, 1976; LaPointe, 1977) but in such cases what is proposed is so close to the Skinnerian or operant position as to make it difficult to conceive that the author (usually a speech therapist rather than a psychologist) has arrived at his stated views entirely independently.

Numerous good accounts exist of the application of operant techniques to clinical problems in general (e.g. Kazdin, 1975) but these usually contain examples taken from almost any other field but aphasia. In the area of aphasia therapy Costello's (1977) description is as good as any. In general the advocates of operant techniques stress such things as the careful analysis of what the patient can and cannot do, the breaking down of what needs to be trained into small steps which successively approximate the desired goal, the use and then the fading of cues, the giving of immediate feedback or reinforcement, and trying to ensure that the patient has mastered each small step before progressing on to the next. In connection with this latter point the aim is to make it possible for the patient to make as few errors as possible; therefore minimizing the chance that an incorrect response will be inadvertently reinforced and so learned.

The general principles underlying the operant approach are much clearer than those involved in the notion of stimulation therapy. It is therefore much easier to decide whether a given therapeutic programme can be legitimately described in this way. Appreciable ambiguity can still arise, especially in such a complex area as language, in that several different and equally operant-based programmes could be devised to achieve a given goal. One therapist using operant principles is therefore not necessarily carrying out an exactly equivalent programme to another who also subscribes to the same rationale even though both may be trying to achieve the same goal from the same starting point.

The linguistic approach

One logical approach to the treatment of aphasia is to try to base interventions on linguistic principles. This has been advocated by a number of authorities (e.g.

Grewel, 1963; Hatfield and Shewell, 1983; Weniger *et al.*, 1980). Linguistic forms of analysis can be used to analyse the nature of the problem as well as to devise interventions. Examples are given by Hatfield and Shewell (1983) and by Weniger *et al.* (1980).

The major difficult with linguistically based approaches to the treatment of aphasia is their variety and generality. Linguistics is a separate discipline which utilizes a number of different sets of principles and theoretical orientations. Since the understanding and treatment of aphasia must inevitably link in with linguistics in some way it is obvious that aphasia therapists should use linguistic work as one source of possible techniques. The problem is that there is no single linguistic approach to aphasia therapy; there are merely a number of possible techniques that are more or less based on different linguistic principles.

Melodic intonation therapy

This form of intervention is based on the observation that even some quite severely dysphasic patients can sing when unable to talk normally (Albert *et al.*, 1973; Sparks and Holland, 1976; Sparks *et al.*, 1974). Its advocates also point to evidence that music is more of a right hemisphere activity. The idea then is that music mediated by the patient's intact right hemisphere can then be used to cue verbal responses. In using this technique the therapist gets the patient to sing phrases and sentences of increasing length in a style rather like operatic recitative. Initially the patient sings in unison with the therapist but later on his own. Finally the melody is faded out.

Unlike the other approaches described so far melodic intonation therapy is not considered suitable for all aphasics. Sparks *et al.* (1974) suggest that the best patients may be those with relatively intact auditory comprehension and impaired verbal expression.

Non-vocal communication systems

This group of procedures is particularly applicable to those with severe dysphasic problems, especially global aphasia. They would be entirely inappropriate for those with relatively mild language difficulties. What they have in common is that their goal is the development of alternative methods of communication and not the restitution of normal speech.

One major source of inspiration for this type of work comes from studies of artificial language learning in chimpanzees (e.g. Premack, 1971). In this well-known series of experiments Premack taught a chimpanzee to communicate by using plastic tokens as 'words' to refer to objects and the relationships between them. It was shown that the subject could use these tokens as a basis for communication and convey simple wants, answer simple questions, etc. by this means. Whether this demonstrates the ability of chimpanzees to learn to use language-like systems in a way that has all the important characteristics of human language is an extremely interesting and controversial issue which need not be dealt with here. In using this work as an inspiration in attempts to develop more effective communication in very severely aphasic patients the aim is modest and falls far short of achieving all the sophistication of normal verbal communication.

Glass *et al.* (1973) describe the use of an artificial language system with globally aphasic subjects which was directly based on the system used by Premack (1971) with chimpanzees. A group based at the Boston VA Hospital (Baker *et al.*, 1975; Gardner *et al.*, 1976) has developed a visual communication system known as VIC. VIC consists of a set of cards containing arbitrary ideographic symbols for nouns, verbs, etc. The system contains a number of basic symbols that most subjects will need to learn but is easily extendable by adding extra symbols to cope with the idiosyncratic communication needs of the individual patient. It appears that even globally aphasic subjects with no worthwhile oral speech can learn to use the elements of such systems (Gardner *et al.*, 1976; Glass *et al.*, 1973).

A rather different non-vocal communication system is provided by 'Amerind'. This is a manually signed communication system closely based on the sign language used by the North American plains indians (Skelly, 1979). Its original advocates considered that learning Amerind might facilitate oral speech in orally apraxic subjects (Skelly *et al.*, 1974). It can equally, and more appropriately, be seen as an alternative communication system for the patient with global aphasia for whom the development of useful oral speech is unlikely.

Amerind has a number of potentially useful features as an alternative communication system. It is simple and based on a relatively small repertoire of signs. In fact it is not a proper language and works in a telegraphic style. The signs can be performed with one hand and this is important since most subjects with global aphasia will also be hemiplegic. Another useful feature is that the meanings of most of the signs are fairly obvious and Skelly *et al.* (1974) claim that normal subjects can understand the meaning of about 80 per cent of the signs with no prior instruction. This of course may not apply to the aphasic subject but a serious limitation of any artificial communication system is that it is valueless if taught to the patient alone. Significant other people in the patient's environment (e.g. spouse and nursing staff) must also be able to use the system, and ease of acquisition is likely to be important for them.

The use of sign languages and other non-vocal systems raises one of the fundamental questions about aphasia. This is the extent to which aphasia is a disturbance in conventional language processes as opposed to being a disruption of all forms of symbolic representation. Again present purposes do not require a firm answer to this question. Aphasia may well affect a wider range of symbolic representation than is involved in conventional language, but all that is required for a technique like Amerind to be useful is that the afflicted individual can learn to use it more effectively than he can utilize normal speech. Reviews of evidence relating to the ability of aphasic patients to use non-verbal means of communication indicate that this is impaired but not usually to such a degree as to preclude the learning of such things as gestures to convey meaning (Feyereisen and Seron, 1982a,b; Peterson and Kirshner, 1981).

As things stand at present non-verbal communication systems are an interesting development in the management of aphasia. An obvious limitation is that they are only of potential value to the small proportion of aphasic patients who are unable to regain a worthwhile level of conventional speech. Amerind may have some advantages over systems like VIC in that it does not require the patient to have available to him special cards or tokens that have to be set out on a flat surface. Amerind is also very easily acquired by those in the patient's environment. It is a less sophisticated means of communication than VIC if the latter is developed to its full potential. However, given the extreme limitations of the populations for which these techniques are applicable it may not be possible to exploit the additional potential sophistication. A final possible limitation of non-verbal systems is that even if the patient can learn to use them with appropriate training, this training may have to be extensive and there is no guarantee that the patient will actually use the technique in his everyday life.

Psychotherapeutic approaches

These are indirect approaches to the problem of aphasia designed to deal with associated problems rather than the basic impairment in communication which will need to be tackled by other means. There is wide agreement (e.g. Benson, 1979b) that aphasia has profound consequences for the sufferer. The brain lesion itself may directly cause emotional and personality changes and the patient will also display emotional reactions to his own handicaps. Given the significance of language in most people's lives it is hardly surprising that many with aphasia become depressed. In addition the emotional reactions to aphasia may cause further limitations in communication by making the patient unwilling to utilize whatever speech capacity does remain.

A number of authors have therefore suggested some form of psychotherapy, which is usually seen as an addition to more conventional speech therapy directed at the language impairment itself. Aronson et al. (1956) used a group situation in which patients could discuss their emotional reactions in adjusting to being dysphasic. Reactions to contacts with other people in everyday life were also dealt with. Other interventions of a similar kind could be cited.

There is little doubt that the patient's emotional response can be a significant factor in the management of aphasia. An important limitation to the use of any form of verbal psychotherapy, whether individual or group, is that the patient's powers of verbal communication are necessarily reduced. These forms of psychotherapy are therefore only applicable to the milder cases. It can be speculated that behaviour therapy techniques might also have something to offer with this aspect of aphasia since they are much less verbal in nature. The obvious sort of case would be where the patient's failure to communicate adequately is partly due to anxiety about the ability of other people to understand him or to worries about making a fool of himself if his speech is not entirely correct.

Other techniques

Numerous other techniques have been suggested (Kertesz, 1971a,b). These include such things as drugs, hypnosis, and hyperbaric oxygen, as well as a range of more specific psychological or linguistic methods. The latter group includes such things as the preventive method whereby the therapist only works on expressions as a whole and not on individual words like the names of objects. This is alleged to help prevent telegraphic speech (Beyn and Shokor-Trotskaya, 1966). Another example is Weigl's (1968) deblocking technique, where the aim is to cue a response via an intact channel before trying to elicit it through an impaired channel. As an example, the patient might be asked to name the actual object, assuming that he can do this fairly reliably, just prior to being required to read the word. Reading in this case would be the impaired 'channel' that required therapeutic attention.

EVALUATION

Although a considerable amount has been written about how aphasia ought to be treated, relatively little attention has been devoted to the problem of deciding whether what has been advocated really does work. There are many like Darley (1975) who accept that therapy does have a beneficial effect despite the poor and uncontrolled nature of the evidence that they cite in support of their belief. There is also a fundamental and even more neglected question in relation to aphasia therapy. This is concerned with whether the ways in which therapeutic programmes are devised, and occasionally evaluated, are really the most sensible. In other words there may be a very good case for approaching aphasia therapy from a radically different direction which has important implications for the development of therapeutic techniques and the ways that these should be evaluated. This latter point will be taken up in a later section.

It would be convenient to be able to take the various therapeutic orientations set out in the previous section one by one and to examine the evidence with regard to the effectiveness of each as considered separately. Given the way that the studies have been done it is probably better to describe the evidence under rather different headings.

Controlled studies

There have been very few of these, given the many different methods of treatment that have been put forward. Even without approaching them in a hypercritical way the studies that have been reported are either poorly described or contain at least one major methodological flaw. Here a major flaw is being defined as a failure to control for, or eliminate the influence of, a factor in the situation that could quite plausibly have a biasing effect on the outcome. This criticism does not include minor potential distortions such as the treated and control groups not being of the same age, where there is little reason to suppose that age differences of the order involved would have a major impact on outcome.

The first investigation to use a control group in evaluating aphasia therapy appears to have been that of Hagen (1973). There were two groups of 10 men who had suffered strokes resulting in aphasia. Both groups were initially followed for 3 months after entering the experimental programme with no special aphasia therapy. Following this members of both groups spent a further 12 months on a long-stay ward with one receiving the standard hospital regime together with both individual and group treatment for aphasia. The other group just received the standard regime with no therapy directed at communication problems.

Detailed results on various communication measures are given for both groups at the start of the experiment and at the end of the initial 3-month period. Both groups showed a similar degree of improvement during this time. Hagen then claims that in the subsequent part of the experiment the treated group showed much better gains than the non-treated on certain measures (e.g. reading comprehension and speech production). Having given an adequate statistical analysis of the first 3-month period such details are omitted from the main part of the experiment. Instead graphs are drawn which give no indication of variability in the data. Other problems with the study are that the nature of the therapy and subject characteristics are too poorly described to allow anyone else to replicate it with confidence.

The most impressive study to offer positive results is that of Basso *et al.* (1979) conducted in Milan. They had data from a total of 281 patients whose aphasia had been initially assessed in a systematic way and who were then reassessed 6 months or more later. About half of these subjects received speech therapy, which was claimed to be of the stimulation type. The other half were untreated, largely because personal circumstances or distance to be travelled precluded attendance at the clinic. Assignment to treated or untreated group was therefore not random but based on administrative reasons. There was a statistically significant difference between the two groups in the amount of improvement shown. Another finding was that despite a failure to find any relationship between type of aphasia and improvement, measures of comprehension showed greater gains than those of expression. There was also a weak, but statistically insignificant, tendency towards a better outcome in subjects who were younger and who had been treated early.

Taken at face value this is encouraging evidence for the efficacy of aphasia therapy and especially that based on the stimulation approach as practised in Milan. As Benson (1979c) points out, the treated and untreated groups could have differed in ways other than the receipt of treatment. Basso *et al.* (1979) did show that the two groups were comparable on the language measures used when they entered the study, which rules out one possible criticism. The possible contaminating factor that Benson draws attention to is that variables outside the control of the experimenter determined which subjects received therapy and which did not. As already indicated, ability to get to the clinic for therapy was a crucial factor. This meant that those living within the city were much more likely to be in the treated group than those in outlying rural areas. It is likely that city-dwellers would come into contact with many more people in their daily lives and may thus have been forced to use their remaining speech capacity much more intensively. This might help to account for their superior rate of recovery. Even if it is accepted that it was the actual therapy that made the difference, this single trial does not show what aspect of therapy is important. It could be that it was just the extra speech practice involved in therapy that was the vital ingredient and not any special techniques that the therapist used. Regardless of these criticisms Basso *et al.* (1979) offer an important and encouraging report, especially if similar findings could be obtained in further studies.

In a previous report from Milan, Vignolo (1964) described a retrospective study in which aphasic patients were divided into two groups according to whether they had received speech therapy (described as 're-education' but possibly inspired as much as anything else by the stimulation approach). Although treated patients did slightly better the difference was definitely not statistically significant. Further analysis suggested that the treated patients who did best with respect to the controls were those treated for longer than 6 months and where the treatment was applied more than 6 months after the ictus. In view of the general trend of findings relating to the timing of intervention this last assertion is surprising. Vignolo argues that spontaneous recovery so dominates the picture over the first 6 months that it is only later that therapy stands a chance of displaying an independent contribution. In the absence of convincing evidence that there really was a true therapeutic effect these further conjectures must be regarded as interesting speculations. Another point about Vignolo's (1964) study is that it was carried out in the same city as that of Basso *et al.* (1979), and Vignolo was one of the authors of the later report. Although this is not made clear in the Basso *et al.* (1979) account it looks as though the later investigation may have been an extension of the former.

In another retrospective study Rose *et al.* (1976) examined hospital records of patients with speech problems after stroke and identified 92 cases of whom 50 had received some form of speech therapy. A number of comparisons were made but the only significant finding was a positive correlation between the amount of treatment and the degree of recovery. This appears hopeful but it might just reflect the fact that speech therapists tend to persist longer in treating patients who appear to be showing good recovery. In other words, good recovery might attract therapist involvement rather than the latter producing the former.

Levita (1978) had 17 patients with aphasia due to stroke treated by speech therapy (the nature of which was inadequately described) and 18 untreated control subjects. The treated subjects had daily therapy sessions over an 8-week period (between 4 and 12 weeks post-ictal). No differences between groups in response to treatment were found although the matching of the groups in terms of age and type of aphasia was not ideal.

What is probably the only attempt to carry out a systematic series of investigations into aphasia therapy has been described by Lincoln (1979) (but see also Lincoln *et al.*, 1982). In the first experiment 24 moderately aphasic subjects (these came between 35th and 65th percentiles in relation to the overall score on the Porch Index of Communicative Ability) were treated for two consecutive 4-week blocks with about 12 treatment sessions per block. They received a different form of treatment for each block with various measures of speech being made initially, after the first block, and at the end of the experiment. Three different types of treatment were used. These consisted of routine speech therapy, an operant training procedure based on Goodkin (1966) and a non-specific control treatment which consisted of the therapist simply trying to hold a conversation with the subject. The basic finding was that none of the treatments was more effective than any other.

One feature of this experiment was that subjects showed an overall improvement over the 8-week period. This improvement might have been the consequence of spontaneous recovery or it could have been some non-specific treatment effect (i.e. a form of 'placebo' effect). Lincoln (1979) checked on this by obtaining a small group of dysphasic subjects from another hospital who received either no speech therapy or an absolutely minimal contact with a therapist. This group was similar to the subjects used in the main experiment in age, time since onset of aphasia and severity. Over an 8-week period this further group showed a similar amount of improvement to that exhibited by the main treatment groups. This suggests that the therapies did not even have a non-specific effect and that all change could be attributed to spontaneous recovery. This latter conclusion is weakened by the fact that subjects in the supplementary group were obtained *post-hoc* from a different hospital and may have differed from the main groups in ways that the experimenters did not assess.

There were two further experiments in this series dealing with severe aphasics rather than the moderate cases used in the investigations described so far. In one of these additional experiments 18 severely aphasic patients in a rehabilitation unit were compared with 11 similar patients in another hospital. The subjects in the rehabilitation unit got regular speech therapy whilst the controls got very little or none. No difference in speech functioning between the two groups emerged after a 4-week period.

In a more rigorously controlled experiment using a cross-over design, severely aphasic subjects received regular speech therapy together with operant training for 4 weeks and speech therapy plus an attention control condition for 4 weeks. Half the subjects received one treatment combination first, and half the other. This is basically a test of the effectiveness of the operant procedure but the results gave no indication that it had any effect. Several different dependent variables were used and the only statistically significant difference that emerged from several tests was in favour of the attention control condition. However, in the context of this investigation it is quite likely that at least one spuriously significant result would arise by chance.

Although impressive in some ways Lincoln's work can be criticized on a number of grounds. One is that the exact nature of the treatments used is not always easy to discern. Four weeks is also a rather short time for a course of speech therapy. This is particularly so if therapeutically worthwhile gains are to be expected. Whether 12 sessions over 4 weeks might be expected to produce a measurable difference on the scales used, even though this may be less than therapeutically useful, is difficult to say. Even though this point is debatable Lincoln's results certainly suggest that the effects of the therapies used were not dramatic.

In some of her studies Lincoln used severe aphasics and operant techniques. The only other controlled trial to use these two features is that of Sarno *et al.* (1970). They used a total of 31 severely aphasic subjects who received up to 40 hours of programmed instruction (using a teaching machine), non-programmed instruction (not well described but probably conventional speech therapy), or who were assigned to a no-treatment control group. The outcome of the three groups was equivalent, thus suggesting that the two main treatments had no effect. The description of this study, both of the subjects and of the kind of things that were taught in the programmed instruction condition, indicates that these really were a severely impaired and probably globally aphasic group. Because subjects of this kind are less likely to show appreciable spontaneous recovery it is also possible that they will be less amenable to any form of therapeutic intervention. For this reason this investigation on its own cannot be regarded as an indication that similar approaches would be of no value if applied to milder forms of aphasia.

The next experiment to be described is rather different from those considered so far, in that it attempts to deal with one common feature rather than with aphasia as a whole. The feature selected for examination was word-finding, which is more or less universally impaired to some degree in all forms of aphasia. Seron *et al.* (1979) argued that there are two alternative strategies for dealing with word-finding difficulties. One involves trying to get the patient to relearn every lexical item that has been lost from vocabulary. The other is to follow the line of thinking set out by Howes (1973) and regard word-finding problems are being a consequence of a disturbance in access mechanisms, thus making all words less available. The therapeutic approach based on this would be to teach the patient strategies for accessing the lexicon.

Seron *et al.* (1979) had two small groups of aphasic subjects (both containing four people). One group was taught by the commonly used extensive method whereby the subject is exposed to a large number of lexical items. The other group was treated along lines described by Wiegel-Crump and Konigsnecht (1973) which stress methods of lexical access. In general the group treated in this way had a better outcome on measures of naming (three subjects in this group showed statistically significant improvement as opposed to only one in the other group). It also appears that on the naming test used as a dependent variable two of the subjects treated by the method emphasizing lexical access strategies showed a significant transfer of improvement from words used in therapy to those used only in the test sessions. Evidence of transfer to situations not used in therapy is, of course, of considerable importance in this kind of study. Unfortunately the number of subjects used was small and the way the data is reported does not make it easy to decide whether transfer was really significantly better on average for one group rather than the other.

The remaining controlled studies are of lesser significance. Although DiCarlo (1980) did use a control group in evaluating the effect of filmed programmed instruction the report is difficult to evaluate because the study is poorly described. Two groups of aphasics both received speech therapy but the experimental group also had at least 80 hours exposure to a filmed programmed instruction package. The programme used was one that had been designed to teach language to the deaf, and so may not have been ideal for aphasics. As it turned out neither group showed any improvement in general communication, lexicon, syntax or semantics. All subjects had suffered a stroke in the territory of the left middle cerebral artery. The fact that no improvement at all was found in either group suggests that the period of spontaneous recovery had passed but the interval between onset of aphasia and therapy commencing is not stated.

The final set of investigations were carried out in Britain and compared the treatment of aphasics by speech therapists as opposed to untrained volunteers. Both David *et al.* (1982) and Lesser and Watt (1978) found that aphasics treated by untrained volunteers improved as much as those treated by qualified speech therapists. The nature of these experiments means that it is impossible to tell whether intervention of some kind had any effect. What they do suggest is that the additional special training given to speech therapists offers little more than can be provided by untrained personnel. In neither of these reports is there an adequate account of the techniques used by the speech therapists.

Uncontrolled studies

There are many accounts of aphasia therapy claiming that some benefit accrued as a result of treatment. In the vast majority of these reports there is no attempt to rule out alternative explanations of change by using control groups or control conditions. There is little point in giving an extensive account of these. However, this does not mean that all uncontrolled studies are without interest and should be discarded out of hand. They can achieve some things such as demonstrating the feasibility of techniques and thus showing that the techniques concerned might be worth further and more systematic investigation. They can also provide interesting hypotheses for further testing and, under some circumstances, give useful negative information. This occurs when a treatment can be shown to produce no change at all in a group of patients to which it is applied. Naturally this is only possible when spontaneous recovery has ceased and it is always possible that the same technique could have a beneficial effect if applied earlier. Despite this it could still be of practical value to know that beyond a certain point a form of treatment is not worth applying.

The studies to be described in this section are therefore those that have some point of interest other than being simply claims that a particular approach is of benefit. Possibly the most interesting reports in this context are those describing the use of artificial language systems. Several reports (Baker *et al.*, 1975; Gardner *et al.*, 1976; Glass *et al.*, 1973; Moody, 1982) show that globally aphasic patients with virtually no useful speech can learn to use some basic symbols to at least the level where they can express and understand simple sentences. Five of the eight subjects described by Gardner *et al.* (1976) were able to use the VIC system at a level which surpassed their ability to communicate orally. What the report does not indicate is whether the subjects actually made use of the system in their normal lives, as opposed to just displaying a certain proficiency in the training sessions.

Skelly *et al.* (1974) used the sign language Amerind not as a means of teaching a new and useful communication system in its own right but because they had observed that gesture facilitated speech. They claim that the six patients taught Amerind, all of whom acquired the first 50 signs within 2 months, did show some improvement in oral speech. The subjects were all judged to have oral apraxia. This apparent relationship between the use of gesture and oral speech is worth following up but the study also demonstrates that Amerind can be learned by speech-impaired subjects. Daniloff *et al.* (1982) have also demonstrated that aphasic subjects can learn to recognize Amerind signs quite easily. So far the indications are that Amerind could prove a useful alternative language system for patients with severe aphasia.

Although there has been no proper controlled trial of melodic intonation therapy Albert *et al.* (1973) and Sparks *et al.* (1974) report its use with right-handed aphasic subjects who had suffered left hemisphere strokes. Six of a total of eight patients showed improvement and the authors claim that all the treated cases had stabilized and were failing to show improvement with more conventional therapies. As discussed in the previous chapter the use of subjects in whom spontaneous recovery is alleged to have ceased is not entirely satisfactory. Nevertheless the findings are encouraging and it would be worth attempting a properly controlled trial.

Holland and Sonderman (1974) describe an interesting attempt to teach comprehension skills. The most commonly used test of comprehension in aphasia is the Token Test (De Renzi and Vignolo, 1962). These authors devised a programmed instruction package based on the Token Test to teach comprehension. This programme was applied to 24 patients with long-standing aphasia (average duration over 5 years). The more moderate aphasics showed appreciable change on the Token Test but little benefit was derived by the more severe cases. That improvement should occur on the Token Test is hardly surprising, since the training procedure was heavily based on this test. Unfortunately training did not show any generalization to another test of comprehension. The lack of generalization means that all that may have occurred is a practice effect on the test.

CONCLUDING COMMENT

On the face of it there is very little evidence that can be offered in an attempt to argue that any form of therapy for aphasia is of proven value. The only major study with anything approaching convincing positive results is that of Basso *et al.*

(1979). As has already been argued, this has defects and limitations. Most other controlled investigations are essentially negative. Some of the uncontrolled investigations offer hints as to procedures that might be of value in some circumstances but certainly could not be offered as strong evidence for effectiveness. The conclusion reached by Darley (1975) after an extensive review of the literature to the effect that 'intensive therapy has a decisive positive effect on recovery from aphasia' is clearly unwarranted.

Equally it would be just as unwarranted at this stage to concude that the treatment of aphasia is a lost cause. Partly this is because there have as yet been very few attempts to evaluate aphasia therapy in a systematic way. Most of the studies have applied vaguely defined techniques to heterogeneous groups of subjects and a rather more careful approach to both these sources of variance is required. There are also a very large number of possible types of treatment that have yet to be tried out properly. Undue pessimism is also not indicated because it can be queried as to whether the general approach to aphasia therapy and its evaluation that has dominated thinking so far is really the most appropriate.

The major approaches to treatment, such as the stimulation approach, the use of operant principles, and the linguistic approach, all represent very general philosophies with regard to how aphasia might best be managed. Whether explicit or implicit one assumption made by advocates of these approaches is that they can be used to deal with any form of aphasic disturbance. They are then tested by being applied to groups of aphasic patients that are either unselected or which fall into relatively broad categories such as those with a certain general level of severity or who have fluent as opposed to non-fluent dysphasia.

Given that aphasia is an extremely complex disturbance with many different manifestations it is not unreasonable to expect that the kind of technique that might prove helpful in, say, assisting a person with naming problems to produce the appropriate word will be very different from that which might be efficacious in dealing with a certain type of comprehension difficulty. Following this argument it might be sensible to begin the quest for effective treatments by starting with very specific problems and then trying to build up some means of positively influencing the selected problem. For example, where the patient has a difficulty in naming common objects the simplest thing might be just to practise naming a set of objects to see if simple practice had any effect. Some advocates of the stimulation approach would probably deny that simple practice could have any effect, but this does not seem to have been tested experimentally. If practice does work it would be necessary to see if there is any generalization to words that had not been practised and, if so, along what dimensions generalization occurs. Various forms of cueing might be introduced to see if this can be used to enhance the rate at which accurate naming is acquired. A large number of other manipulations could be made and their effects tested out.

This style of work is less spectacular than producing a grand therapeutic strategy alleged to cope with a wide range of aphasic disorders. It can be argued that it is likely to produce a much sounder base of established knowledge on which effective therapy could be based. It is also a method of working that is readily adapted to the use of single-case experimental designs which have an important advantage in a situation in which it is difficult to collect large series of subjects with similar characteristics. There is also a wealth of experimental literature on aphasia, such as studies of the influence of different sorts of cues on naming (e.g. Love and Webb, 1977) which can be used to inspire possible therapeutic interventions for use in this approach to the development of effective treatments.

If the arguments in the last chapter are to be applied here it could turn out that it is extremely difficult to improve speech. In contrast therapy might be better if it concentrates more on getting the patient to use his remaining language ability as efficiently as possible. In order to do this therapists would have to move away from artificial situations in the clinic (e.g. working on descriptions of pictures provided by the therapist) to looking at the everyday communication needs of the patient. For example, if the patient lives in the suburbs of a major city and has to travel to work by train then therapy should concentrate on such things as purchasing a ticket, any necessary communication with other travellers, etc. There is a minor school of thought within aphasia therapy which has moved in this direction (e.g. Aten *et al.*, 1980) but this work ought to be extended.

Any reasonably critical reviewer of the evidence must be forced into the view that the evidence for the efficacy of therapeutic interventions for aphasia is less than wholly convincing. Despite this the picture is not wholly black and some encouraging signs can be found. If the arguments presented above have any validity a very different strategy for the development of therapeutic techniques needs to be tried. This may help to put aphasia therapy on a much sounder footing, although this is a field in which success is by no means guaranteed.

CHAPTER EIGHT

Memory disorders

There is a fairly long history of writing and endeavour in the field of aphasia therapy. Apart from certain mainly abortive pharmacological attempts there has been little interest in the treatment and management of memory disorders until relatively recently. From the late 1970s onwards there has been a steadily accumulating literature describing various kinds of psychological intervention aimed at relieving amnesic difficulties.

When considered overall, disturbances of memory are probably the most commonly encountered form of neuropsychological impairment and they can be extremely handicapping to the individuals who suffer them. Memory disorders can arise as a consequence of a wide range of brain pathology and not just from the sorts of clinical condition classically associated with amnesia, such as the Korsakoff syndrome. The latter is only rarely encountered in routine clinical practice despite the extensive research effort that has been put into this condition (inspired by the important consideration that it exhibits a severe amnesia relatively uncontaminated by other impairments). It is important to recognize that many patients with chronic non-progressive brain lesions likely to pose major problems for rehabilitation (e.g. those with severe head injuries, strokes, cerebral anoxia from various causes, and permanent sequelae of encephalitis) are likely to have memory problems. The memory disruption may not be as severe as that usually associated with the Korsakoff syndrome but is nevertheless often serious enough to have an impact on the patient's daily life. It is not possible to go over the various kinds of memory disorder that can be found but extensive accounts do exist (e.g. Butters and Cermak, 1980; Hecaen and Albert, 1978; Miller, 1977; Schacter and Crovitz, 1977; Whitty and Zangwill, 1977). It should also be remembered that the characteristics of a memory disorder due to one cause need not be exactly the same as those associated with another condition that affects memory.

Following the outline of the previous chapter on aphasia the first thing to be examined will be the normal pattern of recovery from memory disorders. The various approaches to treatment will then be described followed by a discussion of the evidence relating to effectiveness. The past few years have seen a sudden surge of interest in possible therapies for memory impairments although much of this work has been fragmented with little in the way of systematic research programmes.

SPONTANEOUS RECOVERY

Despite the considerable concern with amnesic disorders as intriguing psychological phenomena there have been very few attempts to look at the normal course of recovery over time. Much of what does exist in the literature consists of casual observations or incidental findings. The recovery patterns of memory impairments have therefore attracted very much less interest than those of aphasia. This is possibly because attempts to treat aphasia have a much longer history. With the exception of sporadic drug research it is only recently that any appreciable effort has been put into attempts to ameliorate memory disorders. As we have seen, recovery processes do have significant academic and theoretical interest but it may well be that it is the clinical and therapeutic aspect that will bring work on recovery to the fore as far as memory disorders are concerned.

The basic details of what is known can be described fairly succinctly. A perusal of much of the classical work on the neuropsychology of amnesia (e.g. in relation to the Korsakoff syndrome or the few documented cases of bilateral temporal lobe lesions) would reveal very little in the way of comments on recovery. The tendency would be to induce the belief that amnesia is a permanent state with lttle or no recovery. This undoubtedly is the case for some people with very severe amnesias. The best-known of all severely amnesic subjects is the Montreal case H.M. who underwent bilateral mesial temporal lobe resections for the relief of intractable epilepsy and may well have suffered the most severe amnesia ever recorded in detail. H.M. has certainly shown very little change in anterograde amnesia over a considerable number of years (e.g. Milner, 1966). It is unlikely that H.M.'s memory would show further appreciable spontaneous recovery.

Despite this, amnesic disorders, even when severe, can show quite extensive change. In their classic monograph on the Wernicke–Korsakoff syndrome Victor *et al.* (1971) claim that an appreciable proportion of their alcoholic patients presenting with Wernicke's encephalopathy, and who might be expected to have a permanent amnesic syndrome (the Korsakoff stage), do make quite a good recovery. This is probably in response to appropriate vitamin therapy. Similarly the writer has had personal experience of a small number of relatively acute cases (shortly after emerging from Wernicke's encephalopathy) who have exhibited quite severe amnesia on formal neuropsychological examination. Most then revealed a marked improvement in memory performance some months later. Other examples could be cited, but the basic point that even severe amnesia can show at least some recovery is well established. The obvious qualifications are that it may only be the exceptional patient with a severe amnesic syndrome who shows recovery to something like his normal level and that recovery, where it occurs, will begin before the patient has been amnesic for very long. It seems unlikely, once an amnesic syndrome has been established and more or less unchanged for a few months, that any worthwhile additional recovery will occur.

As already noted the vast majority of patients with memory problems do not have the severe amnesic syndrome associated with such rare disorders as the alcoholic Korsakoff syndrome. It is the more frequent and milder memory disorders produced by a wide range of other clinical conditions, and usually accompanied by other neuropsychological impairments, that present the typical clinical problem. Unfortunately evidence is available for very few of these.

Patients with left temporal lobe lesions usually suffer impairments of verbal memory and these have been studied fairly intensively in those undergoing anterior temporal lobectomy for removal of epileptic foci (e.g. Meyer, 1959; Milner, 1966, 1975). The indication in most reports is that the resulting memory impairments are permanent. In one follow-up investigation conducted over a long period Blakemore and Falconer (1967) found that recovery did occur 3–7 years post-operatively with the younger subjects (i.e. young adults) tending to show the earliest recovery. Similar recovery has not been noted by Milner and her colleagues in Montreal. The recovery found by Blakemore and Falconer in London could be attributable to Falconer's different operative technique (giving a slightly different pattern of tissue removal) or to the kinds of memory test used (Newcombe and Ratcliff, 1979). Blakemore and Falconer used tests based on paired associate learning. Since H.M. with his bilateral temporal lesions has not shown recovery, whereas this might be possible under some circumstances for those with unilateral lesions, it could be that bilateral lesions are generally less likely to produce impairments that will recover. The study of more posterior vascular lesions by Benson et al. (1975) would certainly support this contention.

An important group of patients from the point of view of rehabilitation, and who also suffer memory impairments, are those with severe head injuries. There are several aspects to the memory disruption that follows from head injury. The amnesic difficulties occurring during the period of post-traumatic amnesia can be discounted for present purposes since PTA terminates spontaneously in those who are going to make any worthwhile recovery and active rehabilitation cannot proceed very effectively until the patient is out of PTA. This leaves the period of retroactive amnesia (RA) and the longer-term memory deficit that can persist after the end of PTA (Schacter and Crovitz, 1977).

Although RA may initially extend backwards to cover quite an appreciable period prior to the injury this can show considerable shrinkage with the passage of time (Benson and Geschwind, 1967; Russell and Nathan, 1946; Zangwill, 1964). As Benson and Geschwind argue, RA is a phenomenon of considerable theoretical interest but is rarely of much concern in rehabilitation. Of real practical significance is the relative permanence of the memory impairments which remain after emergence from PTA.

A number of relevant studies have been described by Schacter and Crovitz (1977) as part of their more general review of memory changes as a result of head injury. If studies where subjects were tested consecutively over the first few days after injury are discounted as covering too short a period, and as being likely to contaminate PTA effects with post-PTA consequences, then a few early investigations did show some improvement in memory performance with time (Conkey, 1938; Ruesch and Moore, 1943). In a more recent study Groher (1977) also found considerable recovery of memory but it is quite possible that the baseline assessment was within the period of PTA. In two papers Brooks (1972 & 1974) describes the administration of a variety of memory tests to head-injured subjects who were clearly out of PTA. There was no clear relationship between test performance and the time elapsed from the injury, as would be expected if some recovery took place. In a further experiment Brooks (1975) compared head-injured subjects tested around 2–3 months after injury with those tested well over a year afterwards, using measures of both short-term and long-term memory. The later group performed better on the short-term memory task, suggesting that this aspect of memory might well undergo some recovery but long-term memory performance seemed to be static. In a later paper Brooks *et al.* (1980) presented evidence that the severity of the more permanent memory impairment is related to the length of PTA.

The most direct investigation of recovery of memory after head injury has been described by Lezak (1979). She had 24 subjects tested during the first few months after injury and again during their second and third years after the injury. A number of different dependent variables were used to measure different aspects of verbal memory. Only the measures that Lezak regarded as the 'simplest' showed any recovery. These were digit span and a test of immediate recall of verbal material. With regard to the distinction between short-term and long-term memory these measures are, of course, the ones most likely to involve short-term memory and so the results are consistent with Brooks (1975). The one qualification is that initial performance on these measures was relatively better than it was on the others. It could then be that this is another example of the crude generalization to the effect that the most severely affected functions will show least recovery.

There is a small amount of not very adequate evidence with regard to longer-term outcome. Smith (1974) has claimed that memory impairments can remain for one to two decades after head injury. On the other hand, Dencker (1960) examined 36 pairs of monozygotic twins where one had suffered a head injury, and found that at an average of 10 years after injury there was no appreciable difference between those who had and had not suffered head trauma in the recall of prose passages and digit span. The impact of this study is reduced by the fact that the severity of the head injuries in Dencker's group was not generally as high as that found in most of the other work cited.

What emerges from this consideration of a field where the evidence admittedly is scanty and inadequate is that memory impairments are not necessarily fixed. They may show some recovery but recovery is likely to be related to a number of factors including the cause of the memory impairment, its severity, and the particular measures of memory impairment that are used. To date we have not progressed very far in teasing out these variables.

METHODS OF TREATMENT

Distinct methods or philosophies of treatment have not been developed and articulated for use with memory disorders to the same degree as has occurred with aphasia. It is therefore not appropriate to try to force discussion into a set of clearly separate models. Where separate models can be delineated at a conceptual level it is not always clear that they are really different in their practical manifestations.

As Miller (1978) has argued, it is possible to look at the experimental literature on memory for two kinds of information that might be of value in suggesting means of ameliorating memory impairments. Firstly, the literature on normal memory can be examined for evidence of factors that can enhance normal memory performance. Appropriate manipulation of the same variables might assist memory performance in those with impaired memory. A second possible source of techniques is the literature on memory disorder itself. This could also yield cues as to the circumstances under which memory-impaired subjects might learn and retain new information with greater relative efficiency. Unfortunately, as Miller (1978, 1979b) has emphasized, studies of amnesic phenomena have not typically been conducted so as to make it easy to draw such conclusions. The typical experimental design compares amnesic and normal subjects on the same task. What would be of much greater potential value in terms of developing ideas for use in amelioration would be experiments in which the learning and retention of the same material is compared across groups of memory-disordered subjects with each group learning the material in a different way or being asked to remember it under different conditions. Far too little research of the latter type has been carried out.

Another way of getting ideas for possible methods of intervention is to ask what memory aids people actually use in everyday life. Harris (1980) interviewed two samples of normal subjects about the memory props that they actually used in ordinary life. External aids, such as making a list or noting something in a diary, were the most frequently utilized, whereas internal methods, like the use of mnemonics, were resorted to less often.

A final general method of dealing with memory disorders is by pharmacological means. An outline of drug research relating to memory enhancement will be given in a later section.

Psychological techniques

The most commonly used stratagem for the amelioration of memory impairments involves the use of imagery. The role of imagery in normal memory has been extensively studied following Paivio's work (Paivio, 1969, 1971) and it is clear that imagery can enhance the learning and retention of material by normal subjects. It is also interesting to note that psychologists are by no means the first to draw attention to the practical value of imagery. In classical times imagery was used as an aid to oratory (see Patten, 1972). One imagery-based technique was for the speaker to imagine himself walking through a familiar building or house. Words cueing successive sections of his speech could then be imagined written over walls and other prominent features of the building in the order in which they would be encountered. In more modern times stage performers have impressed audiences by the apparently phenomenal amounts of material that could be remembered after a single, brief presentation. Where this has not been based on a magician's illusion it has involved mnemonic techniques which have a high imagery component. One of the best known of such performers, Lorayne, has described the kinds of technique that he uses in popular works (e.g. Lorayne and Lucas, 1974). This is evident, for example, in the technique put forward to assist in the recall of people's names. If the individual is introduced to a Mr Hook, whose name he feels that he ought to remember, then it is suggested that the name, or some derivation of it, be linked to some feature of the owner's face. Thus Mr Hook's face is visualized with a very prominent and exaggerated hook-shaped nose.

Another possible approach to amelioration can be derived from the levels of processing model of memory as set out by Craik and Lockhart (1972). In brief this model suggests that material to be remembered can be processed or elaborated at a number of different levels. A word to be remembered can be processed at the more superficial levels (e.g. in terms of whether or not it was written in capital letters or letters of a certain colour). Processing the word at a rather deeper level might involve its acoustic characteristics (e.g. what words it might rhyme with) and processing it by its semantic characteristics (e.g. what other words have the same or a similar meaning) would be at an even deeper level. Although the theory and its supporting evidence is not above dispute (Baddeley, 1978, 1982) there are a number of findings consistent with the notion that, in normal subjects at least, forcing the subject to consider words at deeper levels of processing does enhance later recall (Craik and Tulving, 1975). It may then be that inducing memory-impaired subjects to process material at the deeper levels will similarly improve their later retention.

Although techniques based on imagery and levels of processing can be clearly separated conceptually they may not be so easily differentiated in practice. This is evident in the one experiment attempting to produce more elaborate and deeper encoding in amnesic subjects (Crovitz, 1979b). The method used could equally have been considered to involve the use of imagery. At a theoretical level it is possible that imagery is effective because it causes deeper encoding and enhances the richness of elaboration. The reverse could also be suggested. Apparently deeper levels of processing may involve a wider imagery and improve memory in this way. However, this latter alternative seems less plausible.

Knight and Wooles (1980) have drawn attention to a number of manipulations that affect normal memory and which also appear to affect the memory of amnesic subjects in the same way. Although most of these have not actually been used in therapeutic interventions they could be of potential value. They include such things as supplying verbal labels for non-verbal material, lengthening rehearsal time, improving rehearsal efficiency, giving some organization to stimulus material and increasing its exposure time. Knight and Wooles also mention the use of retrieval cues and this is something on which there are fairly extensive data.

Warrington and Weiskrantz (1970) showed that subjects with the amnesic syndrome could recall previously learned lists of words with normal, or near-normal, facility if 'partial information' was provided at the time of recall. One partial information condition consisted of providing the initial letters of the words to be recalled and is, of course, a form of cueing. The amnesic subjects were very much worse than normal controls when retention was tested by means of conventional tests of recall and recognition. Similar partial information effects have been reported by Miller (1975) for patients with impaired memories as a result of presenile dementia, and by Squire *et al.* (1978) for subjects suffering a temporary memory deficit after electroconvulsive therapy. The implications of such findings for understanding the nature of amnesic disorders have been challenged by Woods and Piercy (1974), amongst others. but this does not negate the therapeutic potential. Partial cueing of correct responses could be used in learning situations to enhance correct recall and then faded as the correct responses become established.

Another point that is worth noting is that even severely amnesic subjects can retain considerable residual capacity for the learning and retention of certain types of skill (Parkin, 1982). The ability to acquire and remember certain psychomotor skills is one of the things that stays reasonably intact. One obvious strategy would be to try to turn a difficult learning/memory task into a form that could be coped with at a normal level. This will rarely be possible. The evidence reviewed by Parkin is probably important in the sense of giving a reminder that amnesic subjects can learn some things quite well, and this is a fact that can be all too easy to overlook in the presence of severe and obvious deficits.

A final psychological approach that might be used to ameliorate the effects of memory disorders under some circumstances is to manipulate the environment so as to reduce the memory load imposed by critical tasks. This has been suggested by Miller (1978), but there are very few published accounts of the use of this general strategy. One of the few accounts is provided by Davies and Binks (1983). Many complex tasks involve sequences of actions and the person with memory difficulties may break down simply because he loses track of where he is in the sequence or what is demanded next. Altering the environment so that it contains a prominent checklist of the various stages in sequence, together with some sort of cue as to what to do at each stage, might be of considerable assistance.

Drugs

Memory must have some biochemical or physiological basis. It follows from this that memory might be influenced, for better or worse, by pharmacological means. In fact there has been a long history of attempts to derive some useful pharmacological means of treating memory impairments. Very much more effort of this kind has gone into the treatment of memory than any other kind of neuropsychological impairment. This is a topic that basically lies outside the scope of this book but the fact that there is active pharmacological work directed at memory disorders means that advocates of any other type of approach must take some cognizance of it. In the context of a situation where any form of intervention will give, at best, only a small beneficial effect, the possibility of combining different forms of treatment is attractive and merits much more attention than it has received so far. For these reasons some brief comments on memory enhancement by drugs would not be out of place.

There is now considerable evidence that certain drugs, for example stimulants such as strychnine, can have a positive effect on learning and retention in laboratory animals (e.g. Deutsch and Deutsch, 1973). What also seems clear is that even where drugs can be claimed to produce an improvement the size of this is usually small. These drug effects are also dependent upon a number of variables which can include such things as the temporal relationship between the learning trials and drug administration, the particular environmental conditions under which testing is carried out, whether learning is massed or spaced, and the strain of animals used. This more fundamental research does give some support to the notion that useful pharmacological means of modifying memory disorders in man might be developed. On the other hand, it also raises the cautionary note that the benefits of any drug may be small and situation-specific. A single drug that might be of value with a range of memory disorders and under a wide variety of circumstances is probably not a reasonable expectancy at present. It may be that the failure to take this point seriously enough is one reason for the generally disappointing results of human studies.

In human research some positive results have been claimed (e.g. Dimond and Brouwers, 1976) but many studies have been essentially negative (e.g. Britton *et al.* 1972; Fewtrell *et al.*, 1982). This is what might be expected if the animal research findings were to generalize to the human sphere, with effects being small in magnitude and heavily dependent on certain critical experimental conditions. No comprehensive review can be given but some examples of the all-too-typical pattern of clinical research will be described very briefly.

It has been suggested that ribonucleic acid (RNA) might be a substrate of memory (e.g. Hydén, 1970) and this has led to attempts to improve memory by its administration. Some early trials gave positive support using demented patients (e.g. Cameron *et al.*, 1963). Later and methodologically sounder investigations, such as those of Britton *et al.* (1972) and Munch-Petersen *et al.* (1974) failed to find any beneficial effect at all. It has also been claimed that drugs such as cyclandelate (Cyclospasmol), which cause dilatation of cerebral blood vessels and hence increased cortical perfusion rates (e.g. Eichorn, 1965), will affect mental performance, including memory, in mildly demented subjects. As in the case of RNA the initial reports were encouraging (Ball and Taylor, 1967; Fine *et al.*, 1970) but the findings have not been confirmed by later investigators (e.g. Davies *et al.*, 1977).

More recently attention has centred on the use of vasopressin with a variety of conditions resulting in memory impairments and in the use of cholinergic agents.

The latter have come into prominence partly as a result of pathological studies which have revealed well-attested changes in the cholinergic systems of the brain in subjects with dementia of the Alzheimer's type (Rossor, 1982). Again there are positive reports (Drachman and Sahakian, 1980; Goldberg *et al.*, 1982) but negative findings tend to predominate (Fewtrell *et al.*, 1982; Jenkins *et al.*, 1982).

Although there are reasons for believing that useful pharmacological agents might be found, the work so far has not been too encouraging when viewed through eyes that are reasonably critical. As already indicated, the range of usefulness and effect size of any proven drug could well be quite limited. If similar patterns emerge in amnesic humans as are found in laboratory rats then a drug that would improve learning or memory might, for example, have to be administered close in time to the critical learning situation since the time course of its effects might be very restricted. However, it is still possible that the use of such a drug combined with an efficiently designed training programme could have an appreciable effect in assisting a memory-impaired patient to acquire critical new information without it having any appreciable global effect.

EVALUATION

In general evaluation is difficult because of the lack of well-designed trials involving a proper clinical application of techniques. There are some experiments in which clinical subjects learn and remember experimental (i.e. clinically irrelevant) material and a few imperfect studies of real clinical applications. Despite this some useful conclusions can be drawn.

The first report of the use of imagery as a variable in the study of memory disorders came from Patten (1972). He described teaching mnemonic devices of the type used by orators in ancient Greece, and which were based on the use of imagery, to a small group of patients with amnesic problems. There was no proper experimental design and the account given of the actual procedures used is inadequate. Nevertheless Patten claimed that about half of his subjects could derive some benefit from these techniques.

Jones (1974) carried out a more definitive experiment. She used 36 patients who had undergone unilateral temporal lobectomy for the relief of epilepsy. Half of these were left-sided operations and the other half right. Also tested were 36 normal controls and two people with bilateral temporal lesions resulting in severe amnesia. One of these was the well-known Montreal case, H.M. All subjects learned three lists of paired associates with delayed recall 2 hours later. Training in the use of imagery enhanced original learning and later recall of word pairs in the high-imagery lists (i.e. those lists receiving an independent high rating for the number of images that they could evoke). No effect was found for lists with low imagery potential. Subjects with right temporal lesions performed very much like the normal controls, which is what might have been expected since they do not normally have verbal memory impairments (Walsh, 1978). Those with left temporal lesions would be expected to have deficits in verbal memory and they did consistently less well than the controls. However they did show a similar degree of enhancement of learning and memory when utilizing imagery. In contrast the two subjects with bilateral lesions were not assisted at all by imagery.

This experiment gives much more satisfactory evidence that patients with a certain kind of verbal memory impairment (that produced by left temporal lesions) can make use of imagery to improve memory performance, at least under the particular experimental conditions employed. Imagery did not bring their performance up to the level of the controls but it did result in the same degree of improvement. Why imagery should have been ineffective with the two cases suffering from the effects of bilateral temporal lesions is unclear. It could be that the two types of amnesia differ qualitatively and that one is just not amenable to modification by the use of imagery. Another, and possibly more plausible, explanation lies in the fact that the level of amnesia after bilateral lesions is very much more severe than that resulting from unilateral lesions. It seems logical to expect that a certain minimal level of memory performance is required before a technique like imagery can be expected to show any detectable effect, and this may not have been achieved in the two subjects with bilateral lesions.

Whilst allowing that Jones' (1974) experiment had demonstrated a positive effect Lewinsohn *et al.* (1977) criticized it on the grounds that the paired associate lists used were quite short. This allowed some subjects to attain perfect recall and thus produce a ceiling effect. This may explain why in Jones' experiment the beneficial effects of imagery were relatively small. In their experiment Lewinsohn *et al.* used 19 subjects with 'brain injury'. Only very sparse information is provided about the aetiology of the disorders and no details of neuropsychological impairments are recorded other than the fact that they each had some memory difficulty. A slightly larger group of control subjects was also employed.

Two types of learning/memory task were used. One was a conventional form of paired associate learning and the other required subjects to link names to a set of photographs of faces. All subjects initially learned variants of both tasks to a set criterion with a recall test 30 minutes later. Half of the subjects in each of the experimental and control groups then received what appears to have been fairly extensive training in the use of visual imagery. The following day all subjects learned both a list of paired associates and a face-name list to criterion. A test of recall followed by relearning to criterion occurred 30 minutes later. This procedure of testing and relearning was repeated 1 week after initial learning. For both normal controls and brain-injured subjects the use of imagery improved performance on initial acquisition and at the 30-minute recall. The beneficial effects of imagery had disappeared after a week's delay. The effect of imagery was most marked for paired associate learning but was nothing like so impressive on the face-name test.

As Lewinsohn *et al.* themselves point out, there are two disappointing features in the results if they are being considered from the standpoint of the possible use of imagery techniques in clinical settings. Firstly, the gain resulting from imagery present at 30-minute recall had been lost within a week. Inspection of the data also revealed that the failure to find an effect of imagery at 1 week was not the result of recall generally having dropped to such a low level that any true beneficial effect might not have been detected (i.e. there was no 'floor' effect). In any real-life situation the ability to enhance recall for some considerable time later is likely to be important, and a gain only present at 30 minutes may have little practical value. Secondly, the face-name test has much greater 'face validity' than paired associated learning in that patients actually do complain about being unable to remember the names of people. The smallest effects were found on this test. In teaching subjects to use imagery on the face-name task Lewinsohn and his colleagues adapted Lorayne and Lucas' (1974) mnemonic system for associating names with faces. It is possible that better systems for the use of imagery in this context could be derived and so give more encouraging results with the face-name test.

Other investigators have also reported beneficial effects in memory-impaired subjects from the use of imagery based on laboratory type tasks (Binder and Schreiber, 1980; Cermak, 1975; Gianutsos, 1981a; Gianutsos and Gianutsos, 1979). In Cermak's paper it was shown that use of visual imagery enhanced paired associated learning in subjects with an alcoholic Korsakoff's syndrome. Cueing, whereby the subject was supplied with a verbal mediating link between stimulus and response, showed similar benefits to visual imagery when retention was tested by relearning. However, if retention was examined by means of a recognition test then only visual imagery was effective. Cermak has suggested that visual imagery might be more versatile as an aid to learning and memory since it appeared to benefit both acquisition and recall whilst cueing only benefits retrieval.

The reports of Gianutsos (1981a) and Gianutsos and Gianutsos (1979) also merit further comment. The first of these was a single-case experiment, whilst the other utilized four subjects in a 'multiple baseline across cases' design (Hersen and Barlow, 1976). Both these experiments used 'mnemonic training' to assist in the recall of word triplets where the mnemonic training involved the subject in making up a story to link the words. This is probably best construed as a form of imagery. Again the effects of the manipulation were positive.

Certain reservations need to be considered in relation to the work just described. It is possible that the benefits obtained were due to some form of non-specific or 'placebo' effect. If the subject knows that some procedure is supposed to assist his memory, and procedures for training in the use of imagery would be likely to induce this expectation even if this is not stated explicitly, then this may cause him to try harder or to change in some way quite unrelated to the use of imagery. The one experiment that has been specifically designed to examine this issue is that of Gasparrini and Satz (1979). Subjects with left hemisphere strokes were taught paired associates using either visual imagery or a form of verbal mediation as a control technique. The results are more complex than will be revealed here, but it was clear that visual imagery was the most effective technique. It will also be remembered that in Cermak's (1975) experiment visual imagery was effective under a wider range of circumstances than the cueing procedure that was also used. So far the evidence shows that visual imagery is better than the other alternatives that have been tried but this is by no means unequivocal proof that non-specific factors are not operating. To do this it is necessary to show that visual imagery does not appear to the subject to be inherently more plausible a technique for improving memory than the other alternatives (Shapiro, 1981).

Crovitz (1979a) has raised another problem with regard to experiments on imagery. He demonstrated that when using normal subjects the rate of presentation of material has a strong influence on paired associate learning. In the typical experiment with memory-impaired subjects presentation rates have not been strictly controlled (or at least have not been reported as having been carefully controlled) and it is highly likely that subjects using imagery would spend more time inspecting stimuli as they try to derive suitable images. It is interesting that the only negative report of the use of visual imagery to be published so far (Glasgow et al., 1977) is of an experiment where rate of presentation was controlled. On the other hand, close reading of Gianutsos and Gianutsos (1979) gives the impression of a standard rate of presentation for their word triplets regardless of experimental condition, and they found some beneficial effects due to imagery.

The balance of evidence certainly indicates that subjects with amnesic difficulties can benefit from the use of imagery and to approximately the same extent as normal subjects. The memory-impaired subject naturally starts off at a much lower level than the normal controls and, despite the benefit of imagery, does not achieve normal levels of performance under comparable conditions. Unfortunately, the possibility raised by Crovitz (1979a), that imagery may appear to work because it forces subjects to attend to stimuli for longer, cannot be satisfactorily excluded. Crovitz is correct in suggesting that presentation rate is a variable that needs to be carefully controlled in future research of this nature. Whatever the mechanism involved it could be argued from a purely practical point of view that it is the simple fact that imagery has an effect that is important.

The work described so far offers encouragement but there are further obstacles to be overcome before imagery can be regarded as a technique of proven clinical value. Showing that imagery can work with artificial material like paired associates and under laboratory conditions is one thing. It is quite another to claim that it is capable of producing a clinically significant improvement that will have an impact on the patient's everyday life. Even if it can produce a clinically worthwhile effect in helping to recall material that needs to be remembered as part of daily life it does not follow that the patient will actively make use of the technique. The whole history of work on compliance cautions that it is one thing to provide patients with prosthetic devices and quite another to get them properly utilized.

There are very few reports of attempts to treat memory problems clinically in the sense of dealing with a situation that is identified as being of significance by the patient. One such report is that of Glasgow et al. (1977). They describe a subject who was a 23-year-old male student who had previously suffered a head injury. He specifically complained of an inability to remember the names of people that he encountered frequently. Having established that the subject was able to recognize faces that he had seen before, and that the real difficulty did lie in associating names with these faces, a training programme was implemented. This required the subject to use imagery to associate names with pictures of faces. The details of the technique were based on the descriptions given by Lorayne and Lucas (1974). Although initially successful in getting the subject to associate simple names (e.g. Mr Fox and Mrs Apple) with their corresponding pictures there was no benefit when more complex (and presumably more realistic) names were used later. Part of the problem lay in the fact that the subject had difficulty in forming suitable images and took an exceedingly long time over each face–name pair whilst doing so.

Having reached this stage Glasgow *et al.* (1977) decided to use a rather different and much simpler procedure in everyday life. The subject was simply asked to write the name of anyone he encountered onto a record card where he had difficulty in spontaneously producing the name. On three occasions each day he was asked to take out the cards and to try to visualize the person as he read the name. Records kept by the subject indicated that he was forgetting about four people's names each day, in that he could not recall them within a set period when he met the person. During intervention this dropped to less than one name per day being forgotten.

This single-case report suggests that complex strategies based on imagery may not be very effective for clinically relevant material. The procedure that was effective did use a form of imagery but in a much simpler way which was rather different from that envisaged in most of the experimental work on the use of imagery in memory. It also brings out another problem that has been noted elsewhere. Crovitz *et al.* (1979) describe an attempt to teach three memory-impaired subjects to use imagery. As with Glasgow *et al.*'s subject the poor ability of the patients to create suitable images proved a limiting factor. The present writer has also encountered this difficulty in his attempts to use imagery in a clinical setting. Crovitz *et al.* (1979) describe what they call a 'memory retraining practice set', which is a procedure for teaching subjects to derive images. This is only briefly outlined and no evidence as to its effectiveness is offered.

Although it has a number of implications for the amelioration of memory disorders the levels of processing approach to memory originally proposed by Craik and Lockhart (1972) has attracted little attention. McDowall (1979) reported an experiment using patients with the Korsakoff syndrome which has some parallel with the kind of research on depth of processing in normal memory carried out by Craik and Tulving (1975) and others. Subjects were presented with words on cards one at a time, and had to make decisions about each word (e.g. whether the word contained an 'e', or whether it fell into a certain semantic category). Subjects were later asked to recall the words that they had seen. Further experiments followed this up, and introduced a form of cueing at the time of recall by supplying the category names for the different words. In general a depth of processing effect was found in that the Korsakoff subjects gave better recall after being forced to assign the words to semantic categories. Supplying the category cues made the amnesic subjects most like the controls. McDowall (1979) concluded that Korsakoff subjects can code semantically, but are impaired in the ability to generate retrieval cues at the time of recall.

Crovitz (1979b) also looked to the depth of processing model of memory. His two subjects, one an alcoholic Korsakoff syndrome and the other a severe head injury, were required to remember 10 words embedded in a set of sentences linking the words with rather bizarre situations (the 'airplane list'). The idea is that this form of presentation will force the subject to use deeper and more elaborate forms of encoding. Recall of the lists was poor but improved considerably with the provision of cues linked to the original presentation (e.g. the 'moon' was described in the original list as being made of bologna and when asked what was made from bologna the subject could reply 'moon'). As a demonstration this is not very impressive, nor is it stated why the 'airplane list' should be regarded as assisting more elaborate and deeper encoding rather than supplying useful imagery. The apparent value of cueing arises, as in the previously described experiment, and this is taken up in the next study.

Jaffe and Katz (1975) followed up Warrington and Weiskrantz's (1970) demonstration that 'partial cues' could enhance recall in normal subjects to normal or near-normal levels. They had a single case with an alcoholic Korsakoff syndrome and managed to replicate Warrington and Weiskrantz's partial cue effect with this subject. The partial cue given at the time of recall was the initial letter of the word to be recalled. Jaffe and Katz then give an account of an unsystematic attempt to apply this procedure. Their subject had been in hospital for some time but had conspicuously failed to acquire basic information such as the names of commonly encountered staff members. They then used the partial cueing procedure to teach the names of staff members. For example, the subject was told a person's name and then the response prompted by giving the initial letter of the name. According to the account given, this procedure enabled the subject to learn the names of people relatively efficiently but little hard data is provided. In particular it is not shown that the technique used was necessarily better than any other which caused the subject to systematically attempt to learn these names. The use of partial cueing merits further investigation, but Jaffe and Katz's (1975) paper merely demonstrates its feasibility in a clinical setting without proving its effectiveness.

A further account of the use of cueing, but in a purely experimental setting, is provided by Leftoff (1981). All subjects had suffered strokes. One group had left hemisphere involvement and apparent memory disorders. The other consisted of right hemisphere cases. Subjects were required to give immediate recall of lists of words presented either auditorily or visually. Each list was presented 10 times with the same word order on each trial being maintained for half the lists. On the rest of the lists word order was varied from trial to trial. The point of the experiment is that where the word order remains invariant one word in the list can then act as a cue for the next. The main finding of interest was that a consistent order of presentation had a bigger beneficial effect as compared with random ordering in the left hemisphere damaged group with verbal memory problems. This study gives additional evidence as to the possible importance of different types of cue in assisting recall in memory-impaired subjects.

Another interesting description of a clinical intervention with a subject complaining of amnesic difficulties has been reported by Glasgow *et al.* (1977). One of the two cases that they deal with in this paper was a student who had sustained a severe head injury some time previously. Her basic complaint was that she was unable to remember material that she had read or obtained in lectures. Preliminary investigations revealed that the main problem was one of poor retention rather than faulty comprehension. An initial laboratory experiment was then carried out in which two special strategies were compared with a control (i.e. neutral) procedure in terms of their effect on the retention of appropriate stimulus material. One intervention strategy involved immediate active rehearsal of presented material whilst the other was based on the 'PQRST' technique of Robinson (1970). The 'PQRST' sequence involves the subject Previewing the material, asking key Questions about the content, Reading with a view to answering the questions, Stating (or rehearsing) the information, and Testing by finally checking that the questions can be answered.

The results of the laboratory testing using recall intervals of up to a week were very clear. The PQRST procedure (with 96 per cent recall of the main points in the material presented after a week) was superior to simple rehearsal (50 per cent), whilst the neutral control condition came out very badly (8 per cent). The use of the PQRST technique was then transferred to the real-life situation. This could not be evaluated in a very rigorous way but the subject's subjective ratings of ability to remember showed appreciable improvement. Although this intervention was apparently successful it is also worth noting that Glasgow *et al.* (1977) draw attention to the time that was required to implement the PQRST technique. Again this raises the possibility that the technique may owe its effect to making the subject spend more time going over the material that has to be remembered. The other alternative is that the PQRST technique works because it forces the subject to organize the material much better, and it is well established that material that is systematically organized is easier to recall than if no organization is present.

Dolan and Norton (1977) attempted to influence acquisition and retention in memory-impaired subjects by a method obviously inspired by simple clinical applications of operant conditioning. Subjects were repeatedly presented with material consisting of photographs of ward staff and questions about the ward environment in a simple training procedure. A third of the subjects were given material rewards for correct performance, another third received verbal praise, and the rest just experienced pre- and post-testing with no intervening training. If anything, the group receiving material rewards had a better outcome than those getting praise but the difference fell short of statistical significance. It is unfortunate that the control group had no practice at all since this means that it is not clear how much of the experimental groups' improvement could be attributed to the use of rewards. If reinforcers such as praise or material rewards can influence the rate of acquisition or performance on retention tests then this could be a useful finding under some circumstances.

A survey of practices in rehabilitation units in Britain showed that activities like Kim's game and the repeated recall of stories were often used with patients suffering from memory disorders (Harris and Sunderland, 1981). Most of the respondents were not psychologists. What these activities have in common is repeated practice in the recall of different types of material. Gianutsos (1981a) did show some improvement with practice on a short-term memory task with a single subject. However, there is little reason to expect that practice on its own would exert much of a beneficial effect on memory. Any improvement with simple practice is likely to be due to a 'learning to learn' effect (i.e. the subject learning the demands of the situation, what to attend to, etc.) or to the subject acquiring for himself some useful strategy (e.g. use of mnemonics).

Finally, it is worth noting that Davies and Binks (1983) have described the application of principles advocated by Miller (1978) in the management of a single patient with a Korsakoff syndrome. The general approach was to try to alter the environment so that the demands placed on memory were reduced (e.g. by ensuring that only one person spoke to him at a time) and to make maximum use of his residual memory capacity (e.g. by the extensive use of a notebook so that he only has to remember that he has certain information written down rather than what that information actually is). Davies and Binks offer an interesting account of a series of different interventions with a particular case but offer no real evaluation.

COMMENT

The recent years have produced a flurry of work aimed at modifying or ameliorating memory impairments. As far as visual imagery is concerned it is now well established that procedures based on imagery do enhance the retention of memory-disordered subjects (other than those with the most severe amnesic syndromes) when memory is examined under laboratory conditions.

What has yet to be convincingly shown is why these effects are produced and whether they can be usefully applied to clinically relevant settings with the particular problems that actually arise in the patient's everyday life. It still remains a possibility that techniques work simply because they cause the subject to attend to the stimulus material for longer periods. This point was raised by Crovitz (1979a) but it is also worth noting that experimental studies of the alcoholic Korsakoff syndrome have shown that stimulus presentation time can be a crucial variable in determining later recall (Hupper and Piercy, 1977).

There have been few attempts to apply this work to situations of direct relevance to the subject's everyday life. Where such attempts have been reported proper experimental controls have been abandoned (possibly for good practical reasons) and this means that proof of clinical effectiveness is lacking. Even so the results appear to be mixed (e.g. Glasgow et al., 1977) and practical difficulties arise in the use of the techniques (Crovitz et al., 1979). It is interesting that when

Harris and Sunderland (1981) asked their respondents to rate how effective they thought their interventions were in the treatment of memory disorders the median rating corresponded to 'marginally effective'. Under such circumstances ratings by therapists would be expected to err on the side of optimism. In many practical situations it may also turn out to be the case that quite large increases in memory performance are required for the subject to function reasonably adequately. The apparent size of many of the obtained effects is not impressive (Lewinsohn *et al.*, 1977).

Work on the remediation of memory disorders is in its early stages, and the future may well bring much more impressive demonstrations of clinical effectiveness. Until these appear it can only be concluded that the value of psychological interventions in the field of memory disorder is far from proven and optimism with regard to eventual success is premature. Others view this work in a much rosier light (e.g. Powell, 1981) but this is based on a less critical review which takes some rather dubious evidence at face value.

CHAPTER NINE

Other neuropsychological impairments

It is not possible to cover the other neuropsychological impairments in the rather more systematic way that amnesia and aphasia were dealt with. Attempts to ameliorate disorders other than these two have been very fragmentary. This must necessarily be reflected in this chapter, which is in great danger of becoming a rag-bag of different topics. For most of these there is no information about the pattern of spontaneous recovery, there are no well-articulated strategies for treatment, and just a few isolated and often idiosyncratic therapeutic interventions have been reported.

In order to fit this very varied material into some sort of order, no matter how token and arbitrary, it has been decided to begin with disorders of calculation and reading. These come first because they tend to be linked most closely with the dysphasias which have already been covered in Chapter 7. The sequence will then pass on to vision and visuospatial disorders, followed by an examination of the possibility of modifying motor impairments, and conclude with changes in personality, motivation, and related functions.

CALCULATION

Disturbances in arithmetical computation do arise, often in association with dysphasia or left parietal lobe symptoms such as those associated with the Gerstmann syndrome of which acalculia is one element (see Critchley, 1953). As would be expected, dyscalculia has been extensively studied by neuropsychologists (e.g. Levin, 1979) but interest has centred on the nature of the impairment with the questions of recovery and possible treatment failing to attract any significant attention.

One exception is an elegant single-case experiment described by Saan and Schoonbeek (1973). Their client was an accountant who underwent open-heart surgery, following which he developed an ischaemic lesion in the left hemisphere as a result of an embolus in the territory of the left middle cerebral artery. Although the initial impairments were more extensive the persistent problem was a marked dyscalculia. This was quite severe and seriously threatened his continued professional practice. An indication of the initial severity at the start of treatment can be given by the fact that he could not reliably write down two-digit numbers.

The patient was seen frequently with blocks of treatment sessions being devoted to training in different arithmetical skills starting with writing down numbers and proceeding in order of complexity through the various arithmetical operations. The training strategy used appears to have been largely based upon straightforward practice. Matched tests of all aspects of arithmetical performance were given at the beginning and at the end of each treatment block. In general terms the design followed that of a multiple baseline experiment (Hersen and Barlow, 1976).

The results showed a steady increase in all aspects of arithmetical ability throughout the study. For some skills there seemed to be a small increase in the rate of improvement during the period when that particular skill was being featured in the treatment sessions. There was therefore a possible therapeutic benefit but its extent was small as compared to the change due to spontaneous recovery. A considerable amount of therapeutic activity went into these small gains and it is doubtful if the results justified the effort.

READING

Acquired dyslexia (i.e. dyslexia occurring in adults who have previously been able to read) is a topic that is now starting to attract some interest. The recent work on deep dyslexia is of theoretical importance (see Coltheart et al., 1980). Again it is the nature of the disturbances in reading that occur that has been closely examined, and recovery has been largely neglected. As already described in Chapter 2, there has been at least one study of the pattern of recovery. Newcombe et al. (1975) have described recovery curves in individual patients with acquired dyslexia. In most instances the ability to read words in lists improves rapidly in the early stages but the improvement slowly tails off with a smooth recovery curve being produced. In the single exception it is plausible to assume that the discrepant results were due to the subject never having been properly literate in the first place.

There is a single case report of relevance to the question of treatment of dyslexia. Landis et al. (1982) describe a man with a marked impairment of the visual system due to mercury intoxication. In consequence this patient had difficulty in reading. He was able to use kinaesthetic feedback obtained by tracing the outline of letters with his finger in order to identify words that he could not otherwise read. According to Landis et al. their case is very similar to one reported very much earlier by Goldstein and Gelb (1918).

One special strategy for dealing with acquired dyslexia has been described by Gheorghita (1981). The account given is not entirely clear but the following exposition is probably a reasonable approximation of what is intended. Gheorghita suggests that material to be read should be presented in a vertical rather than a horizontal array. Thus the word 'table' would be set out as:

t
a
b
l
e

She argues that dyslexics find things easier to read in this form because it assists them to attend to each letter individually by breaking up the normal tendency to scan quickly from left to right. It is claimed that those with acquired dyslexia can read words in this vertical way better than in the usual horizontal way, and this difference was statistically significant in her simple experiment.

Gheorghita also argues that vertical presentation can be used in assisting such patients to read fluently. The patient can progress from reading words set out vertically by letters to words set out vertically by syllables; e.g.:

can
did
ate

and then to sentences with successive words set out vertically; e.g.:

the
car
sped
down
the
road.

It is claimed that this method of retraining is effective but no data are presented. A similar claim has also been made by Drevillon *et al.* (1977).

An attempt to treat a single case of acquired dyslexia is described by Moyer (1979). His patient suffered a cerebral embolus after open-heart surgery. Most of the initial impairments proved transitory but he was left with a right hemianopia and dyslexia without agraphia. A poorly defined but prolonged training programme was instituted. Because the subject confused similar letters the tactile modality was brought in by getting him to trace letters cut from sandpaper with his finger. Since he could write satisfactorily he was later required to write paragraphs from dictation and then read them back. No attempt was made to obtain any data that could bear upon the effectiveness of these procedures. Some improvement did take place but could well have been due to spontaneous recovery. The main interest in this paper is that it does provide some ideas as to how the problem of acquired dyslexia might be tackled.

Reading can be disturbed for reasons other than dyslexia. This is particularly so in the case of some patients with hemianopias and visual neglect. Quite often people with a hemianopia will learn to adapt by altering their point of fixation so as to bring the observed image into the middle of their intact field. Some may not do this spontaneously, or at least not for some considerable time, and may thus have an apparent reading disturbance because they miss out a portion of each line. Such a phenomenon may also be linked to neglect of anything in the affected hemifield in the absence of any marked hemianopia. The point is that these difficulties in reading are not really due to a dyslexia since the portion of each line of text that is read is read with a normal facility. Approaches to this particular problem belong in a later section dealing with neglect.

WRITING

There is very little relevant literature on dysgraphia. A number of authorities have considered dysgraphia to be especially difficult to treat (e.g. Butfield and Zangwill, 1946). One of the very few accounts of treatment is given by Kapur and Gordon (1975). Their subject was a young man who had suffered a gunshot wound in the left posterior parietal region of the brain. Initial analysis revealed that his main difficulty lay in retrieving from memory the particular spatial movement required to write letters. He could spell aloud a word that he heard spoken.

Two training strategies were used. One was to give the subject extra assistance that was slowly faded out. Thus he was required to trace over letters that had already been written. The second strategy was to induce alternative forms of coding. When he could write a lower case 'n' adequately he was then encouraged to think of 'h' as being an 'n' with an additional stroke on the left-hand side. No systematic evidence as to effectiveness is reported, although the authors claim that there was very little improvement in writing over the first 6 months after the injury. After this time had elapsed the training programme was instituted and appeared to have a definite impact.

VISUAL DISORDERS

A very large number of different visually related disorders can be produced by brain damage and these are described in several sources (e.g. Benton, 1979; Gloning et al., 1968; Hecaen and Albert, 1978). The vast majority of these will not be mentioned since there have been no published attempts to treat them.

Visual field defects

These are undoubtedly the most commonly encountered visual disturbances in patients with brain pathology. The anatomy of the visual pathways is well known and lesions in many places, but especially in the posterior parts of the brain, can disrupt these pathways and so give rise to visual field defects. The pattern of the defect varies reliably with the site of the lesion (Teuber, et al., 1960). There is also well-documented evidence that visual field defects can shrink spontaneously with the passage of time (Teuber, 1974; Zihl et al., 1977).

Zihl (1981), and Zihl and von Cramon (1979), have described an attempt to reduce the size of visual field impairments due to lesions occurring behind the optic chiasm by repeated visual stimulation. Using an accurate perimetric technique light difference thresholds were determined repeatedly along the border between the intact field and the part that was lost. In several subjects this region showed improved contrast sensitivity and the size of the intact field was increased.

The possibility of spontaneous recovery was not controlled for, but the interval between the onset of the field defect and commencing the procedure varied from a few months to over 5 years. Even the patient with the longest interval showed some improvement, which is some argument against the effect being solely due to spontaneous recovery. Another possible artifact is that procedures such as contrast sensitivity may show some small improvement with repeated testing because the subject adapts to the test situation and its demands. The margin of partial impairment between the part of the field that is totally lost and that which is spared might be particularly susceptible to such adaptation effects and thus produce an apparent shrinkage in the field defect. A final possibility is that subjects show no real increase in sensitivity but merely alter their criterion of response so that they become more likely to indicate that they detect a difference under conditions of uncertainty. The method of testing used in the published experiments would not detect this, but Zihl (personal communication) states that a single detection approach was used with some cases and this showed that the improvement was not attributable to this particular cause.

Even if the results do reflect a real shrinkage of the field defect as a result of the procedure used, the size of this effect is not large. It might be speculated that the functional significance of this small change would be of little practical concern since many subjects adapt quite successfully to hemianopias. In fact Zihl hints that the improvement was of some real significance with respect to their subjects' performance in everyday situations but no hard evidence is offered in support of this.

Visual neglect

The phenomenon of neglect is related to field defects since the most extreme manifestations, such as totally ignoring all visual stimuli in one half of space, are invariably associated with hemianopias. Milder forms of neglect, where the subject will occasionally fail to notice some stimuli within one visual field, are not necessarily linked to visual field defects (Weinberg et al., 1977). Neglect can be found after lesions in either hemisphere but is more frequently encountered in right hemisphere lesions. The association between spatial neglect (including neglect in the visual modality) and left hemiplegia has been invoked to explain why left hemiplegics generally recover less satisfactorily than right hemiplegics despite the occurrence of aphasia in the latter. Denes et al. (1982) have suggested that spatial neglect is an important factor in retarding recovery in hemiplegics.

Weinberg, Diller and their colleagues at the Institute of Rehabilitation Medicine in New York have been particularly concerned to retrain those with neglect to attend appropriately to visual stimuli on the affected side (Diller and Gordon, 1981; Weinberg *et al.*, 1977, 1979). In their first report Weinberg *et al.* (1977) used subjects exhibiting neglect who had suffered right hemisphere strokes. Their training package contained several elements. They had a board on which stimuli could appear in different positions. The experimental group practised such things as tracking a target that moved from one side of the board, across the subject's midline, and into the other side. Subjects were also required to search for lights in different parts of the board. Practice was given on cancellation tasks (e.g. crossing out all the '8's on a page with numbers distributed at random over it). Finally graded practice in reading was used.

1 –	Early in life Mr. Harding had found himself	– 1
2 –	located at Barchester. A fine voice and a taste	– 2
3 –	for sacred music had decided the position in	– 3
4 –	which he was to exercise his calling, and for	– 4
5 –	many years he performed the easy but not highly	– 5
6 –	paid duties of a minor canon. At the age of	– 6
7 –	forty a small living in the close vicinity of	– 7
8 –	the town increased both his work and his	– 8
9 –	income and at the age of fifty he became the	– 9

Figure 7. Example of the kind of material used by Weinberg *et al.* (1977) in training patients with visual neglect to read again

The reading practice was of particular interest and is illustrated in Figure 7. In the first stage the subject can use the vertical line on the left as an anchoring point, and the numbers at the beginning and end of each line to ensure that lines are not skipped. These cues are then withdrawn in sequence. The numbers on the right go first, followed by the numbers on the left. Finally the anchoring line is taken away. This procedure is, of course, directed at subjects who tend to omit the first few words of the left-hand side of each line when reading.

In Weinberg *et al.*'s (1977) investigation the treated group received 20 hours total exposure to these special training procedures over a period of about a month. Both this group and an otherwise untreated control group received the unit's standard occupational therapy programme. Both groups were tested before and after on a battery of tests. Some of the tests were very closely related to the tasks used in training (e.g. reading and cancellation tasks) whereas others were less closely related. It was found that the group given the special training procedures improved on a number of visual tasks relating to academic performance (reading, writing, and carrying out arithmetical calculations with pencil and paper). There was some generalization to pictorial tasks (e.g. counting and matching faces) but not to others such as line bisection or locating the body midline.

In a further similar study Weinberg *et al.* (1979) administered a condensed version of the training tasks used in the previous investigation to the experimental group together with two new procedures. Otherwise the design was substantially that of the Weinberg *et al.* (1977) paper. One of the two new procedures was a form of training in sensory awareness. In this the subject sat facing the back of a manikin designed to represent the upper half of the human torso. The subject was repeatedly touched on his back and then had to indicate where he had been touched by pointing to the corresponding position on the manikin. In the second task rods were displayed either directly in front or to one side of the subject. The subject then had to indicate the length of the rod on a horizontal board. In both tasks feedback as to the accuracy of response was provided.

The measures used were based on a larger battery of tests than employed in the previous study, but incorporating most of those that had been used before. Some improvement occurred on most measures with some evidence of generalization to the kinds of task that showed no generalization in the first experiment. The results also indicated that those in the experimental group with severe impairments improved more than those with milder impairments.

An alternative, and often more detailed, account of some of the procedures used to encourage such things as scanning into the affected field in the Weinberg *et al.* (1977, 1979) papers is given by Piasetsky *et al.* (1982). In an experiment with some similarities to those reported by Weinberg and his colleagues, Zihl (1980) showed that it was possible to train three patients with visual field defects to scan to detect stimuli in the region of visual loss.

DISORDERS OF SPATIAL JUDGEMENT

Disorders of spatial awareness and judgement are also quite common. Although they are distinct from the problem of neglect dealt with in the previous section it is quite easy to comprehend that visual neglect is going to cause difficulties in visuospatial awareness. In consequence measures to improve neglect are likely to assist awareness of visuospatial relationships.

There have been very few attempts to try to modify spatial difficulties. One series of experiments based around what is essentially a visuospatial task has again been carried out at the New York Institute of Rehabilitation Medicine (Ben-Yishay *et al.*, 1970a,b; Diller *et al.*, 1974) and summarised by Diller and Gordon (1981). These investigations were built around the Block Design subtest of the Wechsler Adult Intelligence Scale. This subtest was chosen as the point of interest because Ben-Yishay *et al.* (1970c) had found a relationship between initial psychometric assessment and outcome in rehabilitation as judged by length of treatment and final performance of stroke patients with left hemiplegia. Of all the tests used the best single predictor was the Block Design subtest. This task was then analysed and a retraining programme developed through a careful and logical series of steps (Diller and Gordon, 1981).

The initial investigations established the order of difficulty of the various Block Design items for the population under study, and determined the various means of reaching a solution that were employed. A nine-step cueing procedure was developed that would assist all but the most severely afflicted subjects to complete the designs. This cueing procedure was then used as the basis for training the experimental group in an experiment which looked at the effects of training on the performance of subjects with both left and right hemiplegia. The amount of special training amounted to 10 hours spread over 10 days and both the experimental and control groups received the unit's standard rehabilitation programme during the period of the experiment.

The trained group gave unequivocal evidence of improved performance on the Block Design subtest as a result of training. This is of interest in itself as showing that such patients can benefit from a carefully designed and thought-out training programme when carrying out a visuospatial task of this kind. Nevertheless the question of generalization of this training is also of considerable interest. As compared to the control group, that given training on Block Design performance showed gains on a number of other variables. These included the Wechsler Object Assembly subtest, a test of motor impersistence, a blind rating of performance in conventional occupational therapy, and analysis of the visuomotor aspects of eating (Diller et al., 1974).

The main criticism that can be levelled against this series of investigations is that performance on the Block Design subtest is hardly a clinically relevant variable. This should not be allowed to detract from the positive elements of this research programme. The careful analysis of subjects' performance and the design of a training programme based on this analysis represent a level of sophistication not found in many other studies in this field. The fact that training can beneficially affect performance on a visuospatial task, and that some transfer of gains can be found to a practical, everyday task such as eating, is most encouraging.

Miller (1980c) also demonstrated considerable gains as a result of practice on a visuospatial task. The subjects studied were patients with severe head injuries (duration of post-traumatic amnesia in excess of 1 week). These subjects do not exhibit a specific spatial impairment of similar nature to those associated with more focal lesions as studied by Diller and his colleagues. Nevertheless, as judged by their starting levels on the task used, the performance of severely head-injured subjects is considerably below normal levels.

The experimental task was based on the Minnesota Spatial Relations Test. This consists of four boards of approximately equal difficulty with each board containing 58 cut-out shapes. The subject's task is always to fit the 58 different shapes into the correct holes in the board as quickly as he can. In this experiment each subject had five trials on the first board, followed by five on the second, and so on. The order of presentation of the different boards was counterbalanced across subjects to control for the minor differences in difficulty between the four boards.

The results are shown in Figure 8. It can be seen that the experimental group has an extremely poor starting level as compared with the controls. It is also the case that the head-injured subjects make dramatic improvements with practice and show good transfer from one board to the next. At the end of the experiment the control group had more or less reached an asymptote, whereas the

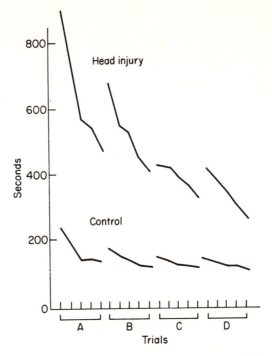

Figure 8. Mean times on successive trials of the four versions of the Minnesota Spatial Relations Test (from Miller, 1980c. Reproduced by permission of the British Medical Journal)

experimental group was still improving and had closed the gap quite considerably. It is possible that further practice would have enabled the experimental group to get even closer to the controls.

It is also interesting to compare relative rates of learning. It is impossible to do this fairly from the data described in Figure 8, since the head-injured subjects with their much poorer starting level have very much more room for improvement. In this experiment it proved possible to match some of the head-injured subjects on the first trial of their fourth board with some of the control subjects starting their first board. Comparative learning curves can then be plotted over five trials and are given in Figure 9. It appears from this that when matched for starting levels head-injured subjects learn more slowly than controls. This is not an unexpected conclusion. The problem is that the data displayed in Figure 9, by controlling for one variable (starting level), immediately confound another. There is evidence from studies of the way in which normal subjects learn skills that the particular aspect of any complex task that is being learned varies with the stage of overall learning (Fleishman, 1968; Fleishman and Fruchter, 1960). It could therefore be that the head-injured subjects with a considerable amount of previous exposure to the task are not learning quite the same thing as the control group over their first five trials. Regardless of these

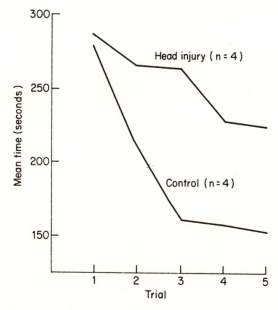

Figure 9. Relative rates of learning in two subgroups when matched for initial performance levels (from Miller, 1980c. Reproduced by permission of the British Medical Journal)

problems of interpretation Miller's (1980c) experiment demonstrates that quite severely brain-damaged subjects can show considerable improvement on a task relying heavily on visuospatial ability when given extensive practice.

It is unfortunate that little further work has been carried out on the amelioration of visuospatial impairments. Luria and Tsvetkova (1964) give what in many ways is an unsatisfactory description of attempts to assist individual patients to carry out visuospatial tasks (including a form of block design task). This was done either by formulating plans for the subject to follow or by providing cues. These authors also make the very valid point that visuospatial performance may be disrupted in a number of different ways (other than as a consequence of visual field defects). In their examples a patient with bilateral frontal lesions failed on block design tests because he could not adequately plan his response to the task and failed to check for errors. Intervention was directed at these aspects of the overall task. A second patient with more posterior lesions exhibited satisfactory planning but required extra spatial cues. What these examples illustrate is not therapeutic interventions of proven effectiveness but the general principle that any intervention will probably need to take into account the reason for task failure. Performance on a task that has any degree of complexity may break down for a number of reasons. Careful analysis of performance will need to precede the design of intervention programmes.

Finally there is a single-case study by Leftoff (1979) that has some bearing on the area under discussion. In this case the subject could make visuospatial judgements with apparent adequacy but could not transfer the information gained to another modality (the tactual modality). Although Leftoff prefers to describe the training procedure in other terms, what amounted to a form of graded practice enabled the subject to improve considerably.

MOTOR BEHAVIOUR

A high proportion of patients with damage to, or disease of, the central nervous system exhibit motor impairments. These may include such things as hemiplegia and quadriplegia but also various forms of tremor or abnormal movements. Despite the very large literature on motor behaviour and motor skills (e.g. Stelmach, 1976; Welford, 1968) neuropsychologists have shown very little interest in disturbed motor behaviour. There has, of course, been some work (e.g. Flowers, 1978; Wyke, 1971) but this is almost so rare as to emphasize the neglect when it does appear.

One approach to motor disorders of neurological origin has been the use of biofeedback techniques. The use of biofeedback in this context has been reviewed by Fernando and Basmajian (1978) and Inglis et al. (1976) in a rather optimistic vein. It is not unreasonable to expect that certain motor disorders might result, at least in part, from impaired proprioceptive feedback, especially where lesions of the somatosensory system are involved. Biofeedback techniques might then be valuable in providing additional information to the patient as to the activity of his muscles and thus assist in relearning motor control. Unfortunately a critical examination of the evidence does not support the overenthusiastic conclusions of some commentators such as Fernando and Basmajian (1978).

Most of the published reports are of uncontrolled clinical studies where EMG biofeedback has been applied to patients with hemiplegia or footdrop (e.g. Amato et al., 1973; Andrews, 1964; Brudny et al., 1974; Swaan et al., 1974). Brudny et al. (1974, 1976) have described the treatment of large numbers of cases with hemiparesis (a total of 45 in the latter paper). Both auditory and visual feedback were given to indicate muscle activity as detected by surface electrodes placed over the appropriate muscle groups. In general these cases had been hemiparetic for some time and the majority were considered to have shown appreciable gains which appeared to persist over time.

Taken as a whole these reports are certainly suggestive. There do appear to be well-documented instances where patients whose condition had seemed to be static produced improvements in motor functioning. Unfortunately the studies cited so far do not involve untreated control groups, and it is not possible to unequivocally exclude the possibility that untreated groups might have shown examples of similar gains. Rather more likely, and therefore more demanding of exclusion, is the hypothesis that the gains following the introduction of biofeedback procedures were just the non-specific or 'placebo' effects of exposing patients to a form of treatment which, from the patient's point of view, must seem to be highly technical and very impressive. There are also a great many possible technical complications and sources of artifact in biofeedback research and these are, at best, only given a token acknowledgement in the vast majority of clinical studies (Gatchel and Price, 1979).

There are very few controlled investigations in the field of biofeedback as applied to neuromuscular retraining. Basmajian *et al.* (1975) had two groups of 10 subjects, each of which had a residual foot dorsiflexion paresis (foot-drop) as a result of a stroke sustained at least 3 months before entering the study. All subjects received three 40-minute treatment sessions a week for 5 weeks. The control group went through the unit's normal therapeutic exercise programme whilst the experimental group did these exercises for only half of each session. For the remainder of the session the experimental group underwent EMG biofeedback training. Dorsiflexion was assessed by a special apparatus at the beginning and end of the treatment regime and several months after the end of treatment. All subjects showed some change but the EMG biofeedback group experienced the greatest improvement. At first sight this is much better evidence for the efficacy of biofeedback but, as Fernando and Basmajian (1978) admit, there is a snag. The interval between the stroke and entering the trial was much shorter on average for the biofeedback group than it was for the controls. Because the minimal interval was only 3 months it is quite possible that many subjects would still be experiencing some spontaneous recovery and this would be most manifest in the EMG biofeedback group.

A rather similar experiment has been carried out by Burnside *et al.* (1982) again using stroke patients with foot-drop. The control group received the usual exercise programme whilst the experimental group had EMG biofeedback in addition. Subjects had blind assessments both before and after treatment and at 6 weeks follow-up. The biofeedback group showed greater improvements and these were maintained at follow-up. This study has avoided the main possible contaminating factor in the Basmajian *et al.* (1975) investigation. What it still leaves open is the mechanism by which the biofeedback exerts its effects. It could produce a better improvement simply because it is seen by the patient to be more impressive and therefore more likely to induce change than basic physiotherapy.

Assuming that EMG biofeedback is effective, and this remains to be clearly proven, there is a further point that merits comment. In their review Inglis *et al.* (1976) describe a number of reports of the biofeedback treatment of hemiplegic patients. A characteristic shown by a number of these reports is that response to biofeedback, where it appears to occur, is quite rapid and dramatic. In other words the response is quick or does not occur at all. Unfortunately not all accounts of treatment comment upon the rapidity of response, so it is not possible to judge how universal this finding is.

It is logical to expect that biofeedback techniques might be of value in neuromuscular rehabilitation. Uncontrolled single-case reports and descriptions of whole series of cases offer many signs of encouragement. What is lacking is a clear demonstration that the apparent benefits really do result from the biofeedback procedure itself and not from non-specific factors. It should also be noted that the history of biofeedback techniques as applied to other kinds of problems has been that of very encouraging early reports followed by the discovery of technical complications and the demonstration that biofeedback is not necessarily any better than simpler alternative treatments (e.g. Gatchel and Price, 1979; Johnston, 1978).

CHANGES IN MOTIVATION, PERSONALITY, AND RELATED PROBLEMS

The problems to be dealt with in this section are difficult to describe and cannot be adequately fitted with a single label. However there is no doubt that changes in personality, motivation, and related functions do occur and that they can present particularly difficult problems in rehabilitation (e.g. Bond, 1975). The spouses of people who have suffered severe head injuries will often complain that their husband 'is not the man that they married'. When pressed they often find it difficult to describe exactly what they mean by this remark, but what they are referring to are alterations in personality and loss of drive or initiative. Employers of such patients may not point to any loss of skills but will comment upon altered attitudes, lack of drive, and slightly inappropriate social behaviour. Brain-damaged patients may also show mood changes. Many people with head injuries become irritable and there is an association between aphasia and depression (e.g. Robinson and Benson, 1981).

Neuropsychologists are mainly interested in cognitive functioning and have failed to show any strong or consistent concern for the effects of brain damage on personality other than to comment upon the rather disinhibited or socially inept behaviour that can be exhibited by patients with lesions in the frontal lobes. Powell (1979, 1981) has attempted to give an overview of this field but the picture he reveals is unsatisfactory. This is largely because of the paucity of good evidence and the considerable conceptual problems inherent in any discussion of personality.

Powell (1981) is also one of the very few authorities who have attempted to present some discussion as to how the adverse personality and motivational changes following brain damage might be ameliorated. He rightly points out that such a complex and varied feature as 'personality' cannot be dealt with as such. It is necessary to specify in detail what behaviour (or lack of behaviour) is causing difficulty and under what circumstances. Powell sets out tables showing how this might be done using two patients as examples. One is a middle-aged man who became unduly introverted after a left hemisphere stroke with transient dysphasia. The other is a younger adult with aggression associated with temporal lobe epilepsy. In the former case the excessive introversion could be seen in reduced social activity resulting in the patient's withdrawal from a football supporters club of which he had been a keen member, his intolerance of visitors to the home, and in not going to the pub with his wife. Appropriate treatment goals can be set based on these things. Unfortunately Powell gives only the briefest description of the techniques used to try to modify behaviour in the desired direction and no indication of success. What Powell's examples do show is that it is possible to approach problems of this kind given determination and ingenuity by breaking them down into a number of more manageable aspects.

Craine (1982) has given a long account of a series of interventions carried out with a patient with frontal lobe dysfunction. One of the problems tackled was impulsivity. This was tackled by means of problem-solving tasks where it was essential to think ahead and not rush in with what might be the most immediately obvious first response. It is difficult to judge the success of this from the account given, but the reader can be forgiven for being sceptical as to whether any improvements on this task generalized to other situations.

One related area which has not been the subject of any formal discussion, but which might be a suitable target for psychological intervention, is assisting people to make use of the skills that they do retain. In clinical work it is not uncommon to be left with the distinct impression that a patient who has, say, a mild dysphasic disturbance will avoid many everyday situations and act so as to minimize social contacts that might necessitate verbal interactions. This is despite a formal examination of language which shows a level of performance that is more than adequate for the patient to understand and be understood in most situations. This situation appears to arise because the patient becomes very sensitive to the occasional error in speech or failure to find the exact word that he needs, and also unduly concerned with the possible adverse reactions to these relatively trivial inadequacies that might be engendered in others.

On an *a priori* basis there is a good chance that well-established techniques, such as those developed by behaviour therapists for anxiety reduction, could help to relieve these secondary handicaps associated with the patient's reactions to his difficulties and his sometimes exaggerated and inaccurate view of their necessary consequences for his life. In some cases it is even possible that an approach along these lines might have a greater benefit than one directed at the primary problem. Relevant reports are awaited.

DISCUSSION

Although most attention has been given to the amelioration of treatment of amnesic and dysphasic disorders there remains a whole range of other psychological changes that may follow brain damage or disease. Many particular defects have not even been mentioned because there is no work on them dealing with their possible rehabilitation. Despite this there is some cause for encouragement. The work by Diller and his associates on visual neglect appears to show real effects which generalize to some degree, and the techniques involved could turn out to be of real clinical significance. Within this particular field, and at this particular stage of its development, this is about as much as can reasonably be hoped for.

CHAPTER TEN

Final comments

In the preceding pages an account has been given of what is known about the pattern of recovery after neuropsychological impairments produced by brain damage or disease. Possible explanations of spontaneous recovery have been described and the evidence that relates to them evaluated. In many ways the overall picture is less than satisfactory. Because of the large numbers of factors that have to be considered as possibly influencing outcome it is not possible to predict recovery with any accuracy. This is particularly so as far as the single case is concerned, although rough-and-ready generalizations about groups can be made. Our understanding of the mechanisms that produce recovery is also inadequate Finally, it would be misleading to claim that there are as yet any psychological techniques of proven clinical usefulness in rehabilitation.

As far as possible means of intervention are concerned it can be argued, as was done by Miller (1980b), that we are in the very early stages of work in this field. In consequence the main interest has to lie in identifying and developing techniques of possible value, leaving rigorous and systematic testing of clinical effectiveness to come later. There is some justification in this argument. Nevertheless it does not excuse the generally poor methodology found in those attempts that have been made to test effectiveness. There is also quite a long history of work on the treatment of aphasia and yet there are very few reasonably competently executed trials of aphasia therapy.

Given that the overall thrust of this book is towards clinical issues, and especially the rehabilitation of those unfortunate enough to suffer neuropsychological impairments, the final question of importance is what can be done to improve the present situation. There are a large number of openings for further development in this field and predicting where the best future pay-off might lie is a hazardous business. The following discussion is therefore somewhat speculative.

An initial point is that the processes underlying recovery, and the factors that conceivably exert some sort of influence over it, are extraordinarily complex. Furthermore they are likely to vary from one situation to another. The kinds of impairment that any intervention might be directed towards ameliorating are very varied, as are the background circumstances of individual patients which determine the context of any intervention. Given this highly complicated background it seems likely that this is not a field in which single advances can be made which will have a dramatic impact over a wide range of situations. Instead individual gains in knowledge and therapeutic efficiency are likely to be small. This does not mean that marked progress is impossible; it is just that this will take time and will be produced as the cumulative effects of many small advances on a number of fronts. It is worth looking at some of these fronts in a little more detail.

FACTORS INFLUENCING RECOVERY

These were reviewed in Chapters 2 to 4. What emerges is that the simple generalizations about recovery that have often been put forward do not withstand scrutiny too well. At best notions like better recovery in younger subjects and those expressed in Ribot's law and Pitres' rule can only be accepted with considerable qualification. Further knowledge concerning the factors influencing recovery would undoubtedly be useful.

Firstly, it would help with the problem of predicting outcome if the relationships between basic subject variables (such as age and background experience), the type and locus of pathology, nature of the resulting handicaps, and the rate and extent of recovery were better understood. Given that many patients will have to face a prolonged period of recovery and rehabilitation, it is of great practical value to be able to make reliable decisions about such things as a possible return to previous employment at a relatively early stage. A second way in which better information about the factors influencing recovery would be of use in contributing to our general understanding of the processes underlying recovery and ways in which recovery might be modified or extended.

Of particular potential value would be more systematic work on the influence of environmental manipulations on recovery. Some intriguing results which merit further investigation have already appeared. For example, Goldman and Mendelson (1977) found that experience with a non-spatial task after orbital prefrontal lesions in monkeys had an effect on later performance with a spatial task. Since no similar effect was found for a task very like that used in the interpolated training this suggests that the benefit was not mediated by ordinary training processes. It would be very interesting if this result could be confirmed and alternative hypotheses with regard to how experience might influence recovery explored. Even if the original finding were shown to be spurious any additional information about the parameters that might determine the effects of experience on recovery or retraining could be of benefit.

It is by exploring problems of this kind that fundamental research on animals might make a significant contribution to the rehabilitation of human patients. Although evidence derived from animal experiments can only be transferred to the human situation with extreme caution, work of this kind could be a very fruitful source of hypotheses for work with clinical populations. The very much greater degree of experimental control that is possible in animal experiments means that possible mechanisms of influence can be studied much more rigorously than would ever be possible in clinical investigations.

MECHANISMS UNDERLYING RECOVERY

Again better understanding of the processes by which spontaneous recovery is achieved could be of value in rehabilitation. This is especially so if it is considered that strategies of intervention will be most efficient if they build upon, or complement, the natural recovery process. As can be seen from the work described in Chapter 5, attention is now starting to be directed at possible mechanisms of recovery, especially in the animal literature.

The biggest gap in knowledge surrounds the kind of mechanism that was described as 'functional adaptation' in Chapter 5. If the analysis given there is reasonably correct then functional adaptation is the general mechanism responsible for a good proportion of longer-term recovery. It is also important as the kind of mechanism that psychological interventions can best build upon, modify, or extend in trying to assist rehabilitation. It is therefore particularly important that the analysis of functional adaptation can get beyond the present state of knowledge where it is an important but largely unexplored general principle.

It is difficult to suggest detailed theories in relation to functional adaptation without resorting to highly specific instances. For example, Gheorghita's (1981) method of dealing with acquired dyslexia by writing material in vertical form is based on the notion that this will break up the normal scanning mechanisms and thus force the subject to pay more attention to each letter or element. This explanation has a certain plausibility. Even if it is eventually proved to be correct, and there is no further evidence on this point, this explanation offers little that would generalize to other situations involving different kinds of tasks and sensory modalities.

Possibly the best way to approach functional adaptation is inductively. This could be done by carefully studying a varied range of situations under which functional adaptation might be expected to occur. The close examination of a number of detailed examples might then enable general principles, if such exist, to be derived. At the very least such an approach might allow the derivation of some rules of thumb as to what submechanisms or subskills can be substituted for others when the latter are rendered inoperative or ineffectual by brain damage. Even this would be information of potential practical value. The obvious limiting factor would be that substituting one means of achieving a given goal for another is dependent upon the kinds of functions that remain relatively intact. This leads to the one clear-cut, if rather low-level, prediction that patients with a given deficit existing in relative isolation are likely to show better compensation for this impairment than those in whom the deficit is only one among many.

Regardless of what is the optimal way of approaching the problem there can be no doubt that functional adaptation is a mechanism that badly needs to be investigated in greater detail. This is, of course, not to argue that investigators should neglect other types of mechanism which also need greater elaboration.

INTERVENTION

It is especially difficult to anticipate what specific forms of intervention will prove to be the most efficacious in rehabilitation. Such predictions will not be attempted here. A more realistic aim is to try to identify certain lines of investigation or broad classes of techniques that might lead to the development of more effective forms of intervention.

One obvious source of ideas for the development of rehabilitation programmes is information about the nature of the impairments that can be found. If, for example, it is necessary to teach a certain skill to patients with a given kind of impairment then it would be useful to know that such patients have great difficulty in acquisition but will retain information and skills quite well once these have been acquired. This would then focus attention on the acquisition process, and this might involve strategies such as breaking the task down into small components so as to ease acquisition. If it was known to be the case that acquisition was difficult, but no matter how well the skill was acquired at any one point in time it would also be rapidly forgotten, then other strategies might be suggested. These could include modifying the environment to make possession of the skill less critical, or building cues into the situation to prompt the correct response.

A major problem in trying to work in this way is that much basic research in abnormal psychology and neuropsychology is not carried out in such a way as to yield information of the most direct value in this context. The typical research design is based on a comparison of performance on a standard measure or task between subjects belonging to the category of interest (e.g. those with visual neglect or a certain type of aphasia) and either normal control subjects or other abnormal groups with the latter selected so as to share some, but not other, features with the group that is of primary interest. The latter type of group is usually chosen so as to control for some possible factor that might contaminate the results of the experiment (e.g. a group with space-occupying lesions in another part of the brain to control for the effects of raised intracranial pressure). The fundamental interest lies in the between-group comparison.

There is another general research paradigm that could be used in abnormal psychology and neuropsychology which is much less frequently used, and which could give a much more direct lead to methods of intervention (Miller, 1979b). Rather than apply the identical task to subjects with, say, visual neglect and subjects forming one or more control groups, it is possible to use a design that systematically varies the task. The different versions of the same task are then applied to groups of subjects with the impairment of interest. Alternatively the same group may do the task under all the different experimental variations if circumstances permit this sort of intensive design. In this way it is possible to study the conditions under which an impairment such as visual neglect is particularly manifest, and under what conditions it causes least interference with ongoing behaviour. This kind of approach can not only give useful information about the nature of the impairments, but it does lead much more naturally into possible methods of intervention. Given the growing interest in rehabilitation and the desirability of linking fundamental research to practice it is unfortunate that this kind of research is rarely carried out.

Given the very varied kinds of impairment that can be encountered, which will no doubt demand an equally varied repertoire of therapeutic responses, it is difficult to identify specific techniques that are likely to be of wide-ranging value. Most of the techniques that have been thought out so far have been dealt with in previous chapters. There is one type of technique that could be of considerable value that has not yet been described.

Gianutsos (1981b) and Lynch (1982) have both drawn attention to the possible use of microcomputers in cognitive rehabilitation. Lynch's paper basically deals with the use of standard computerized games but, in principle, a very wide range of material can be put on a small computer with a visual display unit. This has several advantages. As Gianutsos (1981b) points out, tasks can often be programmed into game form and this makes them more attractive for the subject. The subject can also work largely independently, thus freeing the therapist's time for other things. If carefully programmed, computer-based training procedures can be adapted to the individual's needs, as by varying the size of successive increases in difficulty throughout the program in order to match the subject's rate of progress. Another possible advantage is that a subject working on a particular program on his own (e.g. a form of game like 'Hangman' to help with spelling) can make lots of mistakes without feeling as humiliated as he might be in front of the therapist. A final advantage is that the machine can also be programmed to keep an accurate and objective record of the subject's progress and performance.

One of the major limitations of microcomputers for use in this way lies in the very varied nature of the different problems and impairments that present. It may only be feasible to use microcomputers for fairly standard problems requiring a fairly standard approach to therapy, or for which a fairly standard set of practice tasks might be needed. Not all problems in cognitive rehabilitation may be capable of being tackled in this way either in whole or in part. Nevertheless, as Gianutsos (1981b) shows, it is possible to produce programs relating to a wide range of situations such as searching the visual field, speeded reading of word lists, and various forms of memory training. So far effectiveness has not really been evaluated. Lynch (1982) demonstrates that brain-injured subjects can improve in their performance on certain computer-based games but there was no attempt to show that this improvement was matched by change in any other aspect of behaviour.

There is a further point that needs to be raised with regard to intervention. In the preceding chapters various kinds of neuropsychological impairment were described, together with the various techniques that have been used in remedial interventions. It is difficult to describe all this work otherwise, but the pairing of deficits and techniques can give what is potentially a very misleading impression. There is a strong temptation to regard all forms of psychological intervention or treatment as being linked to certain kinds of problems or the need to attain particular goals in a simple one-to-one relationship. The medical equivalent would be the identification of a specific type of bacterial infection being followed by treatment by a set antibiotic or group of antibiotics. Thus there has been a trend in certain clinical psychologists practising behaviour therapy to rely on corresponding simple relationships such as the identification of a relatively simple and straightforward phobia automatically leading on to desensitization as the treatment. This simple-minded approach is sometimes deprecated in the behaviour therapy literature but is nevertheless the way adopted by all too many practitioners and apparently condoned in many texts on behaviour therapy.

In the case of neuropsychological deficits such simplistic thinking as the identification of a problem in remembering other people's names automatically leading on to attempt to apply imagery techniques like those described in Chapter 8 could be highly counterproductive. The patient may not be able to retrieve the names of acquaintances when socially appropriate for a number of other reasons besides a failure to acquire and retrieve the correct verbal label. Glasgow *et al.* (1977), in their single-case study of a patient with this problem, were careful to begin by ensuring that this really did lie in a failure to acquire or retain names. For example, they checked that the patient did not have something akin to prosopagnosia in that he could recognize faces that he had seen before to a fairly normal degree. This is because a person who cannot recognize a familiar face is unlikely to supply the correct name, even given an almost perfect verbal memory, unless there is some other cue as to the individual's identity. As Mesulam (1981) illustrates with his model of unilateral neglect, most neuropsychological impairments turn out to be very complex, and it is necessary to bear these complexities in mind when devising intervention programmes. Luria and Tsvetkova (1964) also give an example as to how performance on a given task can be disrupted in different ways by patients with lesions in different parts of the brain. The implication of this is that successful intervention is only likely to follow from a very careful analysis of the underlying factors which determine the problem.

It is for this reason that operant techniques that have proved very successful with other severely handicapped groups such as the mentally handicapped (e.g. Kiernan, 1974) may not be quite so universally valuable in dealing with neuropsychological impairments. This is not to reject operant techniques entirely. They undoubtedly have been used with some apparent success in certain contexts (e.g. Wood and Eames, 1981). It is interesting that the cases described by Wood and Eames (1981) involve such things as the use of 'time out' programmes to modify aggressive behaviour in very severely head-injured patients. It is in eliminating undesirable behaviour and teaching very basic self-help skills with very handicapped groups that the operant approach is likely to be of greatest use. Here the situation is very like that of dealing with severely mentally handicapped people and the main difference between the populations lies in the age at which the 'brain damage' was acquired. Patients with more specific impairments, and who are not globally handicapped, are likely to benefit much more from an approach that is more based in cognitive psychology.

As the previous three chapters have illustrated, there has been considerable variety in the attempts that have been made to modify neuropsychological impairments. So far there is not a great deal in the way of firm evidence that psychological intervention is of real value in the rehabilitation of neuropsychological impairments. Partly this is because proper studies have yet to be reported. However those trials that have been carried out often do not reveal very impressive results. It could be that this is a true reflection of the power of the interventions that have been evaluated so far, and it would be foolish to deny this possibility. It is the writer's impression that some forms of intervention may well yield benefits but that these are very rarely of great magnitude. It could be that there is also a contaminating factor which is that most of the studies have just not tested effectiveness in the most appropriate way.

Given that neuropsychological impairments are very complex so that rather different techniques might be appropriate for superficially similar problems and that there are a large number of potentially relevant subject variables, it is difficult to design good group experiments that can control for most of the possible confounding factors. Even quite small groups of relatively homogeneous subjects may take a very long time to collect. This field therefore offers the classic situation for single-case research (e.g. Hersen and Barlow, 1976). There are a few examples of well-conducted single-case investigations that can provide some information about the effectiveness of the interventions used (e.g. Saan and Schoonbeek, 1973) but this approach has not been as extensively exploited as it might be.

There are, of course, disadvantages in single-case research. This is largely because it cannot answer questions of the kind which ask how many of a given group will show an appreciable response to a given treatment or what the average level of response will be. Since these questions are dependent upon the assumption that a response can be obtained, and gaining such knowledge is the prime concern at this stage of development, then this limitation of single-case research is not very important. Single-case investigations also have the advantage that they are easy to dovetail into detailed analyses of the nature of the deficit that is causing concern. As argued above, this latter feature is something that needs to be built carefully into the treatment package.

CONCLUSION

If the picture presented in this book is anything like accurate the reader's response may be one of pessimism. From the point of view of the clinician there are many difficult problems to tackle and there is little that is really secure to hold onto in planning an intervention. On the other hand, these are early days in a very difficult area. Real advances may be slow to emerge, but come they will if psychologists and others with interests in this field are determined to meet the challenge. There are already some signs of achievement that can be built upon, and much can be learned from past failures. The next few years may not see major and dramatic innovations but there is no reason why they should not reveal sound and steady progress.

References

Adams, G. F., and Hurwitz, L. J. (1963). Mental barriers to recovery from strokes. *Lancet*, **2**, 533–537.

Albert, M. L., and Obler, J. (1978). *The Bilingual Brain*. Academic Press, New York.

Albert, M. L., Sparks, R. W., and Helm, H. A. (1973). Melodic intonation therapy for aphasia. *Arch. Neurol.*, **29**, 130–131.

Albert, M. S., Butters, N., and Levin, J. (1979). Temporal gradients in the retrograde amnesia of patients with alcoholic Korsakoff's disease. *Arch. Neurol.*, **36**, 211–216.

Amato, A., Hernsmeyer, C. A., and Kleinman, D. (1973). Use of electromyographic feedback to increase inhibitory control of spastic muscles. *Phys. Ther.*, **53**, 1063–1066.

Andrews, J. M. (1964). Neuromuscular re-education of the hemiplegic with the aid of the electromyograph. *Arch. Phys. Med. Rehab.*, **45**, 530–532.

Aronson, M., Shatin, L., and Cook, J. C. (1956). Socio-psychotherapeutic approach to the treatment of aphasic patients. *J. Speech Hear. Disord.*, **21**, 352–364.

Aten, J. L., Caliguri, M. P., and Holland, A. L. (1980). The efficiency of functional communication therapy for chronic aphasic patients. *J. Speech Hear. Disord.*, **47**, 93–96.

Bach-y-Rita, P. (1981a). Brain plasticity as a basis for development of rehabilitation procedures for hemiplegia. *Scand. J. Rehab. Med.*, **13**, 73–83.

Bach-y-Rita, P. (1981b). Central nervous system lesions: sprouting and unmasking in rehabilitation. *Arch. Phys. Med. Rehab.*, **62**, 413–417.

Baddeley, A. D. (1978). The trouble with levels: a re-examination of Craik and Lockhart's framework for memory research. *Psychol. Rev.*, **85**, 139–152.

Baddeley, A. D. (1982). Domains of recollection. *Psychol. Rev.*, **89**, 708–729.

Baker, E., Berry, T., Gardner, H., Zurif, E., Davis, L., and Veroff, A. (1975). Can linguistic competence be dissociated from natural language functions? *Nature*, **254**, 509–510.

Ball, J. A. C., and Taylor, A. R. (1967). Effects of cyclandelate on mental function and cerebral blood flow in elderly patients. *Br. Med. J.*, **3**, 525–528.

Basmajian, J. V., Kukulka, C. G., Narayan, M. G., and Takebe, K. (1975). Biofeedback treatment of foot-drop after stroke compared with standard rehabilitation technique: effects on voluntary control and strength. *Arch. Phys. Med. Rehab.*, **56**, 231–236.

Basser, L. S. (1962). Hemiplegia of early onset and the faculty of speech with reference to the effect of hemispherectomy. *Brain*, **85**, 427–460.

Basso, A., Capitani, E., Laiacona, F., and Luzatti, C. (1980). Factors influencing type and severity of aphasia. *Cortex*, **16**, 631–636.

Basso, A., Capitani, E., and Vignolo, L. A. (1979). Influence of rehabilitation on language skills in aphasic patients: a controlled study. *Arch. Neurol.*, **36**, 190–196.

Bauman, T. P., and Spear, P. D. (1977). Role of the lateral suprasylvian visual area in behavioural recovery from effects of visual cortex damage in cats. *Brain Res.*, **138**, 445–468.

Benjamin, R. M., and Thompson, R. F. (1959). Differential effects of cortical lesions in infant and adult cats on roughness discrimination. *Exper. Neurol.*, **1**, 305–321.

Benson, D. F. (1979a). Aphasia. In K. M. Heilman and E. Valenstein (eds) *Clinical Neuropsychology*. Oxford University Press, Oxford.

Benson, D. F. (1979b). *Aphasia, Alexia and Agraphia*. Churchill Livingstone, Edinburgh.

Benson, D. F. (1979e). Aphasia rehabilitation. *Arc. Neurol.*, **36**, 187–189.

Benson, D. F. (1980). Psychiatric problems in aphasia. In M. T. Sarne and O. Höök (eds) *Aphasia: Assessment and Treatment*. Almqvist & Wiksell, Stockholm.

Benson, D. F., and Geschwin, N. (1967). Shrinking retrograde amnesia. *J. Neurol. Neurosurg. Psychiatry*, **30**, 539–544.

Benson, D. F., Marsden, C. D., and Meadows, J. C. (1975). The amnesic syndrome of posterior cerebral artery occlusion. *Acta Neurol. Scand.*, **50**, 133–145.

Benton, A. L. (1979). Visuoperceptive, visuospatial, and visuoconstructive disorders. In K. M. Heilman and E. Valenstein (eds) *Clinical Neuropsychology*. Oxford University Press, Oxford.

Ben-Yishay, Y., Diller, L., Gerstman, L., and Gordon, W. (1970a). Relationship between initial competence and ability to profit from cues in brain-damaged individuals. *J. Abnorm. Psychol.*, **75**, 248–259.

Ben-Yishay, Y., Diller, L., and Mandleberg, I. (1970b). Ability to profit from cues as a function of initial competence in normal and brain-injured adults: a replication of previous findings. *J. Abnorm. Psychol.*, **76**, 378–379.

Ben-Yishay, Y., Gerstman, L., Diller, L., and Haas, A. (1970c). Prediction of rehabilitation outcome from psychometric parameters in left hemiplegia. *J. Cons. Clin. Psychol.*, **34**, 436–441.

Beyn, E. S., and Shokor-Trotskaya, M. K. (1966). The preventive method of speech rehabilitation in aphasia. *Cortex*, **11**, 96–108.

Binder, L. M., and Schreiber, V. (1980). Visual imagery and verbal mediation as memory aids in recovering alcoholics. *J. Clin. Neuropsychol.*, **2**, 71–74.

Black, P., Markowitz, R. S., and Cianci, S. (1975). Recovery of motor function after lesions in motor cortex of monkey. In Ciba Foundation Symposium No. 34, *Outcome of Severe Damage to the Central Nervous System*. Elsevier, Amsterdam.

Blakemore, C. B., and Falconer, M. A. (1967). Long-term effects of anterior temporal lobectomy on certain cognitive functions. *J. Neurol. Neurosurg. Psychiatry*, **30**, 364–367.

Bland, B. H., and Cooper, R. M. (1969). Posterior neodecortication in the rat: age at operation and experience. *J. Comp. Physiol. Psychol.*, **69**, 345–354.

Blessed, G., Tomlinson, B. E., and Roth, M. (1968). The association between quantitative measures of dementia and of senile change in the cerebral grey matter of elderly subjects. *Br. J. Psychiatry*, **114**, 797–811.

Bollinger, R. L., and Stout, C. E. (1976). Response contingent small step treatment: performance based communication. *J. Speech Hear. Disord.*, **41**, 40–51.

Bond, M. R. (1975). Assessment of the psychosocial outcome after severe head injury. In Ciba Foundation Symposium No. 34. *Outcome of Severe Damage to the Central Nervous System*. Elsevier, Amsterdam.

Brailowsky, S. (1980). Neuropharmacological aspects of brain plasticity. In P. Bach-y-Rita (ed.) *Recovery of Function: Theoretical Considerations for Brain Injury Rehabilitation*. Hans Huber, Bern.

Braun, J. J. (1975). Neocortex and feeding behavior in the rat. *J. Comp. Physiol. Psychol.*, **89**, 507–522.

Bricolo, A., Turazzi, S., and Feriotti, G. (1980). Prolonged post-traumatic unconsciousness: therapeutic assets and liabilities. *J. Neurosurg.*, **52**, 625–634.

Britton, A., Bernstein, L. L., Brunse, A. J., Buttiglieri, M. W., Cherkin, A., McCormack, J. H., and Lewis, D. J. (1972). Failure of ingestion of RNA to enhance human learning. *J. Geront.*, **27**, 478–481.

Brooks, D. N. (1972). Memory and head injury. *J. Nerv. Ment. Dis.*, **155**, 350–355.

Brooks, D. N. (1974). Recognition memory after head injury: a signal detection analysis. *Cortex*, **10**, 224–230.

Brooks, D. N. (1975). Long and short term memory in head injured patients. *Cortex*, **11**, 329–340.

Brooks, D. N., Aughton, M. E., Bond, M. R., Jones, P., and Rizvi, S. (1980). Cognitive sequelae in relationship to early indices of severity of brain damage after severe blunt head injury. *J. Neurol. Neurosurg. Psychiatry*, **43**, 529–534.

Brookshire, R. H. (1967). Speech pathology and the experimental analysis of behavior. *J. Speech Hear. Dis.*, **32**, 215–227.

Brudny, J., Korein, J., Grynbaum, B. B., Friedmann, L. W., Weinstein, S., Sach-Frankel, G., and Belandres, P. V. (1976). EMG feedback therapy: review of treatment of 114 patients. *Arch. Phys. Med. Rehab.*, **57**, 55–61.

Brudny, J., Korein, J., Levidow, L., Grynbaum, B., Lieberman, A., and Friedman, L. W. (1974). Sensory feedback therapy as a modality of treatment in central nervous system disorders of voluntary movement. *Neurology*, **24**, 925–932.

Buffery, A. W. H. (1976). Clinical neuropsychology: a review and preview. In S. Rachman (ed.) *Contributions to Medical Psychology*. Pergamon Press, Oxford.

Burnside, I. G., Tobias, H. S., and Bursill, D. (1982). Electromyographic feedback in the remobilization of stroke patients: a controlled trial. *Arch. Phys. Med. Rehab.*, **63**, 217–222.

Butfield, E., and Zangwill, O. L. (1946). Re-education in aphasia: a review of 70 cases. *J. Neurol. Neurosurg. Psychiatry*, **9**, 75–79.

Butters, N., and Cermak, L. S. (1980). *Alcoholic Korsakoff's Syndrome: an Information Processing Approach to Amnesia*. Academic Press, New York.

Butters, N., Albert, M. S., and Sax, D. (1979). Investigations of the memory disorders of patients with Huntington's disease. In T. Chase, N. Wexler and A. Barbeau (eds) *Advances in Neurology, Vol. 23, Huntington's Disease*. Raven Press, New York.

Calne, D. B. (1970). *Parkinsonism: Physiology, Pharmacology and Treatment*. Arnold, London.

Cameron, D. E., Sved, S., Solyom, L., Wainrib, B., and Barik, H. (1963). Effects of ribonucleic acid on memory defect in the aged. *Amer. J. Psychiatry*, **120**, 320-325.

Carlsson, C. A., van Essen, C., and Löfren, J. (1968). Factors affecting the clinical course of patients with severe head injuries. Part 1: Influence of biological factors. Part 2: Significance of post-traumatic coma. *J. Neurosurg.*, **29**, 242–251.

Cermak, L. S. (1975) Imagery as an aid to retrieval for Korsakoff patients. *Cortex*, **11**, 163–169.

Chassan, J. B. (1979). *Research Design in Clinical Psychology and Psychiatry*, 2nd edn. Appleton-Century-Crofts, New York.

Chelune, G. J., and Edwards, P. (1981). Early brain lesions: ontogenetic–environmental considerations. *J. Cons. Clin. Psychol.*, **49**, 777–790.

Chomsky, N. (1959). Review of *Verbal Behavior*, by B. F. Skinner. *Language*, **35**, 26–58.

Chorover, S. L., and Schiller, P. H. (1966). Re-examination of prolonged retrograde amnesia in one-trial learning. *J. Comp. Physiol. Psychol.*, **61**, 34–41.

Chow, K. L., and Survis, J. S. (1958). Retention of overlearned visual habits after temporal cortical ablation in monkey. *Arch. Neurol. Psychiatry*, **79**, 640–646.

Coltheart, M., Patterson, K. E., and Marshall, J. C. (1980). *Deep Dyslexia*. Routledge, London.

Conkey, R. C. (1938). Psychological changes associated with head injuries. *Arch. Psychol.*, **33**, No. 232.

Cope, D. N., and Hall, K. (1982). Head injury rehabilitation: benefit of early intervention. *Arch. Phys. Med. Rehab.*, **63**, 433–437.

Corkin, S. (1979). Hidden-figures-test performance: lasting effects of unilateral penetrating head injury and transient effects of bilateral cingulotomy. *Neuropsychologia*, **17**, 585–605.

Costello, J. (1977). Programmed instruction. *J. Speech Hear. Disord.*, **42**, 3–28.

Cotman, C. W. (1978). *Neuronal Plasticity.* Raven Press, New York.

Craik, F. I. M., and Lockhart, R. S. (1972). Levels of processing: a framework for memory research. *J. Verb. Learn. Verb. Behav.*, **11**, 671–684.

Craik, F. I. M., and Tulving, E. (1975). Depth of processing and retention of words in episodic memory. *J. Exp. Psychol. Gen.*, **104**, 268–294.

Craine, J. F. (1982). The retraining of frontal lobe dysfunction. In L. E. Trexler (ed.) *Cognitive Rehabilitation: Conceptualization and Intervention.* Plenum Press, New York.

Critchley, M. (1953). *The Parietal Lobes.* Arnold, London.

Crovitz, H. F. (1979a). Presentation limits on memory retrieval. *Cortex*, **15**, 37–42.

Crovitz, H. F. (1979b). Memory retraining in brain-damaged patients: the airplane list. *Cortex*, **15**, 131–134.

Crovitz, H. F., Harvey, M. T., and Horn, R. W. (1979). Problems in the acquisition of imagery mnemonics: three brain-damaged cases. *Cortex*, **15**, 225–234.

Culton, G. L. (1969). Spontaneous recovery from aphasia. *J. Speech Hear. Disord.*, **12**, 825–832.

Cummings, J. L., Benson, D. F., Walsh, M. J., and Levine, H. L. (1979). Left to right transfer of language dominance: a case study. *Neurology*, **29**, 1547–1550.

Curr, W., and Gourlay, N. (1960). The effect of practice on performance in scholastic tests. *Br. J. Educ. Psychol.*, **30**, 155–167.

Daniloff, J. K., Noll, J. D., Fristoe, M., and Lloyd, L. L. (1982). Gesture recognition in patients with aphasia. *J. Speech Hear. Disord.*, **47**, 43–49.

Darley, F. L. (1975). Treatment of acquired aphasia. In W. J. Friedlander (ed.) *Advances in Neurology*, vol. 7. Raven Press, New York.

David, R., Enderby, P., and Bainton, D. (1982). Treatment of acquired aphasia: speech therapists and volunteers compared. *J. Neurosurg. Psychiatry*, **45**, 957–961.

Davies, A. D. M., and Binks, M. G. (1983). Supporting the residual memory of a Korsakoff patients. *Behav. Psychother.*, **11**, 62–74.

Davies, G., Hamilton, S., Hedrickson, E., Levy, R., and Post, F. (1977). The effect of cyclandelate in depressed and demented patients: a controlled study in psychogeriatric patients. *Age and Ageing*, **6**, 156–162.

Davis, N., and LeVere, T. E. (1979). Recovery of function after brain damage; different processes and the facilitation of one. *Physiol. Psychol.*, **7**, 233–240.

de Leon, M. J., Ferris, S. H., Blau, I., George, A. E., Reisberg, B., Kricheff, I. I., and Gershon, S. (1979). Correlations between computerized tomographic changes and behavioural deficits in senile dementia. *Lancet*, **2**, 589–591.

Dencker, S. J. (1960). A follow-up study of 128 closed head injuries in twins using cotwins as controls. *Acta Psychiat. Neurol. Scand.* (Suppl. No. 123), **33**.

Denes, G., Semenza, C., Stoppa, E., and Lis, A. (1982). Unilateral spatial neglect and recovery from hemiplegia: a follow-up study. *Brain*, **105**, 543–552.

Dennis, M., and Whitaker, H. A. (1976). Language acquisition following hemidecortication: linguistic superiority of the left over the right hemisphere. *Brain Lang.*, **3**, 404–433.

de Renzi, E., and Vignolo, L. A. (1962). The token test: a sensitive test to detect receptive disturbances in aphasics. *Brain*, **85**, 665–678.

de Renzi, E., Faglioni, P., and Ferrari, P. (1980). The influence of sex and age on the incidence and type of aphasia. *Cortex*, **16**, 627–630.

Deutsch, J. A., and Deutsch, D. (1973). *Physiological Psychology.* Dorsey, Homewood, Illinois.

Devor, M. (1982). Plasticity in the adult nervous system. In L. S. Illis, E. M. Sedgwick, and H. J. Glanville (eds) *Rehabilitation of the Neurological Patient.* Blackwell, Oxford.

DiCarlo, L. M. (1980). Language recovery in aphasia: effect of systematic filmed programmed instruction. *Arch. Phys. Med. Rehab.*, **61**, 41–49.

Diller, L., and Gordon, W. A. (1981). Rehabilitation and clinical neuropsychology. In S. B. Filskov and T. J. Boll (eds) *Handbook of Clinical Neuropsychology.* Wiley, New York.

Diller, L., Ben-Yishȧy, Y., Gerstman, L., Goodkin, R., Gordon, W., and Weinberg, J. (1974). *Studies in cognition and rehabilitation in hemiplegia.* Instit. Rehab. Monogr. No. 50. New York University Medical Center.

Dimond, S. J. (1980). *Neuropsychology.* Butterworths, London.

Dimond, S. J., and Brouwers, E. Y. M. (1976). Increase in the power of human memory in normal man through the use of drugs. *Psychopharmacology,* **49,** 307–309.

Dobbing, J. (1974). The later development of the brain and its vulnerability. In J. A. Davis and J. Dobbing (eds) *Scientific Foundations of Paediatrics.* Heinemann, London.

Dolan, M. P., and Norton, J. C. (1977). A programmed technique that uses reinforcement to facilitate acquisition and retention in brain-damaged patients. *J. Clin. Psychol.,* **33,** 496–501.

Drachman, D. A., and Sahakian, B. J. (1980). Memory and cognitive function in the elderly: a preliminary study of physostigmine. *Arch. Neurol.,* **37,** 674–675.

Drevillon, J., Pellault, F., and Perron, M. (1977). Une nouvelle methode de réeducation des troubles severes de la lecture. 'La lecture verticale'. *Les Sciences de l'Education,* **10,** 53–70.

Drewe, E. A., Ettlinger, G., Milner, A. D., and Passingham, R. E. (1970). A comparative review of the results of neuropsychological research on man and monkey. *Cortex,* **6,** 129–163.

Eichorn, O. (1965). The effect of cyclandelate on cerebral circulation. *Vasc. Dis.,* **2,** 303–315.

Eidelberg, E., and Stein, D. G. (1974). Functional recovery after lesions of the nervous system. *Neurosci. Res. Prog. Bull.,* **12,** 191–303.

Eisenson, J. (1949). Prognostic factors related to language rehabilitation in aphasic patients. *J. Speech Hear. Disord.,* **14,** 262–264.

Eslinger, P. J., and Damasio, A. R. (1981). Age and type of aphasia in patients with stroke. *J. Neurol. Neurosurg. Psychiatry,* **44,** 377–381.

Ettlinger, G., Blakemore, C. B., Milner, A. D., and Wilson, J. (1972). Agenesis of the corpus callosum: a behavioural investigation. *Brain,* **95,** 327–346.

Ettlinger, G., Iwai, E., Mishkin, M., and Rosvold, H. E. (1968). Visual discrimination in the monkey following serial ablation of the inferotemporal and preoccipital areas. *J. Comp. Physiol. Psychol.,* **65,** 110–117.

Evans, C. D. (1982). Rehabilitation of head injury. In L. S. Illis, E. M. Sedgwick, and H. J. Glanville (eds) *Rehabilitation of the Neurological Patient.* Blackwell, Oxford.

Fernando, C. K., and Basmajian, J. V. (1978). Biofeedback in physical medicine and rehabilitation. *Biofeed. Self Reg.,* **3,** 435–455.

Fewtrell, W. D., House, A. O., Jamie, P. F., Oates, M. R., and Cooper, J. E. (1982). Effects of vasopressin on memory and new learning in a brain-injured population. *Psychol. Med.,* **12,** 423–425.

Feyereison, P., and Seron, X. (1982a). Non-verbal communication and aphasia: a review. I. Comprehension. *Brain Lang.,* **16,** 191–212.

Feyereison, P., and Seron, X. (1982b). Non-verbal communication and aphasia: a review. II. Expression. *Brain Lang.,* **16,** 213–236.

Fine, E. W., Lewis, D., Villa-Landa, I., and Blakemore, C. B. (1970). The effect of cyclandelate on mental function in patients with arteriosclerotic brain disease. *Br. J. Psychiatry,* **117,** 157–161.

Finger, S. (1978a). *Recovery from Brain Damage.* Plenum Press, New York.

Finger, S. (1978b). Experimental attenuation of brain-lesion symptoms. In S. Finger (ed.) *Recovery from Brain Damage.* Plenum Press, New York.

Finger, S. (1978c). Postweaning environmental stimulation and somesthetic performance in rats sustaining cortical lesions at maturity. *Devel. Psychobiol.,* **11,** 63–74.

Finger, S. (1978d). Lesion momentum and behaviour. In S. Finger (ed.) *Recovery from Brain Damage.* Plenum Press, New York.

Finger, S., Gruenthal, M., and Bell, J. (1981). Some perspectives on the serial lesion effect.

In M. W. van Hof and G. Mohn (eds.). *Functional Recovery from Brain Damage.* Elsevier, Amsterdam.

Finger, S., Hart, T., and Jones, E. (1982). Recovery time and sensorimotor cortex lesion effects. *Physiol. Behav.*, **29**, 73–78.

Fishman, R. A. (1978). The pathology and treatment of brain edema. In W. B. Matthews and G. M. Glaser (eds) *Recent Advances in Clinical Neurology*, No. 2. Churchill-Livingstone, Edinburgh.

Fleishman, E. A. (1968). Individual differences and motor learning. In R. M. Gagne (ed.) *Learning and Individual Differences.* Merrill Books, Columbus, Ohio.

Fleishman, E. A., and Fruchter, B. (1960). Factor structure and predictability of successive stages of learning morse code. *J. Appl. Psychol.*, **44**, 97–101.

Flowers, K. (1978). Lack of prediction in the motor behaviour of Parkinsonism. *Brain*, **101**, 35–52.

Gabriel, S., Freer, B., and Finger, S. (1979). Brain damage and the overlearning reversal effect. *Physiol. Psychol.*, **7**, 327–332.

Gardner, H., Zurif, E. B., Berry, T., and Baker, E. (1976). Visual communication in aphasia. *Neuropsychologia*, **14**, 275–292.

Gasparrini, B., and Satz, P. (1979). A treatment for memory problems in left hemisphere CVA patients. *J. Clin. Neuropsychol.*, **1**, 137–150.

Gatchel, R. J., and Price, K. P. (1970). *Clinical Applications of Biofeedback: Appraisal and Status.* Pergamon, Oxford.

Gazzaniga, M. S. (1978). Is seeing believing: notes on clinical recovery. In S. Finger (ed.) *Recovery from Brain Damage.* Plenum Press, New York.

Gazzaniga, M. S., and Sperry, R. W. (1967). Language after section of the cerebral commissures. *Brain*, **90**, 131–148.

Gazzaniga, M. S., Volpe, B. T., Smylie, C. S., Wilson, D. H., and Le Doux, J. E. (1979). Plasticity in speech organization following commissurotomy. *Brain*, **102**, 805–818.

Gentile, A. M., Green, S., Nieburgs, A., Schmelzer, W., and Stein, D. G. (1978). Disruption and recovery of locomotor and manipulatory behavior following cortical lesions in rats. *Behav. Biol.*, **22**, 417–455.

Geschwind, N. (1974). Late changes in the nervous system. In D. G. Stein, J. J. Rosen, and N. Butters (eds) *Plasticity and Recovery of Function in the Central Nervous System.* Academic Press, New York.

Gheorgita, N. (1981). Vertical reading: a new method of therapy for reading disturbances in aphasics. *J. Clin. Neuropsychol.*, **3**, 161–164.

Gianutsos, R. (1981a). Training the short- and long-term verbal recall of a postencephalitic amnesic. *J. Clin. Neuropsychol.*, **3**, 143–153.

Gianutsos (1981b). Using microcomputers for cognitive rehabilitation. Paper presented to American Psychological Association.

Gianutsos, R., and Gianutsos, J. (1979). Rehabilitating the verbal recall of brain-damaged patients by mnemonic training: an experimental demonstration using single-case methodology. *J. Clin. Neuropsychol.*, **1**, 117–135.

Glasgow, R. E., Zeiss, R. A., Barrera, M., and Lewinsohn, P. M. (1977). Case studies on remediating memory deficits in brain-damaged individuals. *J. Clin. Psychol.*, **33**, 1049–1054.

Glass, A. V., Gazzaniga, M. S., and Premack, D. (1973). Artificial language training in global aphasics. *Neuropsychologia*, **11**, 95–103.

Glendenning, R. L. (1972). Effects of training between two unilateral lesions of visual cortex upon ultimate retention of black–white discrimination habits by rats. *J. Comp. Physiol. Psycho.*, **80**, 216–229.

Glick, S. D., and Greenstein, S. (1972). Facilitation of recovery after lateral hypothalamic damage by prior ablation of frontal cortex. *Nature New Biol.*, **239**, 187–188.

Glick, S. D., and Zimmerberg, B. (1972). Comparative recovery following simultaneous and successive stage frontal brain damage in mice. *J. Comp. Physiol. Psychol*, **79**, 481–487.

156

Glick, S. D., and Zimmerberg, B. (1978). Pharmacological modification of brain lesion syndromes. In S. Finger (ed.) *Recovery from Brain Damage*. Plenum Press, New York.

Gloning, I., Gloning, K., Haub, G., and Quatember, R. (1969). Comparison of verbal behavior in right-handed and non-right-handed patients with anatomically verified lesions of one hemisphere. *Cortex*, **5**, 43–52.

Gloning, I., Gloning, K., and Hoff, H. (1968). *Neuropsychological Symptoms and Syndromes in Lesions of the Occipital Lobe and Adjacent Areas*. Gauthier-Villars, Paris.

Gloning, K., Trappl, R., Heiss, W. S., and Quatember, R. (1976). Programs and speech therapy in aphasia. In Y. Lebrun and R. Hoops (eds) *Recovery in Aphasics*. Swets & Zeitlinger, Amsterdam.

Goldberg, E., Gerstman, L. J., Mattis, S., Hughes, J. E. O., Sirio, C. A., and Bilder, R. M. (1982). Selective effects of cholinergic treatment on verbal memory. *J. Clin. Neuropsychol.*, **4**, 219–234.

Goldberger, M. E., and Murray, M. (1978). Recovery of movement and axonal sprouting may obey some of the same laws. In C. W. Cotman (ed.) *Neuronal Plasticity*. Raven Press, New York.

Golden, C. J. (1978). *Diagnosis and Rehabilitation in Clinical Neuropsychology*. C. C. Thomas, Springfield, Ill.

Goldman, P. S. (1971). Functional development of the prefrontal cortex in early life and the problem of neuronal plasticity. *Exper. Neurol.*, **32**, 366–387.

Goldman, P. S. (1974). Recovery of function after CNS lesions in infant monkeys. *Neurosci. Res. Prog. Bull.*, **12**, 217–222.

Goldman, P. S. (1976). The role of early experience in recovery of function following orbital prefrontal lesions in infant monkeys. *Neuropsychologia*, **14**, 401–412.

Goldman, P. S., and Lewis, M. E. (1978). Developmental biology of brain damage and experience. In C. W. Cotman (ed.) *Neuronal Plasticity*. Raven Press, New York.

Goldman, P. S., and Mendelson, M. J. (1977). Salutary effects of early experience on deficits caused by lesions of frontal association cortex in developing rhesus monkeys. *Exper. Neurol.*, **57**, 588–602.

Goldman, P. S., and Rosvold, H. E. (1972). The effects of selective caudate lesions in infant and juvenile rhesus monkeys. *Brain Res.*, **43**, 53–66.

Goldman, P. S., Rosvold, H. E., and Mishkin, M. (1970). Selective sparing of function following prefrontal lobectomy in infant monkeys. *Exper. Neurol.*, **29**, 221–226.

Goldstein, K., and Gelb, A. (1918). Psychologische analysen hirnpathologischer Fälle auf Grund von Untersuchungen Hirnverletzer. *Zeitschr. Ges. Neurol. Psychiat.*, **41**, 1–142.

Goodkin, R. (1966). Case studies in behavioural research in rehabilitation. *Percept. Motor Skills*, **23**, 171–182.

Goodkin, R. (1969). Changes in word production, sentence production and relevance in an aphasic through verbal conditioning. *Behav. Res. Ther.*, **7**, 93–99.

Gott, P. S., and Saul, R. E. (1978). Agenesis of the corpus callosum: limits of functional compensation. *Neurology*, **28**, 1272–1279.

Greenough, W. T., Fass, B., and De Voogd, T. J. (1976). The influence of experience on recovery following brain damage in rodents: hypotheses based on development research. In R. N. Walsh and W. T. Greenough (eds) *Advances in Behavioral Biology*, vol. 17. Plenum Press, New York.

Gregory, R. L. (1961). The brain as an engineering problem. In W. H. Thorpe and O. L. Zangwill (eds) *Current Problems in Animal Behaviour*. Cambridge University Press, Cambridge.

Grewel, F. (1963). Prologomena to psycholinguistics. In L. Halpern (ed.) *Problems of Dynamic Neurology*. Post Press, Jerusalem.

Groher, M. (1977). Language and memory disorders following closed head trauma. *J. Speech Hear. Res.*, **20**, 212–221.

Gronwall, D., and Wrightson, P. (1974). Delayed recovery of intellectual function after minor head injury. *Lancet*, **2**, 605–609.

Gross, C. G., and Weiskrantz, L. (1962). Evidence for dissociation of impairment in auditory and delayed response following lateral frontal lesions in monkeys. *Exper. Neurol.*, **5**, 453–466.

Guic-Robles, E., Venable, N., Acevedo, I., Aramburu, B., and Pinel-Hamuy, T. (1982). Recovery of visual pattern discrimination by rats without visual cortex when trained by fading procedures. *Physiol. Psychol.*, **10**, 175–185.

Hagen, C. (1973). Communication abilities in hemiplegia: effect of speech therapy. *Arch. Phys. Med. Rehab.*, **54**, 454–463.

Hamlin, R. M. (1970). Intellectual function 14 years after frontal lobe surgery. *Cortex*, **6**, 299–307.

Harlow, H. F., Akert, K., and Schiltz, K. A. (1964). The effects of bilateral prefrontal lesions on learned behavior of neonatal, infant, and pre-adolescent monkeys. In J. M. Warren and K. Akert (eds) *The Frontal Granular Cortex and Behavior*. McGraw-Hill, New York.

Harlow, H. F., Blomquist, A. J., Thompson, C. I., Schiltz, K. A., and Harlow, M. K. (1968). Effects of induction age and size of frontal lobe lesions on learning in rhesus monkeys. In R. L. Isaacson (ed.) *The Neuropathology of Development*. Wiley, New York.

Harris, J. E. (1980). Memory aids people use: two interview studies. *Mem. Cogn.*, **8**, 31–38.

Harris, J. E., and Sunderland, A. (1981). A brief survey of the management of memory disorders in rehabilitation units in Britain. *Int. Rehab. Med.*, **3**, 206–209.

Hatfield, F. M., and Shewell, C. (1983). Some applications of linguistics to aphasia therapy. In C. Code and D. Müller (eds.). *Aphasia Therapy*. Edwin Arnold, London.

Hebb, D. O. (1945). Man's frontal lobes. *Arch. Neurol. Psychiatry*, **54**, 10–24.

Hecaen, H., and Albert, M. (1978). *Human Neuropsychology*. Wiley, New York.

Heilman, K. M., and Valenstein, E. (1979). *Clinical Neuropsychology*. Oxford University Press, Oxford.

Heilman, K. M., Safran, A., and Geschwind, N. (1971). Closed head trauma and aphasia. *J. Neurol. Neurosurg. Psychiatry*, **34**, 265–269.

Heiskanen, O., and Sipponen, P. (1970). Prognosis of severe brain injury. *Acta Neurol. Scand.*, **46**, 343–348.

Hersen, M., and Barlow, D. H. (1976). *Single Case Experimental Designs*. Pergamon, Oxford.

Holland, A. L. (1969). Some current trends in aphasia rehabilitation. *J. Amer. Speech Hear. Assoc.*, **11**, 3–7.

Holland, A. L. (1982). Observing functional communication of aphasic patients. *J. Speech Hear. Disord.*, **47**, 50–56.

Holland, A. L., and Sonderman, J. C. (1974). Effects of a program based on the token test for teaching comprehension skills to aphasics. *J. Speech Hear. Res.*, **17**, 589–598.

Holland, L. K., and Whalley, J. (1981). The work of a psychiatrist in a rehabilitation hospital. *Br. J. Psychiatry*, **138**, 222–229.

Horel, J. A., Bettinger, L. A., Royce, G. J., and Meyer, D. R. (1966). Role of neo-cortex in the learning and relearning of two visual habits by the rat. *J. Comp. Physiol. Psychol.*, **61**, 66–78.

Howes, D. (1973). Some experimental investigations of language in aphasia. In H. Goodglass and S. Blumstein (eds) *Psycholinguistics and Aphasia*. Johns Hopkins University Press, Baltimore.

Hughes, K. R. (1965). Dorsal and ventral hippocampus lesions and maze learning: influence of preoperative environment. *Canad. J. Psychol.*, **19**, 325–332.

Humphrey, M., and Oddy, M. (1980). Return to work after head injury: a review of post-war studies. *Injury*, **12**, 107–114.

Hunter, W. S. (1940). A consideration of Lashley's theory of equipotentiality of cerebral action. *J. Gen. Psychol.*, **3**, 455–467.

Huppert, F. A., and Piercy, M. (1977). Recognition memory in amnesics: a defect of acquisition. *Neuropsychologia*, **15**, 643–652.

Hydén, H. (1970). The question of a molecular basis for the memory trace. In K. H. Pribram and D. E. Broadbent (eds) *Biology of Memory*. Academic Press, New York.

Inglis, J., Campbell, D. and Donald, M. W. (1976). Electromyographic feedback and neuromuscular rehabilitation. *Canad. J. Behav. Sci.*, **8**, 299–323.

Iverson, S. D. (1977). Temporal lobe amnesias. In C. W. M. Whitty and O. L. Zangwill (eds) *Amnesia*, 2nd edn. Butterworths, London.

Jacobsen, C. F. (1936). The functions of the frontal association areas in monkeys. *Comp. Psychol. Monogr.*, **13**, 3–38.

Jaffe, P. G., and Katz, A. N. (1975). Attenuating anterograde amnesia in Korsakoff's psychosis. *J. Abnorm. Psychol.*, **84**, 559–562.

Jeeves, M. A. (1981). Age related effects of agenesis and partial sectioning of the neocortical commissures. In M. W. van Hof and G. Mohn (eds) *Functional Recovery from Brain Damage*. Elsevier, Amsterdam.

Jenkins, J. S., Mather, H. M., and Coughlan, A. K. (1982). Effect of desmopressin on normal and impaired memory. *J. Neurol. Neurosurg. Psychiatry*, **45**, 830–831.

Johnson, D., and Albi, C. R. (1978). Age, brain damage and performance. In S. Finger (ed.) *Recovery from Brain Damage*. Plenum Press, New York.

Johnson, F. N., and Johnson, S. (1977). *Clinical Trials*. Blackwell, Oxford.

Johnston, D. (1978). Clinical applications of biofeedback. *Br. J. Hosp. Med.*, **17**, 561–566.

Jones, M. K. (1974). Imagery as a mnemonic aid after left temporal lobectomy: contrast between material-specific and generalized memory disorders. *Neuropsychologia*, **12**, 21–30.

Kapur, N., and Gordon, D. S. (1975). The retraining of dysgraphia: a case study. *J. Neurol. Neurosurg. Psychiatry*, **38**, 465–468.

Kawaguchi, S., Yamamoto, T., and Samejima, A. (1979). Electrophysiological evidence for axomal sprouting of cerebellothalamic neurons in kittens after hemicerebellectomy. *Exper. Brain Res.*, **36**, 21–37.

Kay, H., Dodd, B., and Sime, M. (1968). *Teaching Machines and Programmed Instruction*. Penguin, Harmondsworth.

Kazdin, A. E. (1975). *Behavior Modification in Applied Settings*. Dorsey Press, Homewood, Illinois.

Kazdin, A. E. (1979). Nonspecific treatment factors in psychotherapy outcome research. *J. Cons. Clin. Psychol.*, **47**, 846–851.

Keenan, J. S., and Brassell, E. G. (1974). A study of factors related to progress for individual aphasic patients. *J. Speech Hear. Disord.*, **39**, 257–269.

Kempinsky, W. H. (1954). Steady potential gradients in experimental cerebral vascular occlusion. *Electroencephal. Clin. Neurophysiol.*, **6**, 375–398.

Kempinsky, W. H. (1958). Experimental study of distant effects of acute focal brain injury. *Arch. Neurol. Psychiatry*, **79**, 376–389.

Kennard, M. A. (1936). Age and other factors in motor recovery from precentral lesions in monkeys. *Amer. J. Physiol.*, **115**, 138–146.

Kennard, M. A. (1940). Relation of age to motor impairment in man and subhuman primates. *Arch. Neurol. Psychiatry*, **44**, 377–397.

Kennard, M. A. (1942). Cortical reorganisation of motor function: studies on series of monkeys of various ages from infancy to maturity. *Arch. Neurol. Psychiatry*, **48**, 227–240.

Kertesz, A. (1979a). *Aphasia and Associated Disorders: Taxonomy, Localization and Recovery*. Grune & Stratton, New York.

Kertesz, A. (1979b). Recovery and treatment. In K. M. Heilman and E. Valenstein (eds) *Clinical Neuropsychology*. Oxford University Press, Oxford.

Kertesz, A., and McCabe, P. (1977). Recovery patterns and prognosis in aphasia. *Brain*, **100**, 1–18.

Kiernan, C. C. (1974). Behaviour modification. In A. M. Clarke and A. D. B. Clarke (eds) *Mental Deficiency: The Changing Outlook*, 3rd edn. Methuen, London.

Kimble, D. P. (1976). Changes in behavior of hippocampal-lesioned rats across a 6 week post-operative period. *Physiol. Psychol.*, **4**, 289–293.

Kircher, K. A., Braun, J. J., Meyer, D. R., and Meyer, P. M. (1970). Equivalence of simultaneous and successive neocortical ablations in production of impairments of retention of black–white habits in rats. *J. Comp. Physiol. Psychol.*, **71**, 420–425.

Knight, R. G., and Wooles, I. M. (1980). Experimental investigation of chronic organic amnesia: a review. *Psychol. Bull.*, **88**, 753–77.

Lambert, W., and Fillenbaum, S. (1959). A pilot study of aphasia among bilinguals. *Canad. J. Psychol.*, **13**, 28–34.

Landis, T., Graves, R., Benson, D. F., and Hebben, N. (1982). Visual recognition through kinaesthetic mediation. *Psychol. Med.*, **12**, 515–531.

Langton-Hewer, R. (1982). Rehabilitation of stroke. In L. S. Illis, E. M. Sedgwick, and H. J. Glanville (eds) *Rehabilitation of the Neurological Patient*. Blackwell, Oxford.

LaPointe, L. L. (1977). Base-10 programmed stimulation: task specification, scoring and plotting performance in aphasia therapy. *J. Speech Hear. Disord.*, **42**, 90–105.

Lashley, K. S. (1921). Studies of cerebral function in learning. II. The effects of long continued practice upon cerebral localization. *J. Comp. Psychol.*, **1**, 453–468.

Lashley, K. S. (1929). *Brain Mechanisms and Intelligence*. University of Chicago Press, Chicago.

Lashley, K. S. (1935). The mechanism of vision. XII. Nervous structures concerned in habits based on reactions to light. *Comp. Psychol. Mongr.*, **11**, 43–79.

Lashley, K. S. (1938). Factors limiting recovery after central nervous lesions. *J. Nerv. Ment. Dis.*, **88**, 733–755.

Lashley, K. S. (1950). In search of the engram. *Society of Experimental Biology Symposium No. 4: Physiological Mechanisms in Animal Behaviour*. Cambridge University Press, Cambridge.

Laurence, S., and Stein, D. G. (1978). Recovery after brain damage and the concept of localization of function. In S. Finger (ed.). *Recovery from Brain Damage*. Plenum Press, New York.

Leftoff, S. (1979). Perceptual retraining in an adult cerebral palsy patient: a case of a deficit in cross-modal equivalence. *J. Clin. Neuropsychol.*, **1**, 227–239.

Leftoff, S. (1981). Learning functions for unilaterally brain-damaged patients for serially and randomly ordered stimulus material: analysis of retrieval strategies and their relationship to rehabilitation. *J. Clin. Neuropsychol.*, **3**, 301–313.

Lenneberg, E. H. (1967). *The Biological Foundations of Language*. Wiley, New York.

Lesser, R., and Watt, M. (1978). Untrained community help in the rehabilitation of stroke sufferers with language disorder. *Lancet*, **2**, 1045–1048.

LeVere, T. E. (1975). Neural stability, sparing, and behavioral recovery following brain damage. *Psychol. Rev.*, **82**, 344–358.

LeVere, T. E. (1980). Recovery of function after brain damage: a theory of the behavioral deficit. *Physiol. Psychol.*, **8**, 297–308.

LeVere, T. E., and Fontaine, L. (1978). A demonstration of the importance of RNA metabolism for the acquisition but not the performance of learned behaviors. *Exper. Neurol.*, **59**, 444–449.

LeVere, T. E., and LeVere, N. D. (1982). Recovery of function after brain damage: support for the compensation theory of the behavioral deficit. *Physiol. Psychol.*, **10**, 165–174.

LeVere, T. E., and Morlock, G. W. (1974). The influence of preoperative learning on the recovery of successive brightness discrimination following posterior neodecortication in the hooded rat. *Bull. Psychonom. Soc.*, **4**, 507–509.

LeVere, T. E., and Weiss, J. (1973). Failure of seriatim dorsal hippocampal lesions to spare spatial reversal behavior in rats. *J. Comp. Physiol. Psychol.*, **82**, 205–210.

LeVere, T. E., Davis, N., and Gonder, L. (1979). Recovery of function after brain damage: toward understanding the deficit. *Physiol. Psychol.*, **7**, 317–326.

Levin, H. S. (1979). The acalculias. In K. M. Heilan and E. Valenstein (eds) *Clinical Neuropsychology*. Oxford University Press, Oxford.

Levin, H. S., Grossman, R. G., and Kelly, P. (1976). Short-term recognition memory in relation to severity of head injury. *Cortex*, **12**, 175–182.

Levita, E. (1978). Effects of speech therapy on aphasic's responses to functional communication profile. *Percept. Motor Skills*, **47**, 151–154.

Lewinsohn, P. M., Danaher, G. B., and Kikel, S. (1977). Visual imagery as a mnemonic aid for brain-injured persons. *J. Cons. Clin. Psychol.*, **45**, 717–723.

Lezak, M. D. (1976). *Neuropsychological Assessment*. Oxford University Press, Oxford.

Lezak, M. D. (1979). Recovery of memory and learning functions following traumatic brain injury. *Cortex*, **15**, 63–72.

Lincoln, N. B. (1979). *An Investigation of the Effectiveness of Language Retraining Methods with Aphasic Stroke Patients*. Unpublished Ph.D. thesis, University of London.

Lincoln, N. B., Pickersgill, M. J., Hankey, A. I., and Hilton, C. R. (1982). An evaluation of operant training and speech therapy in the language rehabilitation of moderate aphasics. *Behav. Psychother.*, **10**, 162–178.

Lishman, W. A. (1978). *Organic Psychiatry*. Blackwell, Oxford.

Loeser, J. D., and Alvord, E. C. (1968a). Agenesis of the corpus callosum. *Brain*, **91**, 553–570.

Loeser, J. D., and Alvord, E.C. (1968b). Clinicopathological correlations in agenesis of the corpus callosum. *Neurology*, **18**, 745–756.

Lorayne, H., and Lucas, J. (1974). *The Memory Book*. Stein & Day, Briarcliff, N.Y.

Love, R. J., and Webb, W. G. (1977). The efficiency of cueing techniques in Broca's aphasia. *J. Speech Hear. Disord.*, **42**, 170–178.

Low, W. C., Lewis, P. R., Bunch, T., Dunnett, S. B., Iverson, S. D., Björklund, A., and Stenevi, Y. (1982). Function recovery following neural transplantation of embryonic septal nuclei in adult rats with septohippocampal lesions. *Nature*, **300**, 260–261.

Luria, A. R. (1963). *Recovery of Function after Brain Injury*. Macmillan, New York.

Luria, A. R. (1966). *Higher Cortical Functions in Man*. Tavistock, London.

Luria, A. R. (1970). *Traumatic Aphasia*. Mouton, The Hague (originally published in Russia).

Luria, A. R., and Tsvetkova, L. S. (1964). The programming of constructive activity in local brain injuries. *Neuropsychologia*, **2**, 95–107.

Luria, A. R., Naydin, V. L., Tsvetkova, L. S., and Vinarskaya, E. N. (1969). Restoration of higher cortical function following local brain damage. In P. J. Vinken and G. W. Bruyn (eds) *Handbook of Clinical Neurology*, vol. 3. North Holland, Amsterdam.

Lynch, W. J. (1982). The use of electronic games in cognitive rehabilitation. In L. E. Trexler (ed.) *Cognitive Rehabilitation: Conceptualization and Intervention*. Plenum Press, New York.

McDowall, J. (1979). Effect of encoding instructions and retrieval cueing on recall in Korsakoff patients. *Mem. Cog.*, **7**, 232–239.

McGlone, J. (1980). Sex differences in human brain asymmetry: a critical survey. *Behav. Brain Sci.*, **3**, 215–263.

Mackintosh, N. J. (1974). *The Psychology of Animal Learning*. Academic Press, London.

Mandelberg, I. A. (1975). Cognitive recovery after severe head injury: 2. Wechsler Adult Intelligence Scale during post-traumatic amnesia. *J. Neurol. Neurosurg. Psychiatry*, **38**, 1127–1132.

Mandelberg, I. A. (1976). Cognitive recovery after severe head injury: 3. WAIS verbal and performance IQs as a function of post-traumatic amnesia duration and time from injury. *J. Neurol. Neurosurg. Psychiatry*, **39**, 1001–1007.

Mandelberg, I. A., and Brooks, D. N. (1975). Cognitive recovery after severe head injury: 1. Serial testing on Wechsler Adult Intelligence Scale. *J. Neurol. Neurosurg. Psychiatry*, **38**, 1121–1126.

Markowitsch, H. J., and Pritzel, M. (1978). Von Monakow's diaschisis concept: comments on West *et al.* (1976). *Behav. Biol.*, **22**, 411–412.

Marquardsen, J. (1969). *The Natural History of Acute Cerebrovascular Disease.* Munksgaard, Copenhagen.

Marslen-Wilson, W., and Teuber, H.-L. (1975). Memory for remote events in anterograde amnesia: recognition of public figures from photographs. *Neuropsychologia*, **13**, 353–364.

Merskey, H., and Woodford, J. M. (1972). Psychiatric sequelae of minor head injury. *Brain*, **95**, 521–528.

Mesulam, M.-M. (1981). A cortical network for directed attention and unilateral neglect. *Ann. Neurol.*, **10**, 309–325.

Mettler, F. A. (1952). *Columbia-Greystone Associates—Second Group.* Routledge & Kegan Paul, London.

Meyer, D. R., and Meyer, P. M. (1977). Dynamics and basis of recoveries of functions after injuring to the cerebral cortex. *Physiol. Psychol.*, **5**, 133–165.

Meyer, J. S., Sakai, F., Yamaguchi, F., Yamamoto, M., and Shaw, T. (1980). Regional changes in cerebral blood flow during standard behavioral activation in patients with disorders of speech and mentation compared to normal volunteers. *Brain Lang.*, **9**, 61–77.

Meyer, V. (1959). Cognitive changes following temporal lobectomy for the relief of epilepsy. *Arch. Neurol. Psychiatry*, **81**, 299–309.

Miller, E. (1972). *Clinical Neuropsychology.* Penguin, Harmondsworth.

Miller, E. (1975). Impaired recall and the memory disturbance in presenile dementia. *Br. J. Soc. Clin. Psychol.*, **14**, 73–79.

Miller, E. (1977). *Abnormal Ageing.* Wiley, Chichester.

Miller, E. (1978). Is amnesia remediable? In M. M. Gruneberg, P. E. Morris, and R. N. Sykes (eds) *Practical Aspects of Memory.* Academic Press, London.

Miller, E. (1979a). The long-term consequences of head injury: a discussion of the evidence with special reference to the preparation of legal reports. *Br. J. Soc. Clin. Psychol.*, **18**, 87–94.

Miller, E. (1979b). Memory and ageing. In M. M. Gruneberg and P. E. Morris (eds) *Applied Problems in Memory.* Academic Press, London.

Miller, E. (1980a). Cognitive assessment of the older adult. In J. E. Birren and R. B. Sloane (eds) *Handbook of Mental Health and Aging.* Prentice-Hall, Englewood Cliffs, N.J.

Miller, E. (1980b). Psychological intervention in the management and rehabilitation of neuropsychological impairments. *Behav. Res. Ther.*, **18**, 527–535.

Miller, E. (1980c). The training characteristics of severely head injured patients: a preliminary study. *J. Neurol. Neurosurg. Psychiatry*, **43**, 525–528.

Miller, E. (1983). Intellectual function and its disorders. In M. Shepherd and O. L. Zangwill (eds) *Handbook of Psychiatry*, vol. 1. Cambridge University Press, Cambridge.

Miller, E. A., Goldman, P. S., and Rosvold, H. E. (1973). Delayed recovery of function following orbital prefrontal lesions in infant monkeys. *Science*, **182**, 304–307.

Miller, H. (1961). Accident neurosis. *Br. Med. J.*, **1**, 919–925.

Milner, B. (1966). Amnesia following operation on the temporal lobes. In C. W. M. Whitty and O. L. Zangwill (eds) *Amnesia.* Butterworths, London.

Milner, B. (1974a). Sparing of language functions after early unilateral brain damage. *Neurosci. Res. Prog. Bull.*, **12**, 213–217.

Milner, B. (1974b). Hemispheric specialization: scope and limits. In F. O. Schmitt and F. G. Worden (eds) *The Neurosciences: Third Study Program.* MIT Press, Cambridge, Mass.

Milner, B. (1975). Psychological aspects of focal epilepsy and its neurosurgical management. *Adv. Neurol.*, **8**, 299–312.

Milner, B., Branch, C., and Rasmussen, T. (1966). Observations on cerebral dominance.

In A. V. S. de Reuck and M. O'Connor (eds.). *Ciba Foundation Symposium: Disorders of Language*. J. & A. Churchill, London.

Mohler, C. W., and Wurtz, R. H. (1977). Role of striate cortex and superior colliculus in visual guidance of saccadic eye movement in monkeys. *J. Neurophysiol.*, **40**, 74–94.

Moody, E. J. (1982). Sign language acquisition by a global aphasic. *J. Nerv. Ment. Dis.*, **170**, 113–116.

Moore, R. Y. (1974). Central regeneration and recovery of function: the problem of collateral reinervation. In D. G. Stein, J. D. Rosen, and N. Butters (eds) *Plasticity and Recovery of Function in the Central Nervous System*. Academic Press, New York.

Moyer, S. (1979). Rehabilitation of alexia: a case study. *Cortex*, **15**, 139–144.

Munch-Petersen, S., Parkenberg, H., Kornerup, H., Ortmann, J., Ipsen, E., Jacobsen, P., and Simmelsgard, H. (1974). RNA treatment of dementia. *Acta Neurol. Scand.*, **50**, 553–572.

Munk, H. (1878). Weitere Mittheilungen zur Physiologie der Grosshirnrinde. *Arch. Anat. Physiol.*, **3**, 581–592.

Netley, C. (1972). Dichotic listening performance of hemispherectomized patients. *Neuropsychologia*, **10**, 233–240.

Newcombe, F., Hiorns, R. W., and Marshall, J. C. (1976). Acquired dyslexia: recovery and retraining. In Y. Lebrun and R. Hoops (eds) *Recovery in Aphasias*. Swets & Zeitlinger, Amsterdam.

Newcombe, F., Marshall, J. C., Caravick, P. J., and Hiorns, R. W. (1975). Recovery curves in acquired dyslexia. *J. Neurol. Sci*, **24**, 127–133. In M. S. Gazzaniga (ed.) *Handbook of Behavioral Neurobiology*, vol. 2: *Neuropsychology*. Plenum Press, New York.

Newcombe, F., and Ratcliff, G. (1979). Long-term psychological consequences of cerebral lesions. In M. S. Gazzaniga (ed.) *Handbook of Behavioral Neurobiology, vol. 2 Neuropsychology*. Plenum Press, New York.

Nieto-Sampedro, M., Lewis, E. R., Cotman, C. W., and Manthorpe, M. (1982). Brain injury causes a time-dependent increase in neuronotrophic activity at the lesion site. *Science*, **217**, 860–861.

Oddy, M., and Humphrey, M. (1980). Social recovery during the year following severe head injury. *J. Neurol. Neurosurg. Psychiatry*, **43**, 798–802.

Oppenheimer, D. R. (1968). Microscopic lesions in the brain following head injury. *J. Neurol. Neurosurg. Psychiatry*, **31**, 299–306.

Orbach, J., and Fantz, R. L. (1958). Differential effects of neocortical resections on overtrained and non-overtrained visual habits in monkeys. *J. Comp. Physiol. Psychol.*, **51**, 126–129.

Paivio, A. (1969). Mental imagery in learning and memory. *Psychol. Rev.*, **76**, 241–263.

Paivio, A. (1971). *Imagery and Verbal Processes*. Holt, Rinehart & Winston, New York.

Paradis, M. (1977). Bilingualism and aphasia. In H. Whitaker and J. Whitaker (eds) *Studies in Neurolinguistics*, vol. 3. Academic Press, New York.

Parkin, A. J. (1982). Residual learning capacity in organic amnesia. *Cortex*, **18**, 417–440.

Patrissi, G., and Stein, D. G. (1975). Temporal factors in recovery of function after brain damage. *Exper. Neurol.*, **47**, 470–480.

Patten, B. M. (1972). The ancient art of memory: usefulness in treatment. *Arch. Neurol.*, **26**, 25–31.

Peterson, L. N., and Kirshner, H. S. (1981). Gestural impairment and gestural ability in aphasia: a review. *Brain Lang.*, **14**, 333–348.

Petrie, A. (1949). Personality changes after prefrontal leucotomy. Report two. *Br. J. Med. Psychol.*, **22**, 200–207.

Pettit, J. M., and Noll, J. D. (1979). Cerebral dominance in aphasia recovery. *Brain Lang.*, **7**, 191–200.

Piasetsky, E. B., Ben-Yishay, Y., Weinberg, J., and Diller, L. (1982). The systematic remediation of specific disorders: selected application of methods derived in a clinical research setting. In L. E. Trexler (ed.) *Cognitive Rehabilitation: Conceptualization and Intervention.* Plenum Press, New York.

Pickett, J. M. (1952). Non-equipotential cortical function in maze learning. *Amer. J. Psychol.,* **65,** 177–195.

Pitres, A. (1895). Etude sur l'aphasie chez les polyglottes. *Rev. Med.,* **15,** 873–899.

Powell, G. E. (1979). *Brain and Personality.* Saxon House, Farnborough.

Powell, G. E. (1981). *Brain Function Therapy.* Gower, Aldershot.

Premack, D. (1971). Language in chimpanzee. *Science,* **172,** 808–822.

Pribram, K. H. (1969). *Brain and Behaviour. 1. Mood States and Mind.* Penguin, Harmondsworth.

Prins, R. S., Snow, C. E., and Wagenaar, E. (1978). Recovery and aphasia: spontaneous speech versus language comprehension. *Brain Lang.,* **6,** 192–211.

Raab, D. H., and Ades, H. W. (1946). Cortical and midbrain mediation of a conditioned discrimination of acoustic intensities. *Amer. J. Psychol.,* **59,** 59–83.

Reid, L. S. (1953). The development of noncontinuity behavior through continuity learning. *J. Exp. Psychol.,* **46,** 107–112.

Reitan, R. M. (1964). Psychological deficits resulting from cerebral lesions in man. In J. M. Warren and K. Akert (eds.) *The Frontal Granular Cortex and Behavior.* McGraw-Hill, New York.

Ribot, T. (1883). *Les Maladies de la Memoire.* Libraire Germer Baillière, Paris.

Roberts, A. H. (1976). Long-term prognosis of severe accidental head injury. *Proc. R. Soc. Med.,* **69,** 137–140.

Robinson, F. P. (1970). *Effective Study.* Harper, New York.

Robinson, R. G., and Benson, D. F. (1981). Depression in aphasic patients: frequency, severity, and clinical–pathological correlations. *Brain Lang.,* **14,** 282–291.

Rose, C., Boby, V., and Capildev, R. (1976). A retrospective survey of speech disorders following stroke with particular reference to the use of speech therapy. In Y. Lebrun and R. Hoops (eds) *Recovery in Aphasics.* Swets & Zeitlinger, Amsterdam.

Rosenzweig, M. R. (1980). Animal models for effects of brain lesions and for rehabilitation. In P. Bach-y-Rita (ed.) *Recovery of Function: Theoretical Considerations for Brain Injury Rehabilitation.* Hans Huber, Berlin.

Rosner, B. S. (1974). Recovery of function and localization of function in historical perspective. In D. G. Stein, J. J. Rosen, and N. Butters (eds) *Plasticity and Recovery of Function in the Central Nervous System.* Academic Press, New York.

Rossor, M. (1982). Dementia. *Lancet,* **2,** 1200–1203.

Rosvold, H. E., and Szwarcbart, M. K. (1964). Neural structures involved in delayed response performance. In J. M. Warren and K. Akert (eds) *The Frontal Granular Cortex and Behavior.* McGraw-Hill, New York.

Ruesch, J., and Moore, B. E. (1943). Measurement of intellectual functions in the acute stage of head injury. *Arch. Neurol. Psychiatry,* **50,** 165–170.

Russell, E. W. (1981). The chronicity effect. *J. Clin. Psychol.,* **37,** 246–253.

Russell, W. R. (1971). *The Traumatic Amnesias.* Oxford University Press, London.

Russell, W. R., and Nathan, P. W. (1946). Traumatic amnesia. *Brain,* **69,** 280–300.

Russell, W. R., and Smith, R. (1961). PTA in closed head injury. *Arch. Neurol.,* **5,** 4–17.

Rylander, G. (1951). Observations on mental changes after total lobotomy and after inferior lobotomy. *Acta Psychiat. Neurol. Scand.,* Suppl. No. 60.

St James-Roberts, I. (1981). A re-interpretation of hemispherectomy data without functional plasticity of the brain. 1. Intellectual function. *Brain Lang.,* **13,** 31–53.

Saan, R. J., and Schoonbeek, H. R. (1973). Problemen bij de behandeligen en de evaluatie van een patient met rekenstoornissen. In A. P. Cassee, P. E. Boeke and J. J. Barendregt (eds) *Kilische Psychologie in Nederland,* Deel 2. Van Loghum Slaterus, Deventer.

Sanders, H. I., and Warrington, E. K. (1971). Memory for remote events in amnesic patients. *Brain,* **94,** 661–668.

Sanders, H. I., and Warrington, E. K. (1975). Retrograde amnesia in organic amnesic patients. *Cortex*, **11**, 397–400.

Sarno, J. (1981). Emotional aspects of aphasia. In M. T. Sarno (ed.) *Acquired Aphasia*. Academic Press, New York.

Sarno, M. T. (1980). Language rehabilitation outcome in the elderly aphasic. In L. K. Obler and M. L. Albert (eds) *Language and Communication in the Elderly*. Lexington Books, Lexington, Mass.

Sarno, M. T. (1981). Recovery and rehabilitation in aphasia. In M. T. Sarno (ed.) *Acquired Aphasia*. Academic Press, New York.

Sarno, M. T., Silverman, M., and Sands, E. (1970). Speech therapy and language recovery in severe aphasia. *J. Speech Hear. Res.*, **13**, 607–623.

Schacter, D. L., and Crovitz, H. F. (1977). Memory function after closed head injury: a review of the quantitative research. *Cortex*, **13**, 150–176.

Schneider, G. E. (1970). Mechanisms of functional recovery following lesions of visual cortex or superior colliculus in neonate and adult hamsters. *Brain Behav. Evol.*, **3**, 295–323.

Schneider, G. E. (1973). Early lesions of superior colliculus: factors affecting the formation of abnormal retinal projections. *Brain Behav. Evol.*, **8**, 73–109.

Schneider, G. E. (1977). Growth of abnormal neural connections following focal brain lesions: constraining factors and functional effects. In W. H. Sweet, S. Obrador, and J. G. Martin-Rodriguez (eds) *Neurosurgical Treatment in Psychiatry, Pain and Epilepsy*. University Park Press, Baltimore.

Schneider, G. E. (1979). Is it really better to have your brain lesion early? A revision of the 'Kennard principle'. *Neuropsychologia*, **17**, 557–583.

Schoenfeld, T. A., and Hamilton, L. W. (1977). Secondary brain changes following lesions: a new paradigm for lesion experimentation. *Physiol. Behav.*, **18**, 951–967.

Schuell, H. M., Carroll, V., and Street, B. S. (1955). Clinical treatment of aphasia. *J. Speech Hear. Disord.*, **20**, 43–53.

Schuell, H. M., Jenkins, J., and Jiminez-Pabon, E. (1964). *Aphasia in Adults*. Harper & Rowe, New York.

Schwartz, S. (1964). Effect of neonatal cortical lesions and early environmental factors on adult rat behavior. *J. Comp. Physiol. Psychol.*, **57**, 72–77.

Seltzer, B., and Benson, D. F. (1974). The temporal pattern of retrograde amnesia in Korsakoff's disease. *Neurology*, **24**, 527–530.

Seron, X., Deloche, G., Bastard, V., Chassin, G., and Hermand, N. (1979). Word finding difficulties and learning transfer in aphasic patients. *Cortex*, **15**, 149–155.

Shallice, T. (1979). Case study approach in neuropsychological research. *J. Clin. Neuropsychol.*, **1**, 183–211.

Shapiro, D. A. (1981). Comparative credibility of treatment rationales: three tests of expectancy theory. *Br. J. Clin. Psychol.*, **20**, 111–122.

Shapiro, M. B. (1970). Intensive assessment of the single case: an unductive-deductive approach. In P. Mittler (ed.) *The Psychological Assessment of Mental and Physical Handicaps*. Methuen, London.

Sidman, M. (1971). The behavioral analysis of aphasia. *J. Psychiat. Res.*, **8**, 413–422.

Skelly, M. (1979). *Amer-Ind Gestural Code Based on Universal American Indian Hand Talk*. Elsevier, New York.

Skelly, M., Schinsky, L., Smith, R. W., and Fust, R. S. (1974). American indian sign (Amerind) as a facilitator of verbalization for the verbal apraxic. *J. Speech Hear. Disord.*, **39**, 445–456.

Skinner, B. F. (1957). *Verbal Behavior*. Appleton-Century-Crofts, New York.

Smith, A. (1960). Changes in Porteus maze scores of brain-damaged schizophrenics after an 8 year interval. *J. Ment. Sci.*, **106**, 967–978.

Smith, A. (1964). Changing effects of frontal lesions in man. *J. Neurol. Neurosurg. Psychiatry*, **27**, 511–515.

Smith, A. (1971). Objective studies of severity of chronic aphasia in stroke patients. *J. Speech Hear. Disord.*, **26**, 167–207.

Smith, C. J. (1959). Mass action and early environment in the rat. *J. Comp. Physiol. Psychol.*, **52**, 154–156.

Smith, E. (1974). Influence of site of impact on cognitive impairment persisting long after severe closed head injury. *J. Neurol. Neurosurg. Psychiatry*, **37**, 719–726.

Sparks, R., and Holland, A. L. (1976). Melodic intonation therapy for aphasia. *J. Speech Hear. Disord.*, **41**, 287–297.

Sparks, R., Helm, N., and Albert, M. (1974). Aphasia rehabilitation resulting from melodic intonation therapy. *Cortex*, **10**, 303–313.

Spear, P. D., and Bauman, T. P. (1979). Neurophysiological mechanisms of recovery from visual cortex damage: properties of lateral suprasylvian visual area neurons following behavioral recovery. *Exper. Brain Res.*, **35**, 177–182.

Sperry, R. W. (1968). Hemisphere deconnection and unity in conscious awareness. *Amer. Psychol.*, **23**, 723–733.

Squire, L. R., Chace, P. M., and Slater, P. C. (1976). Retrograde amnesia following electroconvulsive therapy. *Nature*, **260**, 775–778.

Squire, L. R., Slater, P. C., and Miller, P. L. (1981). Retrograde amnesia and bilateral electroconvulsive therapy. *Arch. Gen. Psychiatry*, **38**, 89–95.

Squire, L. R., Wetzel, C. D., and Slater, P. C. (1978). Anterograde amnesia following ECT: an analysis of the beneficial effects of partial cueing. *Neuropsychologia*, **16**, 339–348.

Steel-Russell, I., and Pereira, S. C. (1981). Visual neglect in rat and monkey: an experimental model for the study of recovery of function following brain damage. In M. W. van Hof and G. Mohn (eds) *Functional Recovery from Brain Damage*. Elsevier, Amsterdam.

Stein, D. G., and Firl, A. (1976). Brain damage and reorganisation of function in old age. *Exper. Neurol.*, **52**, 157–167.

Stelmach, G. E. (1976). *Motor Control: Issues and Trends*. Academic Press, New York.

Stewart, J. W., and Ades, H. W. (1951). The time factor in reintegration of a learned habit after temporal lobe lesions in the monkey (macaca mulatta). *J. Comp. Physiol. Psychol.*, **44**, 479–486.

Strich, S. J. (1961). Shearing of nerve fibres as a cause of brain damage due to head injury. *Lancet*, **2**, 443–448.

Subirana, A. (1958). Prognosis in aphasia in relation to cerebral dominance and handedness. *Brain*, **81**, 415–425.

Subirana, A. (1969). Handedness and cerebral dominance. In P. J. Vinken and G. W. Bruyn (eds) *Handbook of Clinical Neurology*, vol. 4. North Holland, Amsterdam.

Swaan, D., van Wieringer, P. C., and Fokkema, S. D. (1974). Auditory electromyographic feedback therapy to inhibit undesired motor activity. *Arch. Phys. Med. Rehab.*, **55**, 251–254.

Symonds, C. P. (1937). The assessment of symptoms following head injury. *Guys Hosp. Gazette*, November, pp. 1–19.

Taylor, J. (1931). *Selected Writings of John Hughlings Jackson*. Hodder & Stoughton, London.

Taylor, M. T (1964). Language therapy. In H. G. Burr (ed.) *The Aphasic Adult: Evaluation and Rehabilitation*. Wayside Press, Charlottesville.

Teuber, H.-L. (1955). Physiological psychology. *Ann. Rev. Psychol.*, **6**, 267–296.

Teuber, H.-L. (1974). Recovery of function after lesions of the central nervous system: history and prospects. *Neurosci. Res. Prog. Bull.*, **12**, 197–213.

Teuber, H.-L., Battersby, W. S., and Bender, M. B. (1960). *Visual Field Defects after Penetrating Missile Wounds of the Brain*. Harvard University Press, Boston.

Thatcher, R. W., and Kimble, D. P. (1966). Effect of amygdaloid lesions on retention of an avoidance response in overtrained and non-overtrained rats. *Psychon. Sci.*, **6**, 9–10.

Thompson, R., Lukaszewska, I., Schweigerdt, A., and McNew, J. J. (1967). Relation of visual and kinaesthetic discrimination in rats following pretecto-diencephalic and mesencephalic damage. *J. Comp. Physiol. Psychol.*, **63**, 458–468.

Thurstone, L. L. (1944). *A Factorial Study of Perception*. University of Chicago Press, Chicago.

Tomlinson, B. E., Blessed, G., and Roth, M. (1970). Observations on the brains of demented old people. *J. Neurol. Sci.*, **7**, 205–242.

Trexler, L. (1982). *Cognitive Rehabilitation*. Plenum Press, New York.

Ungerstedt, U. (1971). Post synaptic supersensitivity after 6-hydroxy-dopamine induced degeneration of nigro-striatal dopamine system. *Acta Physiol. Scand.*, Suppl. 367, 69–93.

Victor, M., Adams, R. E., and Collins, G. H. (1971). The Wernicke Korsakoff Syndrome. F. A. Davis, Philadelphia.

Vignolo, L. A. (1964). Evaluation of aphasia and language rehabilitation: a retrospective exploratory study. *Cortex*, **1**, 344–367.

von Monakow, C. (1914). Die Lokalisation im Grosshirn und der abbau *der Funktion durch Kortikale Herde*. J. F. Bergmann, Wiesbaden.

Wall, P. D. (1980). Mechanisms of plasticity of connection following damage in adult mammalian nervous system. In P. Bach-y-Rita (ed.) *Recovery of Function: Theoretical Considerations for Brain Injury Rehabilitation*. Hans Huber, Bern.

Walsh, K. W. (1978). *Neuropsychology: A Clinical Approach*. Churchill-Livingstone, Edinburgh.

Ward, A. A., and Kennard, M. A. (1942). Effect of cholinergic drugs on recovery of function following lesions of the central nervous system in monkeys. *Yale J. Biol. Med.*, **15**, 189–228.

Warren, J. M., and Akert, K. (1964). *The Frontal Granular Cortex and Behavior*. McGraw-Hill, New York.

Warrington, E. K., and Weiskrantz, L. (1970). Amnesic syndrome: consolidation or retrieval. *Nature*, **228**, 628–630.

Watson, C. W., and Kennard, M. A. (1945). The effect of anticonvulsant drugs on recovery of function following cerebral cortical lesions. *J. Neurophysiol.*, **8**, 221–231.

Weese, G. D., Neimand, D., and Finger, S. (1973). Cortical lesions and somaesthesis in rats: effects of training and overtraining prior to surgery. *Exper. Brain Res.*, **16**, 542–550.

Weigl, E. (1968). On the problem of cortical syndromes. In M. L. Simmel (ed.) *The Reach of Mind*. Springer, New York.

Weinberg, J., Diller, L., Gordon, W. A., Gerstman, L. J., Lieberman, A., Lakin, P., Hodges, G., and Ezrachi, O. (1977). Visual scanning training effect on reading-related tasks in acquired right brain damage. *Arch. Phys. Med. Rehab.*, **58**, 479–486.

Weinberg, J., Diller, L., Gordon, W. A., Gerstman, L. J., Lieberman, A., Lakin, P., Hodges, G., and Ezrachi, O. (1979). Training sensory awareness and spatial organization in people with right brain damage. *Arch. Phys. Med. Rehab.*, **60**, 491–496.

Weisenberg, T., and McBride, K. (1935). *Aphasia: A Clinical and Psychological Study*. Commonwealth Fund, New York.

Weiskrantz, L. (1968). Some traps and pontifications. In L. Weiskrantz (ed.) *Analysis of Behavioral Change*. Harper & Row, New York.

Welch, K., and Penfield, W. (1950). Paradoxical improvement in hemiplegia following cortical excision. *J. Neurosurg.*, **7**, 414–420.

Welford, A. T. (1968). *Fundamentals of Skill*. Methuen, London.

Weniger, D., Huber, W., Stachowiak, F.-J., and Poeck, K. (1980). Treatment of aphasia on a linguistic basis. In M. T. Sarno and O. Höök (eds) *Aphasia: Assessment and Treatment*. Almqvist & Wiksell, Stockholm.

Wepman, J. M. (1951). *Recovery from Aphasia*. Ronald Press, New York.

West, D. R., Deadwyler, S. A., Cotman, C. W., and Lynch, G. S. (1976). An experimental test of diaschisis. *Behav. Biol.,* **22,** 419–425.

Whitty, C. W. M., and Zangwill, O. L. (1977). *Amnesia,* 2nd edn. Butterworths, London.

Wiegl-Crump, C., and Konigsnecht, R. A. (1973). Tapping the lexical store of the adult aphasic: analysis of the improvement made in word retrieval skills. *Cortex,* **9,** 410–418.

Will, B. E., and Rosenzweig, M. R. (1976). Effets de l'environnement sur la récupération functionnelle après lesions cérébrales chez les rats adultes.*Biol. Behav.,* **1,** 5–16.

Will, B. E., Rosenzweig, M. R., and Bennett, E. L. (1976). Effects of differential environments on recovery from neonatal brain lesions by problem-solving scores and brain dimensions. *Physiol. Behav.,* **16,** 603–611.

Willanger, R. (1970). *Intellectual Impairment in Diffuse Cerebral Lesions.* Munksgaard, Copenhagen.

Williams, M. (1979). *Brain Damage, Behaviour and the Mind.* Wiley, Chichester.

Wood, R., and Eames, P. (1981). Application of behaviour modification in the treatment of traumatically brain-injured adults. In G. Davey (ed.) *Applications of Conditioning Theory.* Methuen, London.

Woods, B. T., and Carey, S. (1979). Language deficits after apparent clinical recovery from childhood aphasia. *Ann. Neurol.,* **6,** 405–409.

Woods, B. T., and Teuber, H.-L. (1978). Mirror movements after childhood hemiparesis. *Neurology,* **28,** 1152–1158.

Woods, R. T., and Piercy, M. (1974). A similarity between amnesic memory and normal forgetting. *Neuropsychologia,* **12,** 437–445.

Wyke, M. (1971). The effects of brain lesions on the performance of bilateral arm movements. *Neuropsychologia,* **9,** 33–42.

Yarnell, P., Monroe, P., and Sobel, L. (1976). Aphasia outcome in stroke: a clinical neuroradiological correlation. *Stroke,* **7,** 514–522.

Zangwill, O. L. (1964). Psychological studies in amnesic states. *Proc. 3rd World Congr. Psychiatry,* **3,** 219–227.

Zangwill, O. L. (1977). The amnesic syndrome. In C. W. M. Whitty and O. L. Zangwill (eds.) *Amnesia,* 2nd edn. Butterworths, London.

Zeaman, D., and House, B. J. (1963). The role of attention in retardate discrimination learning. In N. R. Ellis (ed.) *Handbook of Mental Deficiency.* McGraw-Hill, New York.

Zihl, J., (1980). 'Blindsight': improvement of visually guided eye movements by systematic practice in patients with cerebral blindness. *Neuropsychologia,* **18,** 71–77.

Zihl, J. (1981). Recovery of visual field associated with specific training in patients with cerebral damage. In M. W. van Hof and G. Mohn (eds) *Functional Recovery from Brain Damage.* Elsevier, Amsterdam.

Zihl, J., and von Cramon, D. (1979). Restitution of visual function in patients with cerebral blindness. *J. Neurol. Neurosurg. Psychiatry,* **42,** 312–322.

Zihl, J. von Cramon, D., Brinkmann, R., and Backmund, H. (1977). Verlaufskontrolle und prognose bei Gesichtsfeldausfallen von Pateinten mit cerebrovaskulären störungen. *Nervenarzt,* **48,** 219–224.

Zimmer, J. (1981). Lesion induced reorganization of central nervous connections: with a note on central nervous transplants. In M. W. van Hof and G. Mohn (eds) *Functional Recovery from Brain Damage.* Elsevier, Amsterdam.

Author Index

Subject Index